The Battalion

The Battalion

Citizen Soldiers at War on the Western Front

Ian Andrew Isherwood

Pen & Sword

MILITARY

An imprint of
Pen & Sword Books Ltd
Yorkshire – Philadelphia

Pen & Sword
MILITARY

First published in Great Britain in 2024 by
PEN & SWORD MILITARY
An imprint of
Pen & Sword Books Ltd
Yorkshire – Philadelphia

ISBN 978 1 52677 422 4

Typeset in Chennai, India
by Lapiz Digital Services.

Printed and bound by CPI UK

Pen & Sword Books Ltd incorporates the imprints of Pen & Sword
Archaeology, Atlas, Aviation, Battleground, Discovery, Family History, History, Maritime, Military, Naval, Politics, Social History, Transport, True Crime, Claymore Press, Frontline Books, Praetorian Press, Seaforth Publishing and White Owl

For a complete list of Pen & Sword titles please contact

PEN & SWORD BOOKS LTD
47 Church Street, Barnsley, South Yorkshire, S70 2AS, England
E-mail: enquiries@pen-and-sword.co.uk
Website: www.pen-and-sword.co.uk

or

PEN AND SWORD BOOKS
1950 Lawrence Rd, Havertown, PA 19083, USA
E-mail: uspen-and-sword@casematepublishers.com
Website: www.penandswordbooks.com

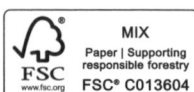

MIX
Paper | Supporting
responsible forestry
FSC
www.fsc.org   FSC® C013604

Dedication

To Marco, Nicholas, Diane, and Team Peirs I offer this book. It would have been impossible to write without you all and it is with heartfelt thanks that I dedicate it to you.

To H.J.C.P., I leave this imperfect reanimation of your battalion's actions in the First World War for posterity.

Contents

Acknowledgements

In my first semester teaching twentieth century world history, an eager and smart undergraduate approached me about his great-grandfather who was the commanding officer of a British Army battalion in the First World War. Later Marco Dracopoli came to class armed with a box containing the letters of his relative, H.J.C. Peirs. I was fortunate to end up as Marco's academic advisor in the history department at Gettysburg College, where in due course, he went on to write a fine paper on his great-grandfather's style of leadership in the First World War.[1] Upon his graduation in 2014, the Dracopoli/Zorich family allowed me to form a small team to digitise and then publish H.J.C. Peirs's letters online.[2] This book would have not have been possible without the endless support given to our project by their family. Without their generosity, we would not have a digital history project; without their support of me, this book would not be possible.

I am grateful to the archives and staff at the following repositories who have helped my research: The National Archives (UK); the Imperial War Museum; the Surrey History Centre; the Liddell Hart Centre for Military Archives; and Special Collections, Musselman Library, Gettysburg College. Historians usually do not discover things in archives; we mostly bring to light materials which have been preserved, stored, and catalogued by archival professionals. To say that a historian is as good as their archivists is not hyperbole, but a simple fact of doing research. I am eternally grateful to the professionalism and skill of the archivists I have known. Of your collections, I have endeavoured to quote from materials within existing copyright guidelines and established practices for fair use; should any copyright holder believe that I have not given proper acknowledgement or attribution, I will correct this in a future edition.

In researching Peirs and the 8th Battalion, I have benefited from many who have reached out to me in the process of writing this book. I am grateful to

---

1   Marco Dracopoli, 'A New Officer for a New Army: The Leadership of Major Hugh J.C. Peirs in the Great War', *The Gettysburg Historical Journal*: Vol. 13, Article 6.
2   https://www.jackpeirs.org.

Dan Re'em and the Fairtlough family for their kindness and help. I am also grateful to Brian Curtis, Allan Hitchcock, Simon Barnard, Michael Lucas, Steve Smith, William Hall, and Richard Novell for providing insights during the writing of the book. Special thanks as well to Sebastian Laudan for his insights into the German sources of the March 1918 offensives. I am grateful to the Severin family in Le Verguier for providing our team with research materials while we were in France. Thanks to Susanna Monseau for offering context and research help concerning her ancestor, Lance Corporal John Sayer VC. Andrew Arnold has lent his keen eye to this manuscript and I am very grateful for his comments and for his professional expertise on all things Surrey at war. Tim Godden's illustration of Peirs and his men at Le Verguier has proved to be inspirational on difficult writing days. My editors with Pen & Sword, Rupert Harding, Harriet Fielding, Lisa Hoosan, and Heather Williams, deserve special mention for their professionalism, persistence, and beyond anything else, patience as I laboured to finish this book.

I am also grateful to the institution where I work, Gettysburg College. Thanks to the Provost's Office which has supported – from the very start – our work on the Peirs project and has supported my research with funding. In particular, Jack Ryan and Rob Bohrer saw to it that our project received funds for overseas travel and to pay our student workers. This research has also benefited from the development department at Gettysburg College, who allowed us to crowdfund a research trip to France and Belgium. Thanks to all of you who donated for our research team to go abroad. I wish to also thank the U.S. WWI Centennial Commission for supporting our project from 2018 onwards.

I was lucky to finish this book while serving as the Harold K. Johnson Chair of Military History at the US Army War College. I am very grateful to the Department of National Security and Strategy and to my chair, Dr Carrie Lee, for this opportunity, which allowed me the time to end the book on a high note while teaching future strategic leaders. Thank you, Seminar 6, for your persistent encouragement as I mopped up the book – learning from all of you this year has been one of the great honours of my career. And thank you Professor Michael Neiberg for being a sage mentor, a kind colleague, and a good friend.

I also have wonderful colleagues at the college who helped with this book. Diane Brennan is an invaluable friend. She helped support this research in countless ways over the last ten years. Tim Shannon, Michael Birkner, and

Bill Bowman's friendship and support in the history department is appreciated. Dave Powell helped steer me through tenure as I was writing this book; his support kept my mind off worrying about that process, as much as possible, so I could do the real work of teaching and scholarship. Chris Fee proved a kind mentor in this regard and has helped me with the idea of a 'work/life' balance in academia. Helping to put that into practice has been Ian Clarke, who made sure that when the virus came, we went fishing. Mornings on the water have kept not only my sanity, but also, my ability to focus; I am writing these acknowledgements after catching two rainbow trout on a difficult spring creek as proof. My pandemic 'therapy sessions' with Kurt Andresen demonstrate that fellowship over a glass and guffaw is good for the soul.

My closest colleagues in writing this book have been those from #TeamPeirs who supported this research and kept me on task. Kevin Lavery helped with early archival research and has been a good friend. I would ask for no better company than Jesse Campana and Meghan O'Donnell should I ever have to relive the anniversary of the Kaiserschlacht again. Both were an indispensable part of the best historical research trip I have ever taken. Ben Roy deserves special mention for his outstanding research and storytelling skills. Lizzie Hobbs was my right hand researcher. No task was too great or too small, and this book would be much less without her help. Without R.C. Miessler we would not even have a digital history project; without his creativity, our website would consist of random letters and a broken timeline; without his friendship, I would be a poorer person. Jenna Fleming transcribed every important document used in this book; she fact checked it to make sure I did not let the side down (all mistakes are mine alone, however!); and she has demonstrated time and time again to be the true expert on our team. This book would be much better had she written it. Amy Lucadamo, for twenty-two years you have listened to me talk about war and that deserves special mention in despatches. Thank you for so much, but most of all, for being my friend. Finally, thank you to all of the students who have workshopped many of the ideas in this book with me over the years – your cleverness and enthusiasm has made me a better scholar. You have proved to me what I have long suspected – that I teach in the best liberal arts college in the country for the study of war.

Writing this book during a pandemic has proved difficult. It did not come out the way I thought it would, but it is now finished. When I began it during the summer of 2019, my mother was battling two forms of cancer. As I was trying to write the book, I watched her diminish and ultimately succumb in January 2020. Then came Covid, lockdown, homeschooling, general upheaval, dread, unbelievable professional stress, and pathos. Though our lives went topsy turvy, I would never have finished this book without the faith and love of my family. I am fairly certain that I would have finished it much sooner had there been no pandemic, but I am certain that I would have never finished it at all without Sam Isherwood's love and support and Henry Isherwood's good cheer through the most difficult three years of our lives. I am profoundly and eternally grateful to you both (and to our dog Bertie, though not all of the time). My mother always wanted to be remembered by the simple epitaph 'I tried'. So it was for her, and so it is for me and this book, written as the world turned upside down and now tries to right itself.

Battle Plan and Maps

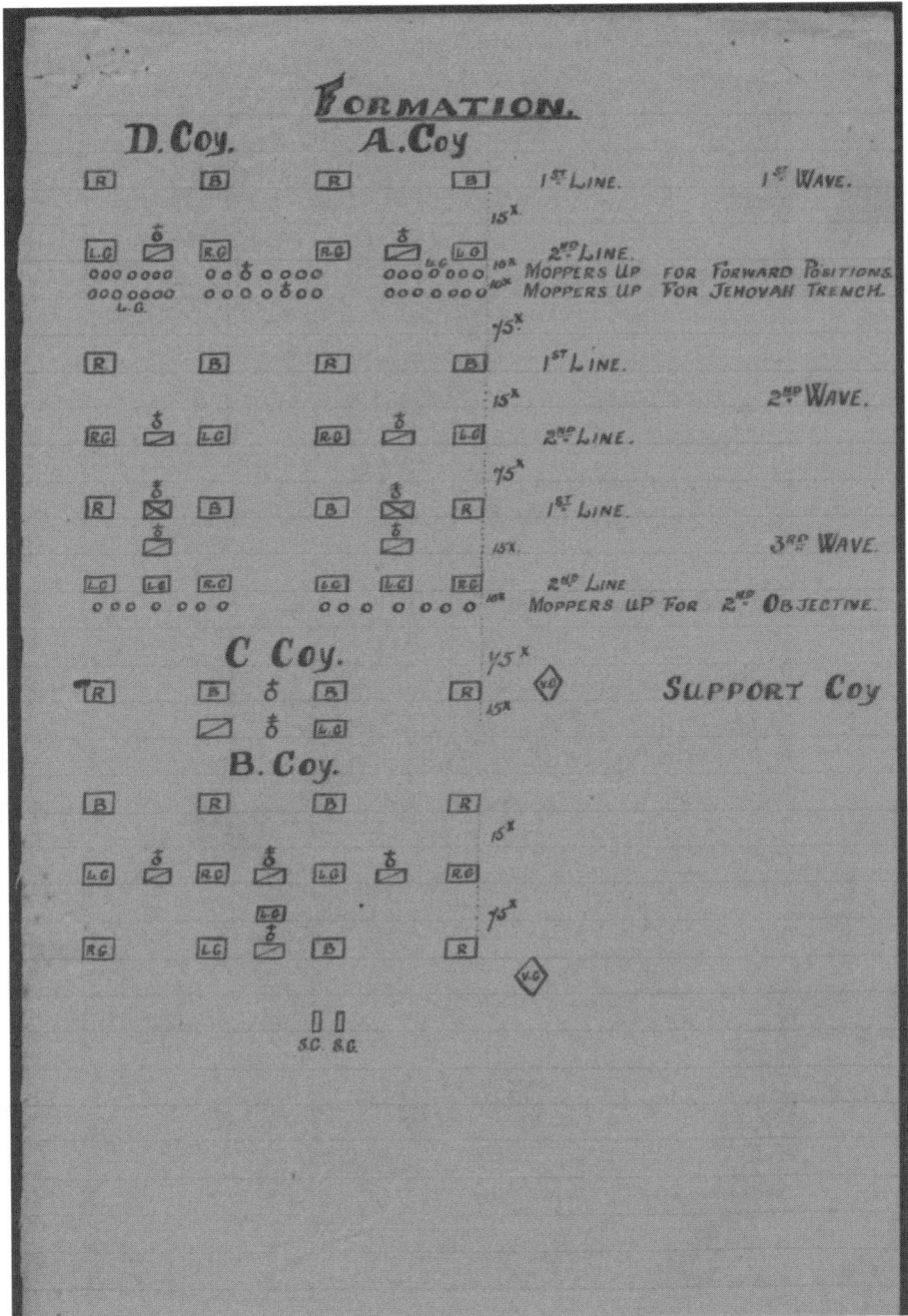

Detailed plan for the 31 July 1917 attack. The plan shows how each company and platoon was to be organized according to their special roles with D and A Company taking the lead. The battalion rehearsed the attack in detail.
Credit: The National Archives, ref. WO 95/2214/4

Map detailing the 31 July 1917 attack against Jehovah and Jordan trenches near Shrewsbury Forest. The map shows the battalion's flanks in pencil with and the center dividing point between A and D Companies.

Credit: The National Archives, ref. WO 95/2214/4

Trench map of the village of Le Verguier showing the direction of attack on 21-22 March 1918. Each circle represents a post held in force by the 8th Queen's, the arrows indicating the direction of assault on their positions. By the morning of 22 March, the village was nearly surrounded, and the battalion withdrew from along the Sunken Road to the south.
Credit: The National Archives, ref. WO 95/2208/2

Introduction

Driving north on the highway from Charles de Gaulle airport, there is no obvious trace of how the landscape suffered a century ago. The fallow fields that now flank the road once bore the deep burdens of war. Carved into chalky soil were thousands of miles of zig-zaggy trenches antagonistically facing off against one another. In between, there were long stretches of no man's land, pockmarked by shelling; an often wet and dismal space cluttered with the detritus of industrialised war. At any given time, there was the rumble of artillery firing somewhere along the line. When the cacophony reached its crescendo during the big bombardments, the great guns rained down destruction and death on men who clutched dearly the sides of their trenches for protection. The land's deep scarring matched the psyches of the men who fought there – their minds were strained, emotionally exhausted, and forever altered by what they felt, saw, and participated in at the front. This was a scale of desolation unseen in the history of war. Even my hometown of Gettysburg, Pennsylvania cannot claim such magnitude of devastation and tragic distinction as this entire *region* of France.

Though three armies waged war here for four bitter years, now what was then the old front line is a place of silence, tranquility, and beauty that is both sombre and ubiquitous in its agrarian banality. The region has proved, like many of the men who fought here, to be resilient to the trauma that was once inflicted upon it. The highway exits, though, do reveal the region's violent heritage, ones that the landscape fails to recognise through its rejuvenation. The exit for Compiègne – about 60 miles north of Paris – reminds us of where and how the war ended with the Armistice in a train car in November 1918. Continuing north are exits for Saint-Quentin, Péronne, and Amiens – land sacred to the British Expeditionary Force (BEF) in their battles of 1916 and 1918. Carrying on are the battlefields of Arras, Cambrai, Vimy Ridge, and just to the west of Lens, the Loos Salient, where the BEF fought and bled in 1915. The exits off the A1 northbound from Paris are a table of contents of the fighting on the western front.

The men and women who survived the war and later grieved in the cemeteries of northern France and western Belgium knew this landscape for its brokenness, but also for what we see now, its recovery. They were the ones who dug the trenches and attacked across no man's land. They were the ones who loaded the guns and fired the shells that destroyed men's bodies and blew up their trenches. They were the ones who grimly faced morning stand-to at the firestep, wondering if the enemy would attack and then wondering about their breakfast if he did not. They were the ones who nursed the wounded and comforted those broken in both mind and spirit. Rather than seeing what we see now – familiar quaint brick villages – instead they saw military targets on maps: redoubts in the rubble ruins of houses and enemy observation points in steeples broken by shelling; forests left as smoldering heaps of felled timber, cut down by high explosive and metal shell fragments. Those that served here were the agents of the vast deliberate destruction of the world's first truly industrialised war.

They were also the generation that restored the land and memorialised the sacrifice of their comrades. The land bears signs, too, of sacrifice and death in the stillness of the cemeteries and grandeur of the war memorials. The cemeteries are deceptive, however; their clean-cut and silent mournfulness is not the story of what happened here during the war, but instead of the importance of the war to the generation who survived it. They are beautiful and well-ordered and stand as reminders of the cost of war, but not of what the war was, what it looked and felt like. For that you have to look much harder; and if you do, you can find the remnants of trenches and shell craters nearby. Nevertheless, the neatly arrayed headstones and perfectly manicured cemeteries are also a tribute to the amazing vitality of a land that is beautiful, despite the war's wreckage. They are a testament of the war generation's loss, but also, of its lasting emotional and spiritual power and vitality.

That word – vitality – is one that people do not usually associate with the First World War. Yet, the landscape obviously reflects this sense of restoration. The once torn-up fields are replenished now with crops and the once ruined villages are painstakingly reconstructed. As proof of the resiliency of the land, as well as one to the efforts of the French to rebuild, there is little from the highway that indicates anything but peacefulness. There are lumbering windmills here and there generating power. There are combines rolling along as the occasional farmer works the land. Reconstructed red brick villages, with their mostly unused churches and closed storefronts, adorn each small ridgeline between the valleys of farmland. In the summer, poppies and cornflowers break up the monotony of chalky soil and greenery with bright blue and red clumps of irritatingly charming wild beauty. It is hard to imagine that here the ground rumbled, the air was poisoned, and that these quiet hamlets became redoubts manned by men who stood ready to kill one another by the thousands.

* * *

Our team came as pilgrims eager to see what secrets the battlefields reveal. With our tour books and trench maps, we drove north on the A1 from the airport, me struggling with the gear stick in our rented Citroën. Relearning a standard transmission came at the expense of a few ground gears and grimaces from my three colleagues, who were too kind to tell me the fear they felt in my driving. We exited at Péronne, navigated the roundabout, and then drove into one of the small cities along the Somme. The scenery immediately changed from pastoral to commercial – from rolling ridges to near instant urbanisation. Suddenly, there were car dealerships, fast food restaurants, and a box supermarket. We pressed along through the southern end of Péronne, adjacent to the River Somme. Within a few minutes we were out of the city. The grey stone and red brick homes grew fewer in number. We jutted out from the city into what the Somme region is and has always been – farms and villages connected by circuitous country roads. Though it was late March, it began to snow, the large and lumpy flakes that come when it is not cold enough to freeze but just cold enough for the clouds above to be confused as to what they should do. The snow then turned to sleet and the sleet to rain. The horizon changed from blue to grey as the sun struggled to burst through heavy clouds.

We made our journey on the first day of spring. The annoyingly inconsistent weather appropriately reflected the cosmic change by ushering in the new season's hopefulness and renewal. For us the day had a darker significance. Our team – a professor, an archivist, and two shining undergraduate research assistants – came to record and to commemorate the centennial of the 1918 German Spring Offensive, the Kaiser's Battle. We came armed with the trappings of a digital humanities project: smartphones, laptops, tablets, and a 360-degree camera. Our mission was to tell the story 100 years to the day of a battalion of British soldiers who fought a heroic last stand in the face of a tremendous German attack. On social media we traced this battalion's actions during the last week of March 1918 on their original battlefields.

Why were four Americans so invested in the story of one British battalion in the First World War? This is a reasonable question considering that we travelled 4,000 miles to relive the story of men for whom we had no direct relation by blood or nationality. The First World War is a largely overlooked conflict in America and we came from Gettysburg College, where we have our own battlefield and our own great war to mull over. The short answer is that we came to France because a student of mine eight years before told me about a Harrods box full of letters in his family's attic. That box, it turned out, held the correspondence of Lieutenant Colonel H.J.C. Peirs CMG DSO, who commanded the 8th Battalion of The Queen's (Royal West Surrey Regiment), a unit that made their stand at Le Verguier on 21 March 1918. With the family's support, we created a digital history project for the centennial of the First World War and published Peirs's correspondence online 100 years to the day in which he wrote each letter home.[1] Three years later, and after much planning and fundraising, we were in France for the centennial of the 8th Queen's most significant battle.

As we drove towards Le Verguier on 21 March 2018, I was conscious of both the burden of history and the fallibility of memory. It was vital that our team got the story right, especially since we were shooting live video from the battlefield. More than the potential for historical embarrassment was our sense of obligation to those who were here in 1918. The fight for this tiny French village was important to the 8th Queen's and we took seriously our duty to tell their story. Like the other units of the 24th Division, the 8th Queen's war experience is one that was remembered by the veterans themselves and their descendants, one of scores of other Kitchener battalions who volunteered in 1914 and served for the duration of the war. Our story was bigger than this one battle; it was about preserving an experience that a century later seems so foreign, but also one so very human and relevant to our age too. Here ordinary men – civilians temporarily in uniform – stood firm and defended a village far from their homes. They did so despite years of fatigue, trauma, and hardship at the front. They did so because it was what they were supposed to do.

---

1   https://www.jackpeirs.org/about.

We drove towards their trenches and through the village of Bernes. This village was wrecked during the war and used as a supply and ammunition dump for an artillery battery on 21 March 1918. From there we retraced the steps of Major H.J.C. Peirs, who that morning walked up from this village to meet his men in Le Verguier. As we retraced his steps, my colleague Amy Lucadamo affixed our 360-degree camera to its monopod and carefully held it out the window, capturing the surrounding countryside until her hand became too cold to hold the camera. Minutes later we arrived at the sunken road that held the 8th Queen's headquarters. There we began reconstructing history from the incomplete information we had collected over years of research into this battalion.

As we did so, we used our Facebook and Twitter accounts to give minute-by-minute updates on the progress of the battle from onsite. One hundred years to the moment in which the village was defended, we broadcast a lecture back to my students in the United States as they held in their hands Peirs's letters and photographs. What we did not expect from our trip was probably the most important part; the town's mayor and local citizens came out to talk with us about its history. They brought us photographs, documents, and mementos for us to use in our research. We met members of a family that had relatives in the village during the war and one of their relations, Charles Severin, had, in fact, corresponded with Peirs in 1919. Through their contact, we had a real life tangible connection with figures of the past.

Our experience of recreating the stand of the 8th Queen's completely changed the way in which we viewed not only our project, but also this battalion and its place in the history of the First World War. We realised again that there was a deep connection between people and the landscape and that the story of the war was far more intimate than many of its histories indicate. The Western Front was enormous – 475 or so miles of trenches, often interlocking and containing multiple lines and redoubts, miles deep in sections. Le Verguier was one of hundreds of fortified villages making up the trench network of the BEF in 1918. Even in terms of the Kaiser's Battle, the actions of the 8th Queen's was a tiny part of a much larger battle. In the greater history of the war, Le Verguier is remote – it is at the very most a footnote to a much larger event taking place around it. Yet for the men who fought in that small French village, their experiences on 21–22 March 1918 were absolutely life altering and foundational to the story of their service.

Their 'face of battle', to borrow John Keegan's most famous phrase, was everything to them; it was *their* history of the First World War.[2]

In the eight years we have worked on the Peirs project, attempting to reconstruct his life and the lives of those in his battalion, I have often thought of the First World War writer Guy Chapman. In his memoir, *A Passionate Prodigality*, he described his task as a 'faint reanimation' of the lives of the men with whom he served.[3] Unlike Chapman, H.J.C. Peirs never wrote his war recollections. He never wrote to make sense of his experiences and memories and to memorialise his unit and men. Instead, he left behind his war letters that were marked on the outside of an envelope by the family with the charmingly quaint moniker 'for posterity'. We have attempted to reanimate a largely forgotten infantry battalion and to show how the war was fought from its perspective.

After our trip, I decided to write this book as a micro-history that reveals broader themes about the war. We are culturally predisposed to see First World War soldiers as victims or as passive sufferers who inhabited a broken landscape in a war of doomed heroism.[4] But that is not really the complete story of the majority of men who fought. Theirs too is a story of endurance, resilience, and comradeship – a story about emotional and physical survival, as well as hardship and suffering. Another often-overshadowed perspective is that of developing military skill: of learning and adaptation at the front. At the battalion level, men became better soldiers as the war was ongoing and their officers became better leaders. When they defended Le Verguier, the veterans of the 8th Queen's had years of bitter trial and error under their belts. Sure, they suffered greatly in their battles, but they also got better at fighting. Leadership and training were two reasons why this was the case, but so was the tenacity of the common soldier, who learned to cope at the front and to do a rough job well. This is a history of the transformation of ordinary citizens into skilled soldiers, an examination of how they survived emotionally as a unit, and a snapshot about what the war was like for the foundational element of the BEF – the infantry battalion.

---

2 John Keegan, *The Face of Battle* (New York: Viking, 1976).
3 Guy Chapman, *A Passionate Prodigality* (London: Ivor Nicholson & Watson, 1933), Dedication.
4 See Helen McCartney, 'The First World War Soldier and his contemporary image in Britain', *International Affairs*, 90:2, 2014, pp.299–315.

Central to this book and to the battalion's history is the correspondence of its longest serving senior officer, Hugh John Chevallier 'Jack' Peirs. It is through his letters that we are introduced to the 8th Queen's and through his eyes that we gain a glimpse of the battalion's *esprit de corps*. It is his correspondence that binds the other historical sources together and it is through his interpretation of the war that we have the most compelling argument for why this story needs to be told. While much of the story of the battalion presented here pertains to the journey of its commander, there was also a unit around him that was learning to fight in an ever-changing war of attrition. Thus, this is both the story of Peirs, but also of those for whom he invested every inch of his paternalistic leadership. Commanding this battalion was the touchstone of his life.

The unit to which he was devoted, the 8th Queen's, was a typical New Army service battalion. The unit served in every major campaign the British Army fought after their arrival in France in 1915. Importantly, the battalion would not be considered an 'elite' unit, though many of their officers and men were awarded medals for gallantry. This is not to say that they did not go through the meatgrinder of hard service – the battalion sustained heavy casualties in each of their major engagements. Still, they were an ordinary unit; they served, they suffered, and for many, they survived. Beyond anything else, their history teaches us about the endurance necessary by temporary soldiers and the leadership characteristics of their officers to see an utterly dehumanising war through to the end. Indeed, this is the partial story of how citizens became soldiers, how a battalion learned to fight, and how eventually the BEF saw to victory on the Western Front at the battalion level.

This book is divided into chapters that reflect the narrative arc of the 8th Queen's service. From a wider perspective, the chapters also reflect a story that would be familiar to most, if not all, Kitchener battalions on the Western Front. The first two chapters pertain to the battalion's training in England and their embarkation to France. Here the men's enthusiasm for doing their bit in the war came in stark contrast with the state's complete inability to clothe, house, and equip them. After these logistical issues were ironed out – after several months – the men trained for overseas service. Nothing could have prepared them for what awaited in battle, but they did go through prolonged military training to make them familiar with army life and to toughen them up physically before being deployed to France.

Once abroad, the 8th Queen's faced an immediate trial through battle at Loos. It is no exaggeration to say that this battle had a profound effect on all members of the 24th Division. The 8th Queen's lost half their number in less than an hour. Their botched attack at the Lens-La Bassée road came not only with a personal price in the heavy casualties they sustained, but the division itself came under blame that resulted from their failure. Though it is the contention here that this stigma was ultimately unjust, it coloured the way that the officers and men in the unit saw their experiences. Loos proved to them that they had a long way to go as soldiers. For Major Peirs personally, this engagement was one in which he was determined not to repeat, but instead one to learn from and to train his men to overcome.

Loos also demonstrates a base line for our understanding of the logic of fighting the First World War. It was a dramatic bloodletting, but through it we can see just how far the battalion evolved over the next few years. In the 8th Queen's, we see a steep learning curve that the men had to climb in training and conditioning. The middle chapters of the book pertain to this story, one that is easily forgotten in the mud and pathos of the war. The 8th Queen's survivors recovered from Loos as the battalion reconstituted. As they settled into trench life, the battalion learned to cope and survive the trials of the front and gain new proficiency in arms. They raided enemy lines, endured and held their line in gas attacks, and went into the Battle of Somme far more tactically experienced for what lay ahead than they were in 1915. By 1917, the battalion had become a sophisticated fighting unit, learning new tactics ingrained in the BEF from the hard lessons of 1914–16. After the Somme, the remaining men could say with confidence that they were hardened soldiers.

All of the lessons learned in the pivotal years of 1916 and 1917 were ones shared by the BEF as a whole and the experience of the 8th Queen's mirrors that of many other units that fought and endured the Western Front. The last third of this book reflects the ultimate trial of Peirs and his men – the battles of 1918 – where they applied their tactical lessons both in the rearguard action of March and during the pursuit of the German army in November. Of course, like all demobilised battalions, the story of the war did not end once the fighting stopped. The final chapter of this book addresses the efforts of Peirs and other members of the 8th Queen's and the 24th Division to memorialise their comrades. Both Peirs and his family had a significant role in preserving the memory of their service.

In addition to the history of the battalion, this book hopes to present a blended approach to the writing of a unit history. As such, I hope to show the war's history on the Western Front through the eyes of a commanding officer and his battalion – what they knew at the time and what did not know – and what they saw and reacted to at the front. Foundational to this story is what is sometimes overlooked in the 'harder' forms of military history – that human beings bear the burdens of fighting and have to live through their experiences and with their memories afterwards. In studying the First World War this factor is a basic, and to my mind, incredibly important aspect to understanding the war. In this book we have the partial story of a few thousand men who came in and out of the battalion in its four years of existence. We have the partial story of over 700 of them who were killed in action. We have the partial story of what it was like to fight, to endure, and to survive the terrible conditions of the Western Front. This theatre of war was undeniably dehumanising, but human beings existed and many carried on despite what had happened to them. That is the story of Peirs and his men, not in partial bits and pieces, but in its narrative total. That is the story this book hopes to tell.

Chapter 1

Volunteers

Few could have anticipated the catastrophic scale wrought by four years of European war. By the time it ended, the war's repercussions registered in the millions. Millions were killed on its various fronts. Millions of civilians were displaced and dislocated. Millions died of disease and tens of thousands were victims of deliberate destruction. Beyond the sobering body count, which was felt locally in communities spanning from London to Mesopotamia, the First World War was also environmentally devastating. Landscapes and villages were ruined by shelling. On the Western Front in particular, armies made northern France and Belgium into a vast militarised zone. For those who fought and survived, they carried forward the physical and mental wounds of their service. Their burdens carried far beyond the trenches, casting a long shadow of suffering into the decades beyond.[1]

The war's grimness meant that many saw it afterwards as a cataclysm, a type of moral and cultural Armageddon.[2] It is no wonder that so many felt deeply disenchanted when it was over; for Europeans raised with ideas of cultural superiority, the war starkly upended those assumptions, and with them, the idea of progress that was firmly engrained in their society before 1914.[3] Especially for those who fought on the Western Front, the notion of

---

1   The war's impact has often been measured in terms of its body count, but it was also a social and cultural event of great magnitude affecting the course of twentieth-century history and beyond for all nations of Europe, the Near and Middle East, and of course, the wider European empires. See David Reynolds, *The Long Shadow* (New York: Simon & Shuster, 2013); Robert Gerwarth, *The Vanquished* (New York: Farrar, Strauss and Giroux, 2016); Alan Kramer, *Dynamic of Destruction* (Oxford: Oxford University Press, 2007); as well as the vast historiography on the war's memory. Stephane Audoin-Rouseau and Annette Becker's book *14–18: Understanding the Great War* (New York: Hill and Wang, 2000) directly engages with the changing concepts of civilization through the war's conduct.

2   See Reynolds, *The Long Shadow*, Chapter 5; Richard Overy, *The Morbid Age* (London: Allen Lane, 2009), pp.10–16.

3   Disenchantment is not a word used lightly, but one that reflects, I think, the complicated feelings of social/political insecurity and the deep feelings of mourning during, and then

civilization itself mocked them in the bitterest of ways by the stalemated character of trench warfare, the moral normalisation of extreme violence and suffering, and the increased lethality of weapons that destroyed the land and poisoned the air. The war was cruel beyond anything that the civilians who queued to join up in the autumn of 1914 could have fathomed. It is no wonder that Britons were haunted by its legacy; the war was the great shock that ushered in a new and uncertain future for the nation and empire.[4] Its great shock continues to this day.

It is hard for us now to look back at the war and see anything but its tragedy. We know how the story goes. In 1914, things were less certain. To the thousands who volunteered, the costs of war were unimaginable. There is complexity to this notion; men who 'rushed to the colours' were not entirely ignorant of the risks of modern war, but certainly were to the ramifications of their decision and of what the Western Front would become. They had no televisions, video games, or war films of any consequence to illuminate their expectations; they had illustrations, popular books, and their imaginations, which could not predict the long, hard road of attrition in which they were about to march.

Thus, in August 1914 'the war' was an event of unknowns. These unknowns were complicated by the desperate situation in France and Flanders as both sides grappled with the emerging stalemate. Year-by-year the conflict metastasised in its violence to the frustration of general staffs who tried to work the calculus of killing to their favour. Aiding generals were new, untested, and untried technologies; bigger guns, tanks, bomber and fighter planes that worked in a trial and error relationship with evolving tactics.[5] New and

particularly, after the war. For one aspect of the word's context before, during, and after the war, see Andrew Frayn's study *Writing Disenchantment* (Manchester: Manchester University Press, 2014).

4   For notions of cultural change and the war generation, specifically, three titles recommend themselves, though they are each works not immune to criticism. Still, the general point of a generation in varying degrees of cultural upheaval is one easily defended. Modris Eksteins, *Rites of Spring* (New York: Mariner Books, 2000); George Mosse, *Fallen Soldiers* (Oxford: Oxford University Press, 1990); Robert Wohl, *The Generation of 1914* (Cambridge: Harvard University Press, 1978).

5   William Philpott's *War of Attrition* (New York: Overlook, 2014) is a good general guide to shifting assumptions in the face of military realities; Aimee Fox's *Learning to Fight* (Cambridge: Cambridge University Press, 2017) demonstrates the ways in which the British Army, specifically, met the intellectual challenges of the war and learned from its experiences. See also Jonathan Boff's *Winning and Losing on the Western Front* (Cambridge: Cambridge University Press, 2012).

horrific ways of killing were dolled-out on infantry who were 'living in holes in the ground, exposed to sun, wind, and rain, surrounded by watchful enemies, forever in the presence of disaster and death'.[6] To the men in the holes, their perception changed as their minds became altered and accustomed to trench life. As the great commentator on soldiers' stories Samuel Hynes wrote of the war, 'it added a new scale of violence and destruction to what was possible – it changed reality'.[7]

That changed reality was not known to the men who volunteered in 1914. To realise the differences between 1914 and 1919 we need to immerse ourselves in a process of unravelling our assumptions about the First World War and of understanding the past on its own terms. This requires a degree of historical imagination. The way we see the First World War now was not the *zeitgeist* of 1914. Further, a century of the war's morbid memory in Britain has made it difficult for us to see past the poppies and to factor the motivations and worldview of real people who went to war, changed because of their experiences, and (for the most) returned home. We have to take turpentine to our assumptions and work through a century of the war's legacy – a legacy of unmitigated doom, victimisation, futility, and tragedy.[8] The mentality of 1914 was very different from the way we see the war now; it requires some heavy lifting to understand why men kept fighting.

For the thousands of men who turned up in Guildford to the regimental depot of The Queen's (Royal West Surrey Regiment) in autumn 1914 to fight the German Empire, these men did not come as lambs to the slaughter. Instead, they came as nascent citizens doing their duty because their nation and empire called on them. They did their duty and as the war evolved, they changed to meet the challenges meted out upon their survival.

Britain Goes to War

Britain officially declared war on Imperial Germany on 4 August 1914. The proximate reason for British intervention was the German army's invasion

---

6 Charles Douie, *The Weary Road* (London: John Murray, 1929), p.12.
7 Samuel Hynes, *A War Imagined*, (London: Pimlico, 1992), p.ix.
8 The counter-point exists with John Terraine's corpus of scholarship and with Gary Sheffield's *Forgotten Victory* (London: Headline, 1991); for details on the war's memory in Britain specifically, see Daniel Todman, *The Great War: Myth and Memory* (London: Hambledon Continuum, 2005), and Helen McCartney, 'The First World War Soldier and his contemporary image in Britain', *International Affairs*, 90:2, 2014, pp.299–315.

and occupation of Belgium.[9] The German government's decision for war and bellicosity confirmed to some in the British government a deep assumption of its aggressive intentions for militaristic hegemony in Europe. Though a majority in the British cabinet eventually supported intervention, the government approached war with a degree of trepidation.[10] Though the British Empire fought more than its share of wars in the nineteenth century, the last major continental war fought against a European adversary had been far away in the Crimean Peninsula in the 1850s. Indeed, the last time Britain engaged in coalition warfare against a European power bent on aspirations of continental hegemony was against Napoléon in 1815. In the ninety-nine years since Waterloo, the character of warfare had drastically changed: industrialisation, imperialism, and increased populations made for a fateful trifecta that increased the scale and stakes of war and wed the outcome of the next conflict to ideas of national and imperial survival.

When Britain went to war in August 1914, the government did not do so lightly. The British public also understood the seriousness of the moment; their nation and empire had sought to avoid major continental wars for a century and now found itself compelled to defend Belgium and France against a German invasion. Though there were public gatherings in London and jingoistic articles in the press in the first weeks of the war, many Britons were sober in their responses. The most that can be said responsibly is that the public eventually became convinced of the need for intervention, which was not akin to being enthusiastic for war. 'It was possible to believe,' historian Adrian Gregory reminds us 'that war in principle was an inglorious evil, and at the same time believe that Britain had a moral commitment to France, implying that Germany had to be opposed even at the price of war.'[11] The invasion of Belgium carried strategic, moral, and humanitarian reasons that the public understood. As Major General Wilkinson Bird wrote, Britain was at war to 'to defend the weak, and to uphold the freedom of Belgium, even though this involved them in a bitter conflict with a great nation which was already most strong in arms'.[12]

---

9   Richard Hamilton and Holger Herwig, *Decisions for War* (Cambridge: Cambridge University Press, 2004), pp.144–5.
10 Ibid.
11 Adrian Gregory, *The Last Great War* (Cambridge: Cambridge University Press, 2008), p.25.
12 H.C. Wylly, *History of the Queen's Royal (West Surrey) Regiment in the Great War.* (Uckfield, UK: Naval and Military Press, 2009), p.v.

In 1914, however, Britain was not comparatively strong in arms. The BEF was the smallest army of any great power. Professional and well-trained, the British Army numbered at 250,000 men on home service, 150,000 of whom were ready for embarkation abroad. On paper, Britain had a further 750,000 men in the Territorial Army and 340,000 in the reserves.[13] This was not enough men to fight a protracted conflict against a major power. From the outset, the Secretary of State for War, Field Marshal Lord Kitchener, speculated that the war would likely be a long one, and that Britain would have to pull its weight alongside its French ally. Two days after the declaration of war, Parliament authorised the recruitment of 500,000 men to join the ranks of established British regiments. Rather than amalgamating volunteers into existing battalions, the War Office decided to put them into new 'service' battalions for the duration of the war only. These New Army battalions were to be made up of volunteers and commanded by officers with temporary commissions.

Kitchener decided to raise service battalions that bore his name. He believed that it was better for volunteers to start from scratch in new units rather than be brought through the part-time Territorial Army, of which he had a low opinion.[14] Though thousands volunteered in the first weeks of the war, the real boom in recruitment came in late August and September. That was when the BEF first saw combat and the spike in recruitment can be tied to the retreat from Mons, where British forces were pushed back by the invading German army.[15] With the old army in retreat, tens of thousands of men volunteered to aid in the war effort. The last week of August and first of September yielded the highest number of men enlisting – 174,901 – and by mid-September there were 478,893 swamping recruiting depots.[16] Temporary camps were built in a haphazard fashion as the War Office proved completely unprepared to meet the rush.[17] To some degree, the biggest challenge on the Home Front was not the recruiting of a new army to meet the threat, but instead, what to do with the hundreds of thousands of men who were volunteering. The War Office had made little provision for food, shelter, clothing,

13 Ian Beckett, Timothy Bowman and Mark Connelly, *The British Army and the First World War* (Cambridge: Cambridge University Press, 2017), pp.89–90.

14 Ibid, pp.90–91.

15 Alexander Watson, *Enduring the Great War* (Cambridge: Cambridge University Press, 2008), pp.48–9.

16 Becket, Bowman and Connolly, *The British Army*, p.97; Peter Simkins, *Kitchener's Army* (Barnsley, South Yorkshire: Pen & Sword, 2014), p.75.

17 Simkins, *Kitchener's Army*, pp.66–72.

equipment, or even enough officers to command the mob of civilians who now joined the fight.

Surrey Responds to War

Mass enlistment was a national phenomenon that played out locally through regimental depots.[18] Local recruitment did not mean that Kitchener battalions were uniformly 'local' in their composition, but instead that men tended to drift towards regiments that were nearby or ones that had a certain cache for joining. In West Surrey, men signed up with The Queen's (Royal West Surrey Regiment), a regiment with a martial tradition dating back to the seventeenth century.[19] The Queen's had a long list of battle honours in its three centuries of service; it had both local character and prestige. Nicknamed 'the mutton lancers' for their regimental symbol of the pascal lamb, the Queen's traditionally recruited men from West Surrey and nearby London.[20] Over the course of the war, Surrey men served across the world; they were deployed to France, Belgium, India, Afghanistan, Palestine, Gallipoli, Italy, and Mesopotamia.[21] In the first months of the war, there were three service battalions (6–8th) of the Queen's raised of volunteers at Guildford.

The 8th Queen's mustered into service in September 1914. By the second week of September, there were nearly 1,000 recruits corralled at the Exam Field in Shoreham. The first volunteers made their own rough accommodation.[22] They gathered as a strange amalgamation of classes and occupations; there were city men, country farmers, gamekeepers, servants, and industrial workers. The new recruits were hemmed in an open field where hastily erected army tents provided basic shelter. At the start, there was very little to suggest that these men were anything other than civilian squatters camping on a green in Shoreham. They were a vast unequipped mob of civilians.

The first great challenge of their military service was one of basic amenities: by mid–September thousands more volunteers arrived as part of the newly constituted 24th Division. These men needed tents, adequate sanitation, and

---

18 For a history of volunteering in the late Victorian and Edwardian periods, see David French, *Military Identities* (Oxford: Oxford University Press, 2008), Chapter 8.
19 Referred to from here on out as 'The Queen's'.
20 'Regiment Nicknames', https://www.queensroyalsurreys.org.uk/1661to1966/regimental-nicknames/nicknames.shtml.
21 See H.C. Wylly, *History of the Queen's Royal (West Surrey) Regiment in the Great War*, Preface for a summary of the fighting battalions of The Queen's.
22 Simpkins, *Kitchener's Army*, p.238.

food. The regimental historians of the sister 8th Battalion, Royal West Kent Regiment described the situation:

> bell tents were eventually pitched, the men being told off ten to a tent. Later some wet blankets and equally wet loaves were distributed. No feeding utensils were issued for some days, and a piece of wood or newspaper had to serve as a plate, and the fingers as knife, fork, and spoon. The tea invariably had half an inch of grease on the top while the food was almost uneatable.[23]

The second challenge was to make these civilians look like soldiers. They wore their own clothes on their backs for weeks before receiving their temporary uniforms. The men were entirely civilian in their look and disposition: 'at Shoreham the infantry of a whole division, all in mufti, and all, with the exception of a very few officers and a few N.C.O.'s, absolutely untrained.'[24] The third – and by far the most daunting task – was to get the men to act like soldiers. This would take months of hard training outlined in a War Office course of instruction, much of which they were not able to fulfil due to a lack of rifles and equipment. Any casual military observer in the first weeks would have recognised the herculean effort in taking a mass of civilians in mufti and making it into a fit unit.[25]

Most of the first volunteers hailed from nearby villages and towns in Surrey. Beyond this local core, there was a contingent from London and according to the battalion's history, nearly one full company – B Company – from Kent.[26] These men were from Ramsgate and Margate and originally intended to enlist in The Buffs but ended up in the Queen's.[27] The average age of the original battalion at Shoreham was 24.5, but there was a wide spectrum,

---

23 H.J. Wenyon and H.S. Brown, *The Eighth Battalion The Queen's Own Royal West Kent Regiment 1914–1919* (Naval and Military Press, 2021), p.2. Originally published in 1921.
24 Ibid., p.3.
25 Surrey History Centre (SHC), QRWS/18/2, 'Unpublished anonymous history of the 8th Service Battalion, 1914–1919'. Quoted by permission of the Surrey History Centre. Copyright of the Surrey History Centre. These details are from an unpublished battalion history found in the Surrey History Centre, which contains a number of colourful anecdotes. Hereafter, for brevity's sake it will be referred to as 'SHC, Unpublished Battalion History'.
26 SHC, Unpublished Battalion History, 1.
27 Ibid.

from teenagers who lied about their age to those firmly in middle-age.[28] There was a mix of those who knew something of the world, that is men with professions and families, and those who knew little beyond school and their parents' rules. Like other Kitchener battalions, many came from working-class backgrounds, yet there were also middle-class men in the ranks and a wide variety of occupations represented. Though a local 'Surrey' battalion, there were also soldiers from all over the United Kingdom and of varying occupations; there were farmers, factory workers, houseboys, gardeners, shopkeepers, dockworkers, clerks, and even a few former soldiers who came back to the colours.

Just as there was not one kind of soldier who joined in 1914, there was no universal motivation for enlisting. Though the 'rush to the colours' has been interpreted by some since with a sense of implied tragedy – of young men drawn by the state ignorant of the ramifications of their enlistment – the motivations of Kitchener volunteers were complicated. In his landmark study *Kitchener's Army*, Peter Simkins writes, 'the social, political, and economic forces which drove men to enlist were far more varied and complex than these writers have implied. Patriotism in 1914 encompassed many subtle shades and nuances.'[29] Among motivations of those enlisting were genuine enthusiasm, patriotic duty, outrage at the German army's actions in Belgium, and a belief that vital British national security was at risk.[30] Like all wars, some enlisted because of a crowd mentality, the social pressures whether they be jingoism or of the martial burden of manhood, factors that were often felt but usually unspoken.[31] For many there was also an authentic hope that war was adventurous or exciting, particularly compared to the complacency of working as a clerk or the dangerous difficulty of industrial work. Walter Hitchcock, a gamekeeper at Lord Ashcombe's large estate at Denbies, recalled that he wanted to enlist from the start and that 'most fellows did not think it would

---

28 This has been calculated from the battalion's casualties at Loos. The battalion's casualties are a large and random sampling of men across all four companies.

29 Simkins, *Kitchener's Army*, p.165.

30 Alexander Watson, *Enduring the Great War*, pp.47–9; See also Adrian Gregory, 'British "War Enthusiasm" in 1914: A Reassessment', in G. Braybon (ed.), *Evidence, History, and the Great War* (New York: Berghahn Books, 2003).

31 Toby Thacker, '"Your country needs you": why did so many volunteer in 1914', *The Conversation*, https://theconversation.com/your-country-needs-you-why-did-so-many-volunteer-in-1914–30443.

be a bad job.'[32] Some also sought to escape underemployment or unemployment, two factors that often forced young men to emigrate to the dominions or to the United States to find opportunity before the war.[33] Those men now sought opportunity and adventure in France. For many there were multiple motivations at play in their minds at the same time; humans, then just as now, are capable of having consistent, conflicted, and even contradictory reasons to take the king's shilling and go to war.

Once arriving in camp and under canvas, the men had to be controlled, conditioned, and commanded by commissioned and non-commissioned officers. In this regard, the 8th Queen's benefited by having senior officers who had some military experience. In September 1914, the War Office 'dug out' of retirement Colonel Frederick Howard Fairtlough CMG, as the battalion's first commanding officer. Born in 1860 to a military family, Fairtlough was a career army officer in the Queen's. He commanded the regiment's 3rd Battalion in the South African War, where he distinguished himself as an effective leader of volunteers. After South Africa, he continued to command the regiment's militia until his retirement. He had vast experience training men and had a talent for turning civilians into soldiers. Fairtlough was also a part of the West Surrey establishment, living at Catteshall Manor near Goldalming. He was a devoted husband and father and was committed to his children's education and moral upbringing.[34] Fairtlough's son Eric followed his father into the army. In August 1914, while his father was putting on his old uniform, his son was serving in France as an officer in the BEF. The battalion could have done far worse and little better in their selection of a tried-and-true local officer with experience training volunteers.

Fairtlough was lucky to be joined by other officers who had varying degrees of military experience. His most trusted lieutenant was his adjutant, Hugh John Chevallier 'Jack' Peirs, who had served with Fairtlough as a subaltern in the militia before the war. Peirs was a 28-year-old solicitor who lived with his parents in a well-to-do named house, Queen's Well, in Carshalton. His father, Hugh Vaughan Peirs, was a partner in a profitable

---

32 Walter Hitchcock, Oral History, https://walterhitchcock-ww1.blogspot.com/search?updated-max=2015–11–05T13:09:00–08:00&max-results=7&start=1&by-date=false.

33 Jay Winter, *The Great War and the British People* (New York: Palgrave, 2003), pp.266–70.

34 IWM, Doc. 12610, Papers of Major General E.V.H. Fairtlough, DSO, MC. This collection contains Fairtlough's intimate correspondence to his family from both the Boer War as well as the first year of the First World War.

London law firm that had a fashionable address at 17 Albemarle Street in Mayfair. The elder Hugh Peirs married Charlotte Sophia Paull and they had four children – three daughters and a son, Jack. Peirs had a typical upbringing for a member of his class; he was educated at Charterhouse and then New College, Oxford, where he read law and played football. After Oxford, Peirs was commissioned into the militia and then followed in his father's footsteps as a clerk in his firm. At the outbreak of war, Peirs was a practising solicitor with a few years of parade-ground military experience in the militia; he was given a temporary commission as a lieutenant and he followed his old colonel's lead into the 8th Queen's. Peirs was quickly promoted to captain and then appointed adjutant. In 1915, he was promoted to major and became Fairtlough's second-in-command.

Though they had a close working relationship, there was a generational difference between the two senior officers of the battalion, one that did not create any noticeable tension, but was surely present. Fairtlough was a middle-aged man with a military career behind him. He was used to the way the British Army did things and he had the mentality of a career soldier. This is not to say that Fairtlough was stuck in his ways or past his prime, but it is to indicate that he bore similarity with the hundreds of other early-war battalion commanders upon whom the rigors of war would be keenly felt; change often comes slower to those who have lived an entire life or career doing things one particular way. This new war would be one of many changes and adaptations, ones with which many career officers struggled. Peter Hodkinson's study of British battalion commanders in the First World War indicates that the early war colonels were a mixed bag of varying effectiveness. The most significant impediments to an middle-aged reactivated officer's ability to command were attitude, physical stamina, and up-to-date knowledge of tactics/modern warfare.[35] Though many early commanders failed the test in one or all of these areas, Fairtlough worked against the limitations in all three.[36] Yet, his age also meant that he was less resilient both physically and mentally than his younger officers; in a war of attrition fought in often appalling conditions, resilience and stamina were key aspects of consistent command. Like other competent senior commanders

---

35 Peter Hodkinson, *British Battalion Commanders in the First World War* (London: Ashgate, 2015), pp.36–8.

36 In the next chapter on Loos, the question concerning the difficulties of command is addressed.

dug out of retirement, it is possible that had Fairtlough lived beyond 1915, there was a chance he would have been promoted to brigade command or – especially with his militia experience – given a role training new recruits back in England. Moreover, in addition to being an efficient officer, he was deeply respected by the men under his command. As Peirs wrote of him in reflection, 'I cannot imagine any better man being given a battalion to raise & train. He was ceaselessly at work on his men's behalf & he practically never took a holiday and only occasionally did he even go away for a Sunday. It was entirely due to his energy and perseverance that the Battalion reached the standard it did.'[37]

Training in England was fundamentally different than surviving the rigors of active service abroad. Peirs was a young-ish and eager volunteer who maintained close connections with home throughout the war. Though he had some military training and appears in his photographs and written demeanor to be every inch the British Army officer, Peirs was a civilian first and foremost. A former militia officer, he did not seek a regular commission before the war and instead went into the law where he was a clubby solicitor with a stylish address in Mayfair. He was one of the thousands of temporary officers who became a new type of commander for a new type of citizen-soldier.[38] As Hodkinson's study indicates, Peirs's background was typical of the eventual 'Citizen CO'. He came from an upper-middle class background, went to public school where he excelled in team sports, and had a stable profession before the war.[39] Though not raised specifically to be a warrior, he was indoctrinated through his background for leadership. At 28 years of age in 1914, he was young enough to be healthy and adaptable; if he did not get killed or break down under the strain, Peirs could grow into his command.

Unlike many other Kitchener battalions, the 8th Queen's had some officers of previous service. Major Alfred Grylls served as an officer in the Middlesex Regiment in the Boer War and was commissioned in the Queen's at 39 years of age to command C Company in 1915.[40] Captain Cyril Cooke also had expe-

---

37 IWM, Doc. 12610, Papers of Major General E.V.H. Fairtlough DSO MC, Vol. 7, Letter 479, H.J.C. Peirs to Maud Fairtlough, 10 October 1915.
38 See Marco Dracopoli, 'A New Officer for a New Army: The Leadership of Major Hugh J.C. Peirs in the Great War', *The Gettysburg Historical Journal*: Vol. 13, Article 6. Available at: https://cupola.gettysburg.edu/ghj/vol13/iss1/6.
39 Hodkinson, *British Battalion Commanders*, pp.161–5.
40 'O.M. Obituary,' *The Malvernian*, December 1941, No. CCCCLXXX.

rience in South Africa.[41] Captain (later Major) George Fox had previously been a second lieutenant in the Queen's and had resigned his commission in 1906, before then returning to take command of B Company in 1914.[42] The rest of the subalterns who commanded its platoons were of more limited experience, though some had training in Officer Training Corps (OTC) from their public schools. As far as Kitchener battalions went, the 8th Queen's had a good foundation and were not starting entirely from scratch.

Similar to units in the pre-war army, the battalion's first cohort of officers came from privileged backgrounds and there was a class division between officers and many of the men under their command. The classism of the British Army at the time might seem jarring, but it reflected existing social divisions. Many of the middle-class officers of the Queen's had been born into privilege and were educated in a system that indoctrinated boys to be future leaders of the nation and empire.[43] Lord Kitchener and his staff at the War Office believed that the need for officers could be accommodated through the public schools and university Officer Training Corps.[44] At the start of the war in particular, officers were commissioned largely because of their position in society, their family background, and their education at the right sort of schools. As such, they came from the same social demographic – the upper-middle class – and consisted of men who had been through the same educational system.[45] Officers shared a background and a culture; they sounded largely the same, used the same slang, read similar books, wrote with similar styles of handwriting, had their uniforms tailored and their equipment purchased from the same providers, and they placed social emphasis on a certain standard of mess life and comradeship.

Though officers were certainly privileged, this did not mean that they were soft. In many ways upper-class officers were emotionally prepared for hardship, though this is not the same thing as being desensitised to mass violence. Public school life was often harsh in its discipline, draconian in its

---

41 'Canadian War Graves Project', https://canadiangreatwarproject.com/person.php?pid=41548

42 *The London Gazette*, 21 April 1903, 2529; *The Civil & Military Gazette*, 10 April 1906, p.8.

43 See Michael Roper, 'Between Manliness and Masculinity: The "War Generation" and the Psychology of Fear in Britain, 1914–1950', *Journal of British Studies* 44 (April 2005) and Peter Parker's book *The Old Lie: The Great War and the Public School Ethos* (London: Continuum, 2007).

44 Simpkins, *Kitchener's Army*, pp.212–13.

45 Ibid., pp.212–23.

rules and customs, and frequently spartan in terms of its living conditions.[46] In such an environment, boys learned emotional control and to repress their feelings. In Edwardian England, public schools were perceived to be an important part of molding and indoctrinating the next generation of men to lead the Empire with martial spirit and emotional endurance.[47] As the war continued, there were not enough upper-middle class public school-educated men left, and more and more men were promoted from the ranks. This created a different cadre of officers who largely earned their place in command and who understood the lives of the men they commanded more intimately. The surviving officers' service records of the 8th Queen's indicate that after 1916, many of the battalion's junior officers came from a broader social demographic, many of whom had spent some time in the ranks.

The Western Front – Winter 1914–15

As the 8th Battalion began their training in the autumn of 1914, the war raged in France and Belgium with horrendous brutality. In the opening campaigns, the French, German, and British armies suffered terrible casualties due to manoeuvre warfare. High casualties necessitated the beginnings of trench warfare; rudimentary field fortifications initially thwarted increasingly costly assaults. The first trenches on the Western Front emerged from shallow fire-pits dug to protect infantry while firing prone or kneeling behind hastily dug ramparts. Concentrated and rapid artillery fire drove men deeper into the ground; the Western Front, as it would be known, was scraped into existence out of the soil of northern France by infantry desperate to protect themselves. By December 1914, trench lines stretched across northern France and Belgium. It was in Ypres that the last desperate and terrible battle of the year raged, as the German army attempted to regain the advantage before the year's ending.

It is difficult to imagine the shock of those first few months of war to the men fighting on the Western Front. Rank and file British infantry training focussed on musketry – in particular rapid aimed fire – and tactical movement, skills which were ingrained in army doctrine and that proved

---

46 Peter Parker, *The Old Lie*, pp.36–8.
47 Michael Roper, 'Between Manliness and Masculinity: The "War Generation" and the Psychology of Fear in Britain, 1914–1950', *Journal of British Studies* 44 (April 2005), pp.344–8.

important on the Western Front.[48] Tactically, the BEF was not much worse off than their German or French counterparts – indeed likely much better off in fact – but defensive firepower from machine guns and especially from artillery, changed the dynamic of movement and severely tested its training. Simply put, high casualties, in particular officers and NCOs, meant that battalions were reduced rapidly to skeletons, their combat effectiveness diminishing by the day. In all armies, the casualties meted out in the first months of the war could not be sustained over the long term; there would be no functional armies left unless a defensive solution was found.

Among the first units in the BEF to be deployed to the Western Front was the 1st Queen's, the parent unit of the 8th Battalion. The 1st Queen's was professional to its core and led by career officers. Both its senior commissioned officers and NCOs were of long service and the men in the battalion were well trained. In August 1914, the battalion was at the parade ground at Bordon after coming off brigade manoeuvres near Aldershot. The battalion mobilised on 5 August and three days later was ready for war.[49] Their mobilisation complete, the battalion embarked on 12 August with 998 regular army officers and men.

In France, the 1st Queen's marched towards Mons in Belgium and encountered the invading German army. Outnumbered and outflanked, the British Army began a general retirement south towards the French army. Pursued and retreating, the 1st Queen's marched 200 miles until their situation stabilised in the first week of September.[50] The 1st Battalion participated in the big battles of the war's opening act: the First Battle of the Marne, the Battle of the Aisne, and the First Battle of Ypres. The latter proved catastrophic. Through open warfare and then in bloody desperate actions with rudimentary field fortifications, the small professional core of the old British Army was bled white.

The 1st Queen's fared badly. Arriving back in Belgium in October, the battalion had already been badly battered through two months of campaigning. On 23 October, the battalion lost a further 135 men near Langemark. The next week the battalion took to trenches near Gheluvelt at a crucial junction on the Menin Road outside of Ypres. In two days of fighting, the battalion

---

48 Spencer Jones, *From Boer War to Great War* (Norman, OK: University of Oklahoma Press, 2012), pp.87–8.
49 Wylly, *History of the Queen's*, p.8.
50 Ibid., pp.14–15.

lost nine officers and 624 men killed, wounded, or missing.[51] Only thirty-two men were accounted the next day.[52] Ten days later, the battalion mustered only 179 survivors, fewer than the regular complement of an infantry company.[53] By the end of 1914, twenty-six out of twenty-seven of their officers were casualties and the battalion as a whole was reduced to a few platoons.[54] The ordeal of the 1st Queen's was typical for the old contemptables that fought for their lives to thwart the German invasion. The deterioration of the old army necessitated the training and deployment of the new army as soon as possible.

Training the Battalion

The first task of that new army was to equip and train men who were at their core civilians and who knew nothing of the tactical challenges faced at the front in December 1914. As mentioned earlier, the first volunteers of the 8th Queen's arrived by train at the 24th Division's mobilisation site, Oxen Field, outside of Shoreham, in the second week of September. Volunteers were sorted into companies and platoons and put under the command of their new subalterns and NCOs. For nearly two months they learned rudimentary drill during the days and slept under blankets in the chilly nights of the early autumn. In November – two months after their enlistment – they were issued their first uniforms in Kitchener blue. The battalion still lacked proper equipment and had no rifles. The men's first impression of army life was shambolic.

By November, it was apparent that the tent city at Shoreham had become a hinderance to the health of the men. Huts were being built for winter accommodation, but they took time to construct. As the weather turned, the men patiently waited for better shelter. The situation proved dire when, on 1 December, heavy rains flooded the camp.[55] Mudslides had turned the camp into a vast bog.[56] As the winter weather would only get worse, the divi-

---

51 Ibid., p.24.

52 A detailed look at their ordeal can be found through Andrew Arnold's scholarship on his website: https://ww1geek.com/2012/10/31/1st-queens-at-gheluvelt/.

53 Wylly, *History of the Queen's*, p.26.

54 Ibid., p.9.

55 SHC, Unpublished Battalion History, p.2.

56 Peirs claimed that the mud on the Western Front was not as bad as that at Shoreham. See Special Collections, Musselman Library, Gettysburg College, MS-250 The First World War Letters of H.J.C. Peirs, Peirs to his father, 26 October 1915. Subsequent correspondence from Peirs comes from this collection unless otherwise noted.

sion broke up to find better accommodation. The 8th Queen's moved to more suitable billets in Worthing. So far, their first three months of service had demonstrated the limitations of the War Office to supply its volunteers. Yet, despite the haphazard way in which these men were mustered into service, they were adjusting to army life. As 1915 approached, the men had the vague appearance of soldiers in uniform and were capable of basic parade ground drill by platoon and company.

By the New Year the battalion was fully formed, clothed, and commanded by a full complement of officers. The battalion, now in the 24th Division, consisted of just over 1,000 men subdivided into four companies. Each company had 227 men in it and was led by 6 officers. Each company was then subdivided into four platoons, each commanded by a lieutenant and then further divided into four sections under a lance corporal. The 8th Queen's joined three other New Army battalions to form the 72nd Brigade. All these 'sister' battalions were all raised from the southeastern counties of Surrey and Kent and were made up of the same cohort of men – K3 – or the third 100,000-men cohort to volunteer for service.[57] Surrey became something of a garrison county; it not only hosted 72nd Brigade, but also the rest of the 24th Division, consisting of the 71st and 73rd brigades as well as the divisional artillery, medical, and logistical support arms – 18,000 men in the division alone – training for deployment as desperately needed reinforcements for the campaigns of 1915.

The battalion trained in earnest while they were in Worthing. After Christmas, they received their first khaki uniforms and a few rifles to begin basic musketry at the range. The men were billeted in civilian homes, some enjoying their landlords, while others felt the arrangement was an awkward one. Walter Hitchcock recalled:

> I got a rotten billet, some of these blokes got billets and they used to say 'Oh we had bacon and eggs for breakfast and we had this, that and the other', you know, and the old woman that I was billeted with – it was corned beef and bread and butter and skilly, you

---

57 In addition to the 8th Queen's, the 72nd Brigade consisted of the 9th East Surreys, the 8th Buffs, and the 8th Queen's Own (West Kent) battalions.

know, and, er, we got there – she reckoned that her old man was running about after her niece.[58]

In the evenings, the men enjoyed themselves and appear to have been generally treated well by locals; during their service, many of the original battalion returned to visit Worthing on leave from the front.[59] The officers were billeted comfortably at the Warne's Hotel, an elegant tourist hostelry. In Worthing, the men began to look and feel like soldiers.

Though the winter precluded serious training, better weather in the spring led to route marches and training with their arms. Most of this was at company rather than battalion level. Notably, the battalion went on their first forced march of 30 miles and became proficient at the range. Their first historian wrote:

> every man had been through a course of musketry on the miniature range and had been thoroughly instructed in the first principles of shooting, officers & NCOs had been taught to pick up targets and deliver passable fire orders, and all ranks had been instructed in trench digging and above all everyone was thoroughly fit and learnt to work in unison and their keenness had not been abated.[60]

Their spadework was put to the test when the battalion transferred on Good Friday 1915 to Reigate, where they spent two weeks digging defenses for London. From there they went back to Shoreham, to their new huts. There they joined the rest of the division for their most serious training in the late spring and summer of 1915.

How did the training of the 8th Queen's fare with other Kitchener battalions? And was it adequate for the task allotted to them? The army planned for a six-month training regimen in August 1914 for New Army volunteers. The emphasis was on physical conditioning, acclimation to army life, and elementary drill in the first few weeks, followed by more sophisticated training in arms and in company/battalion manouevres later. The sheer fact that the 8th Queen's did not have uniforms or equipment for the first two months

---

58 Walter Hitchcock, Oral History, https://walterhitchcock-ww1.blogspot.com/search?updated-max=2015-11-05T13:09:00-08:00&max-results=7&start=1&by-date=false.
59 SHC, Unofficial Battalion History, pp.2–3.
60 Ibid., p.3.

of their existence indicates that the army's training regimen, while logical, was hopelessly optimistic. Moreover, most of the junior officers and NCOs were also learning their jobs as they went along, further compounding the hopes of the army for men to master their craft in small units – at the squad or platoon level – before then branching out to company and battalion-sized training; the most experienced officers in the Queen's were at the top of the battalion's command structure, the least experienced at platoon level. The Queen's did, however, have an advantage in their core component of senior officers that some other New Army battalions did not; they had a colonel who had spent most of his career training citizen-soldiers.

By spring, the men were in khaki and finally had their rifles. Seven months after enlisting, they were able to train in all areas of the army curriculum. Time was not wasted that winter. The men were physically conditioned, had mastered small-scale drill, and were reasonably acclimated to army life. Once they had their rifles, they trained in marksmanship, which was the bedrock of British infantry tactics. James Norman Hall, a recruit in the 9th Royal Fusiliers, defined musketry as 'instructed in the description and recognition of targets, the use of cover, but chiefly in the use of our rifles. Through constant handling they became a part of us, a third arm which we grew to use quite instinctively.'[61] He recalled that when men had mastered the 'mad minute' of firing fifteen aimed rounds a minute, they ceased to be recruits and were considered soldiers.[62] In reality, training was more complex than just popping off fifteen rounds. 'Marksmanship did not simply consist of shooting on the range, but also included judging distance and understanding enough theory of small-arms fire to be able to aim off for wind or at a moving target,' wrote Richard Holmes.[63] Like Hall's battalion, the Queen's were 'thoroughly' instructed in musketry in the spring of 1915 and began learning basic infantry tactics.[64]

One of the great clichés of the First World War soldier was that he fought a twentieth-century war with nineteenth-century tactics. The training of Kitchener's Army reflects a different reality. Coming out of the Boer War, the British Army reconsidered its infantry tactics and applied lessons learned in South Africa. They emphasised fire and movement and extended order

---

61 James Norman Hall, *Kitchener's Mob*, p.27.
62 Ibid., p.28.
63 Richard Holmes, *Tommy* (London: Harper Perennial, 2005), pp.377–8.
64 SHC, Unofficial Battalion History, pp.4–5.

assaults rather than dense offensive formations. Spencer Jones writes that 'combining extension tactics with the use of cover and rapid, irregular rushes from point to point, the British infantry was among the best prepared in Europe to face modern rifle fire on a tactical level.'[65] Recruits learned rapid, aimed fire and how to assault positions in rushes under covering fire from supporting units. The system of fire and movement was the foundation of British infantry tactics throughout the war, with some tactical modifications to meet the changing character of war on the Western Front. In 1914–15, the 8th Queen's were trained in this manner; they learned musketry and unit drill from the squad to the battalion level. They drilled in extension order advances over open ground and learned to attack in rushes to overcome an enemy position.[66] As their training progressed and became more sophisticated, the men drilled and did 'mock' attacks in larger formations. They also learned how to entrench and defend positions.

In June 1915, the battalion moved back to Shoreham. The men now billeted in huts spaced apart from one another by dusty streets that created a drab scene. Officers and men took to planting flowers and gardened to make their environment look more presentable. Over the next two months they entered a more strenuous and extensive period of training, notably going on longer and longer forced marches as the weather improved. In July, the division marched to Blackdown, near Farnborough, their last training camp in England before they embarked for France. In Blackdown, they trained in both day and night operations at brigade level.[67] In July, the 24th Division were inspected by Lord Kitchener and later by King George V as they dug a mock trench in Chobham Common.[68] Their inspection by the secretary of state for war, as well as the king, was the last notable event for the division before they received their orders for France.

There was a huge difference in the battalion that paraded before the king and the mob that assembled in Shoreham ten months before. The men looked and carried themselves as soldiers. They drilled at company, battalion, and brigade level. They trained in tactics and musketry. Officers attended staff rides, listened to countless lectures, and learned how to command their men. The men marched and marched and marched; they learned how best

---

65 Spencer Jones, *From Boer War to World War*, p.88.
66 Ibid., pp.87–8.
67 SHC, Unofficial Battalion History, p.6.
68 *Western Daily Press*, 21 August 1915, p.5.

to carry their equipment, when to drink from their water bottles, how to function as a collective unit, and how to support one another. They were also physically fit; the 'same physical standard was practically never again reached.'[69] Hauntingly, they would also never be as healthy again, mentally and physically, as they were in England.

Parade ground training and the firing range were very different than real combat on the Western Front. This is not to diminish from the job in which the officers and the NCOs of the Queen's did, but only to reveal a basic but important part of their story – that virtually none of them knew how they would act under the stress of battle and whether their training had adequately prepared them for life on campaign or in the trenches. Combat removes all veneers; the moment when men feel crippling fear, when their mettle would be tested against soldiers who had more than parade ground confidence. The first great casualty was the battalion's optimistic belief in their own abilities, which for the moment ran as high as their spirits, as they waited for their deployment to France.

Embarkation

It was only a matter of time before the battalion went to France. They had trained for ten months and worked hard to get fit for life on campaign; the day was coming fast when their marching, their digging, and their musketry training would be put to use. Both of the New Army divisions training in southeastern England – the 21st and 24th respectively – were badly needed at the front, where the British Army was planning its largest military operation of the war so far. This offensive would take place in the Artois region in late September. Both the 21st and 24th divisions formed the bulk of the general reserve for the army; once their training was complete, they were to embark to France.

The day was fast approaching. In the third week of August, the men were granted a few days' leave and encouraged to visit their families. This was a clear signal that deployment was coming soon. The men scattered across southern England, most to their homes in Surrey, Kent or London, where they said their farewells to friends and family, mothers, and sweethearts. Men ate familiar meals and sipped beer at their local pubs. Their relatives noted their martial bearing in the physically fit specimens that these men

---

69 SHC, Unofficial Battalion History, p.8

had become. For more adventurous soldiers, the many temptations for soldiers on leave in London called. On 27 August 1915 the men were recalled. Embarkation was merely days away.

On the morning of 28 August, the battalion paraded at Blackdown. Most were tired from leave and many were suffering from, if not an actual, then certainly an emotional hangover. Some, no doubt, also had bleary eyes from the last few days of revelry, barely making the midnight curfew the night before, and sleeping the beery sleep of young men's overindulgence before parade. Yet, they stood at attention that morning in their neat platoon and company formations. Their uniforms were cleaner than they would be at any point in the next few months.

One thousand men with the appearance of ubiquity, a fighting unit made from a mob in eleven months. Their heights varied, as did their physical form, but each man wore the same khaki uniform, which they had learned by the bellowing of NCOs how to keep them clean. Upon their caps all wore the regimental badge, inheritors of one of the oldest regimental symbols in England. Through stubborn conditioning over eleven months, each man bore his pack confidently, as he learned to do on forced marches. Unlike a year before, each could now bear the weight of his kit and knew the tricks of carrying it correctly and comfortably. Each man held in his hand a Short Magazine Lee-Enfield rifle, with measured confidence.

If the men looked smart divided into their companies, then their officers looked even smarter. There were young(ish) lieutenants and captains wearing uniforms that separated them by both rank and class from their men. At the front was their colonel, distinguished, grayed, mustachioed and broad-chested, a fine martial figure on his horse. The officers wore tailored tunics, breeches, puttees and boots, the silhouette of the British infantry officer looking more like a man about to go foxhunting rather than sitting in a muddy dugout. Another important part of regimental life was their field music. The band was a particular source of delight to both Colonel Fairtlough and Major Peirs. Both men had a sense of historical pride in their regiment that was manifested and demonstrated by all that they had done over the past year to turn this motley crew into soldiers. If they had any reservations about their training or performance, it was too late now; the battalion was set to be in France in four days' time.

On Saturday, 28 August 1915 the battalion packed for war. On the Monday, Peirs left Blackdown with two lieutenants and 106 men in advance of their deployment. This small command consisted of pioneers and drivers that bore the battalion's baggage, carts, and mules. Before leaving, Peirs quickly visited his mother to say goodbye.[70] With his men and the battalion's baggage, he then boarded a railway coach to Southampton. They crossed to Le Havre on an old passenger ship. Below, his men and beasts were housed together as they lumbered under warship escort towards the French coast. They disembarked in darkness with the usual military disorganisation and delays. Some of their ammunition was thrown overboard and their pack saddles 'disappeared'.[71] The harbor was a messy scene of men and beasts, not all of whom were cooperative. They forced their horses and mules on trains and then embarked northwards to meet the rest of the battalion at Boulogne. Their journey from Surrey managed to be two contradictory things – it was both painfully slow and anxiously hectic.

While Peirs was in France fighting with mules and arguing with inspectors and quartermasters about lost stores, the rest of the 900 men in the battalion marched through Guildford with their band playing. The town turned out to cheer them before they embarked via Folkestone. The battalion arrived at Boulogne shortly after midnight on 31 August. They rested the following day and then met Peirs and their transport. They marched 12 miles to Herly, where they billeted on a farm. The men were put into 'filthy' barns and their company commanders in houses nearby. The battalion HQ set up in the local mayor's house. The men adjusted, it seems, relatively quickly. They cleaned out their billets and scrounged food from the locals.[72] The weather was bad and too wet to do anything. When the weather broke on Sunday, they had their first church service in an orchard, the smell of fruit ripening in the early autumn all around, the men receiving their holy rite in the bucolic countryside of rural France, now militarised with the presence of a brigade of foreign infantry. Their crossing safe, their first days uneventful, the battalion went to 'the war' with a carefree sense of their own purpose and the confidence of soldiers who had prepared the better part of a year for this moment to prove their courage.

---

70 Peirs to his mother, 4 September 1915.
71 Ibid.
72 Ibid.

Chapter 2

On Active Service

The officer stood about twenty paces from his target. He lifted his service revolver and pulled the trigger. The pistol kicked as the heavy .455 slug shot off into the void, wild of its target. He lifted the weighty Webley once more and fired with the same poor result. It certainly did not help his shooting that his second-in-command was next to him. His subordinate was twenty-five years younger and had the keen aim of a West Surrey local rifle club champion.[1] His eyes were young and his hands steady when he levelled his pistol. Peirs aimed his weapon and his shot came home.

The Commanding Officer (CO) had not been to war for fifteen years. In South Africa, Howard Fairtlough had commanded a battalion of volunteers at mostly garrison and guard duty. A photograph in his family papers shows a handsome soldier at the prime of his service. Now, at 54, Fairtlough was firmly in middle-age and in the sore-in-the-saddle phase of his military career. Though substantially older than his other officers, in 1915 he was not too old to fight, but he was perhaps past his prime for sustained campaigning, with its bad food, restless nights, and raw conditions. Commanding a battalion was difficult physically; it was also hard emotionally, especially for a career soldier who had a reputation to uphold. Unlike South Africa, this volunteer battalion was going into action against one of the finest armies in the world and on a vastly different battlefield.

The battalion had only been in France for two weeks, but Major Peirs noticed the fatigue on his commanding officer's face and his increasing irritability. More substantial, perhaps, was that Fairtlough seemed to be overwhelmed. Peirs wrote home after shooting with him that he 'gets so awfully nervous & rattled nowadays that Lord only knows what he will be like when we get further up. I suppose it will be my job to keep him soothed, though

---

1 'Shooting: Carshalton v. Warlingham,' *Dorking and Leatherhead Advertiser,* 1 November 1913.

I don't fancy it very much.'[2] Though his tone here might seem sophomoric or uncharitable, Peirs had known Fairtlough for eight years. And Fairtlough had every reason to worry. He was a life-long army officer, but his experience training volunteer militiamen did not exactly prepare him for what awaited the battalion as it went up the line. Indeed, there was very little that could have prepared him – or any other battalion commander – for what would happen once they came under fire.

Somewhere in France

In the first year of the war the Western Front changed significantly. Within weeks in August 1914, generals faced a conundrum as they commanded mass armies in indecisive battles that yielded tens of thousands of casualties. Martin Gilbert wrote of the opening months that 'the war of rapid victories became a strategy of the past, and a dream for the future.'[3] The failed open attacks of 1914, with their staggering losses, did not inspire confidence in the ability of commanders and their staffs to prepare and manage major engagements. The hope of commanders in 1915 lay within the ability to break through the enemy's trench lines and force a return to open warfare. This was a challenge taken up by both the British and French general staffs.

At BEF headquarters, Field Marshal Sir John French and his staff attempted to understand the changing war and to adapt accordingly through trial-and-error efforts to break the deadlock. These attempts were met with limited successes, but more often with failure and tragically high loss of life. 'Any study of the British Army on the Western Front in 1915 makes for bleak reading,' summarises historian Spencer Jones.[4] The strategic situation facing the British proved dismal and the army was still painfully inadequate in terms of manpower and material to wage a sustained effort on the Western Front.[5] More directly, in this theatre of war there were two crises: one was of shells, a matter of industrial production; the other was of manpower, a matter of raising and training a mass army for deployment abroad. Both came to a head in 1915. It is perhaps too much to say that the war in 1915 devolved into

---

2   Peirs to his family, 17 September 1915.

3   Martin Gilbert, *The First World War*, (New York: Henry Holt and Company, 1994), p.77.

4   Spencer Jones, 'To make war as we must, and not as we should like': The British Army and the Problem of the Western Front, 1915' in Spencer Jones (ed.), *Courage without Glory*, p.31.

5   Ibid., pp.31–2.

a crisis of military thinking; but it is not too much to say that it was a year of discouragement and disappointments at all levels and along all fronts.

When the 8th Queen's deployed to France in September 1915 they were aware of the deadlock in front of them, but were still optimistic in their own part to play. Like other New Army battalions, they confidently wanted to play their part in the show that was coming. The battalion had parade ground experience, but little advanced tactical training in brigade or divisional manoeuvres. Without combat experience as a guide, battalion and brigade staff had only theoretical knowledge of how their men would conduct themselves under fire for the first time. One of the many hard lessons learned in France during the First World War was the cost of inexperience, whether at the level of the general staff, or that of the lance corporal in charge of a section. Experience proved the great genesis of change in military thinking from 1914 to 1918, but it did so at an enormous cost as battalions learned painful lessons and slowly adapted to the evolving war.

Inexperience is not the same thing as ignorance. It is hard to imagine that any man in the 24th Division expected anything other than hard service once they arrived in France. But there is a vast difference in anticipatory knowledge and the wisdom gleaned through action and experience. What most knew of the war came from the British press, which was firmly within the orbit of propagandists, but still endeavoured to report realities of the front: the trenches, the casualty numbers, the difficult and dirty work done over the last year. These temporal details were all well known. For soldiers who had relatives serving abroad, they also had a glimpse of the front from their letters home, depending upon the frankness of the correspondent.

For example, Colonel Fairtlough's son Eric served as an artillery officer from August 1914 and wrote home regularly to his father. He witnessed the opening battles of the war and wrote about the conditions he faced. Describing a German attack being thwarted by British machine guns, he wrote instructionally of a 'few things the war has shown that may be helpful to you …'

1. It is impossible to advance in any close formation under modern artillery fire.
2. Trenches must be narrow, & about 4 ft deep. The narrower the better.

3. The importance of accurate shooting & good fire discipline. This is where we have a great pull over the Germans.
4. Trenches must always be dug as soon as [a] position is taken.[6]

Officers like Eric Fairtlough learned to adapt to the new style of warfare, but this learning took time. His father knew that it was his task to take a cheerful and green lot of civilian-soldiers and prepare them for their first battle where his son's tactical warnings were to be realised.

The future was, of course, unknown to Peirs and Fairtlough as they practised their pistolry together. What they did know was the task in front of them. Since arriving, the battalion trained further with their entrenching tools. Peirs described to his family the men scratching about in the dirt. The men noticed the morbid irony of their grave-like firepits and Peirs wrote, 'When they had dug their holes, which of course look like a line of graves when finished, they have to be filled in & I noticed to-day that each grave has been finished with a little + or tombstone at the head. It was most pathetic till you realised what the young devils were like, who treat such topics so lightly.'[7]

Of course, Peirs, too, was treating the war lightly in his own way with his anthropological observations about the men and the French 'natives' with whom they were billeted. In the same letter he wrote of how his only entertainment of late was tormenting a brigade staff officer who had gotten 'too big for his boots', treating him like he would a nosy prefect at Charterhouse.[8] Indeed, there is something schoolboyish about his first month's letters home, where he relishes in teasing the staff, complains about his billets, and writes of the French as though they were a nuisance to his enjoyment of their country. He received packages and hampers from Fortnum's and requested his father send deflated footballs so that he could organise matches for the men. While his colonel fretted about the men's preparedness and his own fears of living up to the expectations of his duty, Peirs seemed to be enjoying his time in rural France.

Indeed, Peirs's account of the battalion's early weeks in France is full of humorous moments. The men were billeted near orchards and 'accidentally'

---

6 IWM, Doc. 12610, Fairtlough Papers, Eric Fairtlough to Frederick Howard Fairtlough, 28 October 1914, p.44
7 Peirs to his family, 17 September 1915.
8 Ibid.

bumped into apple trees, taking the fallen, bruised apples.[9] With no degree of ironic awareness, in his own long letters home he complained about the men's voluminous correspondence. 'They write reams daily,' Peirs wrote. Which all has to be censored by the Coy [company] officers before it goes off. We encourage football & such to keep them from writing but it appears to have no effect.'[10] Such a dull job as censorship did have its amusing moments. 'I was doing some the other day & I came across one young devil who wrote 2 love letters by the same post to 2 different young ladies, one in Worthing & the other in Brighton so he had not been wasting his time.[11]

The 8th Battalion's early weeks in France featured good weather, mischievous moments by officers and men, and a general sense of an extended field day or camping trip by men who, by appearances, were playing at war. Even a source as official as the battalion war diary had an air of chattiness. The author, the adjutant Lieutenant Walter Roderick Griffith 'Peter' Bye, was a 25-year-old son of a schoolmaster, who before the war excelled at science at St Catherine's College, Oxford. Bye's entries in the war diary have an element of civilian observation to them; they include details that would be lost in later war diary entries. Fretting about the locals, editorialising about the food, complaining about the weather, and anxieties about spies in their midst are not a strictly a matter of record of the battalion's movements and duties, but are things that Bye found interesting about their first few weeks in France. [12] Like the men of the battalion, he too was getting used to his job.

One incident, however, proved prescient and should have caused a degree of pause among the officers of the division. The 8th Queen's had very little experience with brigade or divisional manoeuvres before they arrived in France. In mid-September, the 24th Division attempted a night concentration after a forced march and then a divisional mock attack. On 17 September, the men went to bed early in the evening and woke at 1:30 am with orders to move. They marched all night to arrive where the division was supposed to concentrate; however, due to a staff error no simulated attack took place. Instead, the men had their breakfast idly and 'strolled rather aimlessly across country for three hours' before then cutting their losses and marching the

9   Peirs to his family, 14 September 1915

10 Peirs his family, 19 September 1915.

11 Peirs to his family, 19 September 1915.

12 Sincere thanks to Jenna Fleming for this observation.

8 miles back to billets.[13] The day was hot and the men were exhausted. Even worse, the staff failed to account for food so the brigade and battalion had only one meal in twelve hours after a forced march.[14] When they arrived back in their billets they were tired, hungry, and dehydrated. They accomplished nothing other than fatigue. It is hard now not to see this as a brutal foreshadowing of what would later happen as they marched towards the looming offensive at Loos.

Loos – Context and Background

The arrival of the 8th Queen's in France coincided with a new allied offensive for the autumn of 1915. The previous year had been a bitter disappointment as all three armies on the Western Front attempted – and failed – to break the deadlock. The French army failed to expel the enemy who occupied the rich industrial areas of the north. The German army, frustrated in the north at Ypres, sought a breakthrough against the British using the new weapon of chlorine gas in April 1915. Pushed by their allies, the BEF also sought a decisive battle. In March, General Douglas Haig implemented what appeared to be a successful plan for an attack at Neuve Chapelle. Through careful planning and a rapid artillery bombardment, British and Indian soldiers attacked and took their objectives from a surprised and dazed enemy, demonstrating that effective preparations could lead to results for attacking infantry.[15] This would be the case of so many successes over the next three years, with limited tactical successes in various offensives, but no significant strategic shift. Casualties mounted as the year wore on and by the summer, the seeds of attritional warfare began to germinate and root into the mud.

The French general-in-chief Joseph Joffre leaned upon the BEF's commander Sir John French to attack. He believed that a solution to their strategic dilemma was a coordinated Anglo-French offensive in 1915 to keep pressure on Germany. If the BEF attacked in Artois and the French army in Champagne, then the combined pressure could force a breakthrough, most likely by the French army. [16]

---

13 Peirs to his family, 19 September 1915.
14 The National Archives (TNA), WO 95/2214/1, 8th Queen's War Diary, 17–18 September 1915.
15 William Philpott, *War of Attrition* (New York: Overlook, 2014), pp.144–5.
16 For a summary of the challenge of 1915 on the Western Front, see Michael Neiberg, *Fighting the Great War*, Chapter 3 and Hew Strachan, *The First World War*, Chapter 6.

The overall strategy of mutual support and coordinated offensives was sound. It was also overly optimistic as to what could be realistically achieved. As Hew Strachan indicates, the lessons of fighting so far, 'had convinced the French, like the British, that if they had enough artillery and attacked on a sufficiently broad front they could break through; the key was to have supporting formations ready to carry the attack beyond the first line and so to enable the breakthrough to be achieved in one bound.'[17] By 1915, they had learned it was possible to achieve a temporary breakthrough, but it was exceptionally hard to force a penetration in depth with the resources at hand. As the allies were absorbing these lessons, the Germans were also learning. Their conclusions focused on the advantages of defence; better trenches, more intricate uses of wire and impediments, artillery support, and more effective machine gun placements.

Joffre's plan was for the British to attack in Artois near Lens in the industrial north of France between La Bassée and Loos. There the German army had multiple lines of trenches and commanded higher ground overlooking vast sections of mostly flat landscape. The landscape raised eyebrows: the ground was unforgiving to the attacker. The plan invited significant risks and the exposed terrain almost guaranteed high casualties. Both French and Haig met their task with skepticism.[18]

There were, however, greater strategic considerations that came into play as the summer waned. The first was the maintenance of the Anglo-French alliance, which depended upon the very junior partner BEF pulling their weight. The second was a belief held by the British general staff that the French army was growing war weary. Though bearing little foundation in reality, the myth persisted; the British acquiesced to Joffre's strategy as a way to bolster allied morale.[19] The third major consideration was the massive Russian retreat over the summer of 1915 as a result of the German Gornice-Tarnow offensive. Reports from Russia were particularly dire and played on

---

17 Hew Strachan, *The First World War*, p.180.

18 For the overall strategic situation in 1915, see Robert Doughty *Pyrrhic Victory: French Strategy and Operations in the Great War* (Cambridge, MA: The Belknap Press, 2005, Chapter 4) and William Philpott, *Anglo-French Relations and Strategy on the Western Front, 1914–1918* (London: Macmillan, 1996, Chapter 5).

19 Rhodri Williams, 'Lord Kitchener and the Battle of Loos: French Politics and British Strategy in the Summer of 1915', in *War Strategy, and International Politics: Essays in Honour of Sir Michael Howard* by Lawrence Freedman, Paul Hayes, and Robert O'Neill, eds. (Oxford: Clarendon Press, 1992), pp.117–32.

the mind of the War Office's dominant strategist, Lord Kitchener, who had long been skeptical of Sir John French's ability to command of the BEF.[20] It was Kitchener who persuaded both French and Haig to begin planning for Loos.

Operational planning for Loos fell to First Army commander, General Haig. He was a more than capable officer and had been on the Western Front in command of both a corps and an army by 1915. Haig had an esteemed early career; though his reputation would ebb in the post-war decades, he was a determined general and well respected within the army. Haig approached his task with concentration and professionalism and was the perhaps the only man in the BEF with enough experience on the Western Front to execute a battle of this size.[21]

Haig's staff developed a plan in four weeks. As historian Nick Lloyd writes, 'The preparations that preceded the Battle of Loos were unprecedented, being the largest and most complex logistical operation that had been conducted by the BEF up to that time.'[22] Though detailed, Lloyd also argues that Haig's staff work was still insufficient for the task and his general plan was not subject to adequate scrutiny. The plan itself was fairly conventional: a preliminary bombardment of four days duration to weaken German positions followed by an infantry assault. It was to be the largest British offensive so far on the Western Front – 70,000 men. Aiding the attackers was chlorine gas, never before used by the BEF and the only novel aspect of the battle's planning. Haig had great faith in gas and hoped it could mitigate German resistance, forcing a breakthrough. Gas required a heavy logistical burden to bring the thousands of toxic and bulky cylinders into position. Cylinder gas was a finicky weapon; it depended upon a favorable wind to waft the poisonous cloud towards the enemy. Haig's plan was both optimistic and grand, yet much of the staff work beyond the opening phases of the battle proved insufficient.

An example of poor planning was the handling of XI Corps, also known as the general reserve. After Neuve Chappelle the BEF realised the need for better battlefield communications. Commanders needed to know which

20 See Nick Lloyd, 'Lord Kitchener and "the Russian News'": Reconsidering the Origins of the Battle of Loos', in *Defence Studies*, Vol. 5, No. 3, September 2005, pp.346–65.
21 Brian Curragh 'The Battle of Loos: 1915', in Spencer Jones (ed.), *Courage without Glory*, pp.370–6.
22 Nick Lloyd, *Loos: 1915* (Stroud, Gloucestershire: The History Press, 2008), p.74.

areas should be reinforced and have the means to do so at their disposal quickly to exploit a breakthrough.[23] As such, a key component to success or failure at Loos was how to exploit gains, a difficult task especially with so many men engaged attacking multiple objectives. Haig realised it was crucial to keep a general reserve close to the front to move it as quickly as possible. Regrettably, Sir John French wanted to keep the general reserve under his control.[24]

The general reserve consisted of two New Army divisions – the 21st and 24th – and the elite Guards Division. In command of XI Corps was one of Haig's protégés, General Richard Haking, appointed just three weeks before Loos. Until the very start of the battle, Haig did not have control over XI Corps, which remained firmly in the grip of general headquarters. Haig favoured having the reserve close at hand while French was cautious of manpower and wanted to protect the reserve. This meant that these divisions were too far back. The potential danger of this approach was that the reserve would have to march a significant distance to get to the battlefield before then directly going into action, thereby tiring the men and diminishing their ability to fight.

The disagreement over the handling of the reserve came within a wider context of inadequate planning for the battle. Haig's other corps commanders – Hubert Gough (I Corps) and Henry Rawlinson (IV Corps) – planned the opening phases of the assault throughout September. Haking's XI Corps had only just arrived in France and did not have sufficient training in divisional/corps level attacks. Though Haig envisioned a role for the reserve to play, their training, and in particular the staff work at the division and corps level remained unsatisfactory. Indeed, having only arrived in France weeks before, the New Army divisions had not been hardened by service and were particularly naïve to the rigours of campaigning, trench duty, and battle. They also had not performed any extensive manoeuvres with other divisions and had no experience fighting in France. Though enthusiastic, the New Army divisions faced a steep learning curve. Now they were thrust immediately into battle upon their arrival in France.

---

23 Ibid., p.85.
24 Sir J.E. Edmonds, *History of the Great War: Military Operations in France & Belgium, 1915, Vol. 2* (Uckfield, East Sussex: The Naval & Military Press/Imperial War Museum), pp.272–6.

The March Up Country

On 18 September, Colonel Howard Fairtlough led his ragged battalion back to their billets after their failed divisional training attack. Like his officers and men, he was exhausted after twenty-four hours of meandering. Ever the dutiful husband and father, he sat down in his billet and wrote to his daughter Victoire on a piece of field notebook paper. This was his custom and his habit; in his three weeks in France he wrote home almost daily, often small missives to his wife Maud. To his daughter he was instructional, particularly this evening after he had marched through the countryside and had seen French civilians bearing the burdens of war. He wrote of the women and children working in their fields. He saw great courage in a nation under duress and a people stressed by war, emphasising that it would do many of the 'lazy people' at home 'good if they could come out here and see what France is suffering and how brave the people are.'[25] He was not scolding his daughter or admonishing her for idleness; instead, he was reminding a young woman with a martial name of the cruelty inflicted upon a nation and a people by the invading German army.

Despite being exhausted both emotionally and physically, he was a career soldier and had the determination to see the job through. Fairtlough did not hide the ardours of campaign in his correspondence with his wife, but noted that all felt the burden of war. After several nights of marching, he wrote that 'two or three of my young officers have been rather knocked up, but so far your old man has kept going.'[26] No doubt there was a small degree of pride in his own stamina compared to his subalterns, who were nearly all half his age. Endurance and fortitude were pillars of his generation's sense of martial manhood. Whatever worries Fairtlough felt about the battalion's future at the front, to his family he remained dutiful as father, husband, and soldier.

The 8th Queen's were in France only three weeks before they marched to Loos. The battalion's first historian captured the mood, writing they 'felt that ease & comfort had been left in England and that the more uncomfortable they were the more efficient soldiers they would become.'[27] Though cheerfully uncomfortable in their billets, the men were hardly strained by their training. Of the seventeen days between their arrival on 3 September

---

25 IWM, Doc. 12610, Fairtlough Papers, F.H. Fairtlough to Victoire Fairtlough, 18 September 1915.
26 IWM, Doc. 12610, Fairtlough Papers, F.H. Fairtlough to Maud Fairtlough, 22 September 1915.
27 SHC, Unpublished Battalion History, p.8.

and the march to Loos, the battalion only spent ten days training. Two days of marching, three on field days, three in musketry, and two lively days of bombing made up the bulk of their in-theatre conditioning.[28] They also had two 'practice alarms' where they were to hurry-up and get ready to break camp on one hour's notice. This was the extent of their preparation.

For the common soldier in the battalion, their lives were of quiet military routine, the same as their training in England. Now in France, the men interacted with the locals, speaking in Franglais, while their officers tried to keep them out of trouble. Peirs recalled that 'the British Tommy is very amusing to watch. He is quite at home & armed with a small phrase book can get most of the things he wants. A lot of them are helping to milk the cows etc & generally making themselves useful & I expect it pays them.'[29] His father, a former schoolmaster who understood the importance of keeping boys busy and cheerful, supplied a cache of harmonicas so that the men could keep their spirits up. The harmonicas both entertained and annoyed. 'Father's mouth organs are a tremendous boon & I heard most dismal noises proceeding from a farm last night which proceeded from one of them, while the platoon sat round & howled in unison.'[30] Though their training in France so far was hardly difficult, a year of soldiery meant that the men were fit and in good spirits. Moreover, their light training and nightly music and sing-alongs in the orchards demonstrated a sense of cheerfulness, one that is tempting to ascribe to blissful naivete towards their future. When their new corps commander, Lieutenant General Richard Haking, attempted to break the spell by addressing them with a speech, 'a trifle gloomy, its main theme being the pleasantness of dying for one's Country', he was speaking to men who knew quite a bit about their country but very little about seeing men die for it.[31]

The idyllic monotony of their French country existence could not last forever. The day after their failed divisional manoeuvres, 19 September, staff officer Major Sir William Kay briefed the battalion's officers about the big push planned for the coming week.[32] The division was then put on twenty-four-hour's notice. The battalion packed up its tents and baggage and moved

---

28 TNA, WO 95/2214/1, 8th Queen's War Diary, September 1915.
29 Peirs his mother, 4 September 1915.
30 Ibid.
31 SHC, Unpublished Battalion History, p.9.
32 Ibid. Sir William Algernon Ireland Kay was a noted soldier and staff officer. He was killed in action as a Brigadier General in October 1918.

at 7:00 pm on the 21st. They reached Glem at 11:30 pm. The four-hour march was hot and dirty. The next day the battalion bathed in a river near their billets and rested. The sight of 800 naked men splashing and playing near a mill must have been one of some amusement, though Peirs recalled it was not as scandalous as we might suppose, writing 'it was a beautiful morning & I spent part of it sleeping out on the riverbank. The natives both male & female were strolling up & down while our fellows were bathing but no one minds these little things here.'[33] Whether nude bathing was scandalous or not, it was certainly an indication of how far the men had come towards functioning as a cohesive unit since their enlistment. The bonds of comradeship were not only sewn together through drill and battle, but also through daily domestic routines like messing and maintaining personal hygiene. As Joanna Bourke argues, the intimacy of soldier life meant that men became accustomed to one another's bodies and bodily functions as an important part of their group identity and *esprit de corps*.[34] Splashing about in the water, the men showed how they had come together as a battalion.

The men bathed and their officers lounged on the banks; the men stole apples from the locals and tried their best to romance their girls; the officers messed on hampers from Fortnum's, smoked their pipes like schoolmasters as they walked among their men, and amusingly shared anecdotes in censoring their letters, etc. – there is something blissful and idyllic in their ignorance of the war. They knew nothing of the fate that awaited them beyond the stereotypes they carried about combat in their imaginations. The immense gap between imagination and reality is one that all soldiers confront. For the time being, the 8th Queen's had known discomfort and a little of the dirt of campaign, but as they marched now towards an active combat zone, it was different. Nothing could restore the men of this battalion to their ignorant cheerfulness as they bathed in the water. Nothing could restore their confidence and hope in their martial abilities, nor restore the men's emotional and physical vitality, which was now at its peak. For all the clichés about the First World War, the idea of a vanished world remains one of the hardest myths to disprove because it hinges upon the feelings of people whose lives were fundamentally altered by the war's unquestionable brutality. Here, for a few hours brazenly naked and lazily lounging on the banks of a French river,

---

33 Peirs to his family, 23 September 1915.
34 Joanna Bourke, *Dismembering the Male*, pp.129–31.

the men of the 8th Queen's had a moment of absolute idyll, one of their last moments of peace.

The next day the drums of the battalion beat and the men marched towards the distant rumble of artillery at Loos. It would take the 72nd Brigade five days to march up country. General Haking planned night marches to avoid enemy observation and to protect the soldiers from artillery. After a day of rest, the men set out on 22 September at 6:00 pm for a 19-mile march to Berguettes. They did so in full kit. The battalion had marched like this before and each man was reasonably fit by the standards of the day, but they were unused to marching at night and doing so on French roads. Luckily, they had good weather and moonlight, conditions that Peirs recalled as being 'ideal for a march of reasonable distance.'[35] The men arrived in Berguettes around 2:00 am after eight hours of marching. Their pace was nearly 2.5 miles per hour, though if one accounts for periodic breaks, then their pace was a bit quicker, a good clip for men under heavy packs.

They settled in at 3:00 am on the 23rd and took to bed on their blankets in the orchards and fields around a farmhouse that was home to their battalion staff. The farm had an artillery shell dump on it and was subject to periodic strafing by German airplanes, though none were reported that night.[36] The morning broke to a fine day and the men were ordered to rest for another day and night where they were. The choice to rest the men for a full day proved unwise in hindsight, but it was understandable at the time as the men were quite fatigued from their over-night march. The battalion's historian wrote afterwards of the justification for this decision:

> Without any knowledge of the Divisional or Corps Commanders' reports it is of course impossible to speak of the wisdom of the decision but certainly on the face of it it would appear better to have rested the troops in Bethune on the 24th a proceeding which would probably have averted the breakdown of the Supply Service and enabled the troops to go into battle after a night's rest instead of without one.[37]

---

35 Peirs to his family, 23 Sept 1915.
36 Ibid.
37 SHC, Unpublished Battalion History, p.10.

Fairtlough was frank to his wife on the 24th that it had been a 'most trying march' and that 'dirt and want of good food' was particularly straining.[38] Also, there was another factor – the rising dew point meant that rain was coming, which would have made marching especially unpleasant. As the clouds darkened, the battalion struggled to put up enough canvas to keep their men sheltered before the rain. For those who had a dry spot to sleep, the rain and fatigue may have contributed to a night of rest under shelter. For those soaked and cold, undoubtedly their sleep was intermittent. This was the last chance for the men of the 8th Queen's to rest before they went into battle.

The thunderstorm marked the end of their pleasant nightly marches. From then onwards, what could go wrong did. The battalion demonstrated that they were certainly capable of marching for long periods at a good pace provided there were clear roads and fine weather. Most of the men were in shape after a year of drill, marches, and full meals in England. Indeed, marching was one of the few things in which these men had ample training. Trench conditions had not yet taken their toll; so far, they had borne their fatigue well. However, the change in weather and road congestion – as well as their ignorance of the region – all factored into unpleasant days ahead.[39]

The next evening, they packed up their soggy canvas and blankets and marched towards Bethune overnight. The 11-mile march should have only taken them four hours at their previous pace, but the roads were severely congested and there were many halts. Arriving near dawn, the men were frustrated at the slow pace, their feelings compounded by a 'scratch' breakfast as the rations had not come up. Sergeant Walter Hitchcock recalled the tortuous march and discomfort from the weather:

> we marched, and we marched, and we marched, and the day before we actually went into action, we marched to a place called Bethune – if my memory's right – and we went into a field and the rain was pouring down. The Colonel said [impersonating an upper class voice] 'We shall be staying here for about four or five hours.

---

38 IWM, Doc 12610, Fairtlough Papers, F.H. Fairtlough to Maud Fairtlough, 24 September 1915.
39 Lloyd, *Loos*, pp.92–3.

You men must get some sleep. We shall be going into action tomorrow morning.'[40]

After a few hours' rest, the battalion departed for Vermelles, but was halted, this time for three hours, behind artillery batteries firing in support of attacking units further on. For those who had any food remaining, they ate it while waiting for the roads to clear.

The men were now close enough to the front to see what was ahead of them. They marched along roads pock-marked by shelling. They passed dead and dying men who had participated in the morning assault on the 25th and were confronted by 'columns of wounded, not a cheerful sight for absolutely untried troops.'[41] The landscape now was brutal and industrial; Loos is smack in the centre of French mining country, with its pitheads and waste piles of coal. Equal parts jarring and encouraging were the artillery batteries they passed; great guns firing in support of infantry assaulting to their front. As afternoon bled into evening, the closer they got to the front, the more realistic the war became. The wounded and dead increased in numbers along the road, the former being evacuated on ambulances. Every man in the battalion knew they were going towards the same dangers that had mutilated these men. In the early evening, they finally arrived in Vermelles and were ordered to trenches near Le Rutoine Farm, their pace still painfully slow as they had little indication as to where they were going or what they were supposed to do there. 'Dusk had now fallen, the country was unknown, the whereabouts of the enemy & of our own troops was uncertain and there were many trenches over which there were bridges for cavalry & transport if they could be located.'[42]

This was hardly encouraging. Upon arriving at Le Rutoine Farm, the battalion commanders were briefed – very briefly – that they would be going into action the next day. The manner of receiving their orders did not inspire confidence. There were no detailed maps for their assault, nor was there any mention of an artillery plan. Peirs indicated afterwards that he was not able to figure out their location until the next day, even then with some difficulty.

---

40 Walter Hitchcock, Oral History, https://walterhitchcock-ww1.blogspot.com/2015/05/walter-hitchcock-interview-transcript.html.
41 SHC, Unpublished Battalion History, p.10.
42 Ibid.

Fairtlough never knew exactly where they were.[43] There was no discussion of tactics or information about their objectives. They were merely given verbal orders and a compass bearing towards the enemy's second line of trenches as their only specific information – what amounted to the general direction of an attack that would be conducted at an unspecified time in the near future. There was no indication of the ground to cover and zero intelligence as to what they might be up against. Fairtlough and the other battalion commanders went back to their men and assembled their companies to march up the line at nightfall.

It was no easy task to get into their intended position. They were to advance and occupy a captured line of trenches and to use these as cover for their attack. These trenches had only just been captured by the 1st Division earlier in the day. The battalion struggled their way forward overland. Their experience was further complicated by vague orders, the terrain, and the darkness. The situation grew tense as the battalion came under shellfire for the first time at 11:00 pm. There were no casualties, but the men were tired, hungry, thirsty, and now some of them were frightened. They had been up and moving – however slowly – for more than twenty-four hours without a sustained rest. In that time, they had only eaten two scratch meals. For many, their water bottles were dry, and the men were undoubtedly dehydrated after days of marching. Every man who began the march did so at the height of their physical abilities; now they were putting their stamina to the test.

---

43 TNA, CAB 145/121/193, H.J.C. Peirs to Sir James Edmonds, 18 February 1927.

Chapter 3

In Action

When the 8th Queen's came up the line on 25 September, they entered the battle of Loos. Only hours before, the 1st Division captured the German first line of defenses at great cost. The task now for the 21st and 24th divisions was to build on this momentum and to push forward and take the German second line between the village of Hulluch and Hill 70. It was assumed by the British staff that the Germans were weakened after taking a thorough beating earlier in the day. The Official History records the sense of optimism from hindsight: 'The Germans were on the run, and it seemed only to require another vigorous push to clear them from their second position.'[1] The general reserve divisions were expected to face with little resistance.

In reality, the German position remained strong. Initially, Haig's plan was for the 1st Division to take both the German first and second lines in their opening attack. This proved overly optimistic as the German first line remained a formidable obstacle that was not overcome until late afternoon.[2] They had difficulty keeping men in contact and sustained high casualties. Out of the 6,000 men of 1st Division who attacked, barely 1,500 remained to hold their positions by nightfall.[3] These were significant losses; yet it was thought that their progress could be exploited with another attack in force later in the day. Haig believed that the second line was within grasp if pressed. As they moved up the line, the 24th Division understood at the time 'that the enemy had been heavily defeated and was everywhere retiring, and that no organised resistance need be expected.'[4] Indeed, one of the working assumptions by staff officers in Haking's XI Corps was that the reserve

---

1 Edmonds, *Military Operations in France & Belgium, 1915, Vol. 2*, p.266.
2 Ibid., pp.208–28.
3 Ibid., p.222. Not all these men were casualties; some had lost their way in the confusion of the attack.
4 Ibid., p.284

divisions would not be committed to battle unless the enemy was 'absolutely smashed'.[5]

Though the enemy had taken a beating, they still commanded a substantial network of defences beyond their first line. After the initial shock of the British attack, they proved more elastic in their ability to reinforce and defend their ground than anticipated. Overnight, as the British struggled to get the men of XI Corps up the line – indeed as Haig and his generals did not fully understand the extent of their gains the day before – the enemy was strengthening their position. In particular, they reinforced their second line of trenches with a hodgepodge of German battalions out of their reserve.[6] These reinforcements unrolled their barbed wire into a dense thicket in front of the line. 'What had the day before been an incomplete trench system with, in many parts, a single strand of wire in front, now had a strong entanglement, well-staked, 4ft high and twenty feet deep.'[7] Considering that a small wooden fence can slow, stall, and breakup an infantry assault with catastrophic results, barbed wire strung in deep layers was practically impregnable without careful artillery preparation before an assault over exposed ground. At Loos, the barrage was too small in scale and too spread out along a broad front to inflict much damage upon the German second line, which on the early morning of the 26th remained intact, formidable, and practically untouched by British shells.

Of course, the exact strength of the German position was not known to Haig or his staff. They were also ignorant of the state of XI Corps or the arduousness of their march up country. Haig's staff had an overly-optimistic view of what the men of the 21st and 24th divisions were capable of doing. To some degree this is understandable. Loos was the largest attack waged by the BEF to date. It severely tested their command and control of GHQ, and the situation on the ground was only being ascertained in real time on the evening of the 25th. There simply was not a system in place to provide accurate information about their gains, losses, and intelligence towards what remained to be done. Still, even by rather low 1915 standards of operational planning, to order reserve divisions with no combat experience into a situation in which the general staff did not fully understand and had no adequate

---

5   Ibid.
6   Lloyd, *Loos*, p.170.
7   Philip Warner, *The Battle of Loos*, p.27.

plan for supporting was to run a significant risk to the lives of the men in these divisions. The Official History presents a dire situation: 'Without having been in action before or having seen a shot fired, these troops were actually confronted with a difficult situation on unknown ground, without guidance from the commanders and staffs who had been in the sector and had studied its features for months past.'[8] More strongly, it was, in the words of one former senior officer, 'nothing short of criminal' to bring these divisions into battle under these circumstances.[9]

The Attack

In the failing daylight of 25 September, the battalions of the 72nd Brigade formed up at Le Rutoire Farm to continue their advance. Their orders were to march overland towards the Lens-La Bassée road, 3 miles distant. As the men readied themselves, the skies opened up drenching the men as they stood in their ranks. Their brigade commander recalled:

> Until midnight the scene was a weird one, especially for troops launching into the blue on a night march over country they were totally ignorant of, with the possibility of meeting the enemy in some indefinite position. A black night, rain falling steadily; flashes of guns around, especially to the N.E. where there was much artillery and infantry fire; Verey lights showing for a moment. And then would come a wave of mist, and all was hidden. The only landmark and guiding light were the burning 'pylons' of Loos, and even they at times were obscured by the mist. Consequently, one had to watch one's compass very closely.[10]

As General Mitford indicates, they knew little of where they were going. They had no accurate maps; indeed, Fairtlough and the other battalion commanders were only given a compass bearing of 112 degrees by which the brigade was to orient itself forward. The Official History indicates that 'progress was exceedingly wearisome and slow owing to the state of the ground and the obstacles encountered.'[11] The rain continued.

---

8   Edmonds, *Military Operations in France & Belgium, 1915, Vol. 2*, pp.284–5.
9   TNA, CAB 45/120, Major General Forestier-Walker to Sir James Edmonds, 24 January 1927.
10   TNA, CAB 45/120, Major General Mitford to Sir James Edmonds, 23 January 1926, p.2.
11   Edmonds, *Military Operations in France & Belgium, 1915, Vol. 2*, p.288.

As they moved forward, the brigade confronted, essentially, three imped-iments. The first was the terrain itself, which had been chewed up, thus making progress forward wearisome. The second was the darkness, though this was somewhat menacingly helped by artillery flashes and the burning village of Loos in the distance to the south. Finally, and most importantly, the brigade encountered many obstacles as they worked their way forward. These included some battlefield detritus, ambulance and ammunition wag-ons moving forward and back from the front lines, and most significant of all, British and German trenches that had to be traversed by makeshift bridges, or climbed in and out of, as they advanced overland.[12] Nevertheless, it was slow and awkward going forward as they moved at a pace of less than 1 mile per hour.

At 1:10 am the brigade halted. It was very dark, though there were occa-sional very lights, and the distant burning of pylons from Loos.[13] Moonlight now peeked through the clouds. Upon hearing that Hulluch on his left was still in enemy hands, General Mitford sent one battalion towards the village to secure their flank before continuing the brigade's advance under moon-light.[14] He did not know that the German second line was held in force (and was being actively reinforced) but was merely following his orders earlier in the evening to press the day's advance. Before the brigade could move, the divisional staff intervened.[15] The brigade halted west of the Lens-La Bassée road. Mitford ordered the men to dig in as they were, some in the open, meaning they would thus be exposed to enemy fire upon daybreak.[16]

The 8th Queen's took position in an unfinished German communications trench that was about 2 feet deep.[17] They reached for their entrenching tools and began deepening their trench and creating a parapet to their front. They had been on their feet for an entire day and must have been exhausted.

---

12 TNA, WO 95/2214/1, 8th Queen's War Diary, 25 September 1915.

13 TNA, CAB 45/120, Major General Mitford to Sir James Edmonds, 23 January 1926, p.2.

14 Edmonds, *Military Operations in France & Belgium, 1915, Vol. 2*, p.290.

15 Ibid.

16 In both the battalion war diary, as well as the 'unofficial' anonymous battalion history, it is only mentioned that the Queen's spent the night in captured German communication trenches from 2:00 am onwards, however, the official history is quite specific about the brigade digging into the front of Alley 4. See Edmonds, *Military Operations in France & Belgium, 1915, Vol. 2*, p.290. Lieutenant Duke's letter to Sir James Edmonds clears up some confusion, positioning the Queen's in an unfinished German communications trench.

17 TNA, CAB 45/120, 'Information received from Officers interned in Holland,' statement of Lieutenant L.G. Duke, 20 November 1918.

Additionally, there was no opportunity for a hot meal or to fill their water bottles. Coming under shellfire earlier – their first experience – increased their anxiety and irritability, regardless of whether they took casualties. To add insult to injury, they were thoroughly drenched and now digging. They scraped at the ground in wet wool uniforms, the very action of digging into the soil chafing their bodies, and the very act of lifting and throwing wet earth caking them in gluey clay mud; new layers of misery on a day that seemed to have no shortage of it. To a man they were sore, drowsy, and wet. After attempting to entrench with their tools, the brigade withdrew to better trenches in their rear before daybreak.[18]

The last few hours had the men of the battalion staggeringly tired. 'That night march in the wet on top of several other night marches 'cooked' the men, wrote an officer afterwards.[19] The men had been on their feet for a day.[20] Their exhaustion was compounded by the deep anxiety that comes from anticipation and fear, both of which were abundantly real as the first shells exploded nearby. Their position now was less than ideal, though relatively safe. Taking cover in a communication trench, they were surrounded by wastage of the opening phase of the battle. There were a few British and German dead, some of the latter having choked on chlorine gas.[21] For men who had experienced nothing of trench warfare yet, the first things that probably hit them were the different smells of the battlefield, which would become all too familiar in the coming years, but at the time had to have been foreboding in its olfactory harshness. They were insecure and worried about the future – they had no idea what the day would bring – and had no clue as to how they would react to being under fire. The men must have felt great fear, but also a sense of urgency in their ignorance. The tension had to be excruciating and the sensory impact and discomfort from fatigue had to have been profoundly disturbing.

Dawn came with mist blanketing no man's land and the men moved about. When the mist dissipated, German soldiers began sniping and shells

---

18 Edmonds, *Military Operations in France & Belgium, 1915, Vol. 2*, p.290.
19 TNA, CAB 45/120, Brigadier General A.J. Craven to Sir James Edmonds, 16 February 1926.
20 TNA, CAB 45/120, Major General Forestier-Walker to Sir James Edmonds, 24 January 1927.
21 Walter Hitchcock mentions British dead on barbed wire in no man's land as well. See Walter Hitchcock, Oral History, https://walterhitchcock-ww1.blogspot.com/search?updated-max=2015-11-05T13:09:00-08:00&max-results=7&start=1&by-date=false. General Mitford recalled some bodies, but not many. See TNA, CAB 45/120, Major General Bertram Mitford to Sir James Edmonds, 23 January 1926.

fell on their position.[22] Some attempted to get a scant amount of rest and a bit of food as the morning broke. The 72nd Brigade appeared to be the only one of their division who ate that morning, but they did not have a chance to get water up and the men's bottles were dry.[23] At 9:45 am, brigade head-quarters summoned Colonel Fairtlough, along with the other three battalion commanders.[24] He made his way back to HQ.[25] What Fairtlough saw and heard could not have been encouraging. Mitford, who himself had only just been briefed by staff officer Sir William Kay, indicated the brigade was to attack the German second line at precisely 11:00 am. The brigade's flanks were to be protected by movement on Hulluch, by the 1st Division on the left, and an attack on Chalk Pit Wood and Bois Hugo on their right by the 21st Division. Between the two positions and attacking the centre was to be the 72nd Brigade, advancing on the German second line of trenches. The 9th East Surreys and the 8th Royal West Kents were to take the lead, with the 8th Queen's and 8th Buffs in support. Part of the 2nd Welch went towards the southern end of Hulluch on the brigade's left flank. Mitford himself had no written orders yet from division, there was no adequate intelligence briefing, no indication as to what they were attacking, and no idea as to whether or how his men would be supported by artillery. Once again, they had only a compass bearing to guide them.

The crescent-shaped German second line offered the defender many advantages. If either Hulluch on the left or Bois Hugo on the right flank remained in German hands, then the 72nd Brigade would be subject to fire from three directions over a distance of about 700 yards. The terrain itself provided a further challenge. German trenches were dug into a gentle slop-ing grass-covered field. There was no cover for assaulting infantry and the German machine gunners had an unobstructed field of fire. The only way to attack the position head on was to expose soldiers to direct fire, particularly in the zone between the Lens-La Bassée road and the German wire. Unlike the German first line of trenches, which had been taken with great cost on 25 September, the second line had not been weakened by preliminary

---

22 TNA, CAB 45/120, 'Information received from Officers interned in Holland,' statement of Lieutenant L.G. Duke, 20 November 1918.

23 TNA, CAB 45/121, Cosmo Stewart to James Edmonds, 'Diary' p.3; TNA, CAB 45/120, Major General Bertram Mitford to Sir James Edmonds, 23 January 1926, p.2.

24 TNA, WO 95/2214/1, 8th Queen's War Diary, 26 September 1915.

25 TNO, CAB 45/121, Colonel Eden Vansittart to War Office, 7 October 1917.

bombardment.[26] It remained as the Germans designed it; a fine position to defend against a massed frontal assault by unsupported infantry.

Of course, Haig believed the second line was a weakened position and he did not know the full extent of the high casualties sustained by men of the 1st Division the day before.[27] When General Mitford briefed his battalion commanders on the attack, he was following verbal orders that had been filtered down to him.[28] The past twenty-four hours revealed just how muddled the situation was. Mitford's orders to attack a formidable line of defences with exhausted and untried soldiers merely confirmed what the rest of the division had been through in the last few days in their disorganised, at times chaotic, and certainly unlucky advance into battle. It also reflected the haphazard and downright poor planning for the general reserve.

After the battalion commander's briefing, Fairtlough hustled back to the battalion and instructed his company commanders as to their task with only minutes to spare before they had to form up and follow the 8th West Kents into battle.[29] While he had been in his briefing, the battalion's position was shelled with both shrapnel and high explosive; their first significant experience under fire.[30] At 11:00 am promptly, the 8th Royal West Kents and 9th East Surreys formed into position in extended order – two companies in front and two behind – each platoon in lines led by their officers.[31] At the front of the West Kents was their CO Eden Vansittart, who had his compass in his hand, fixing the bearing he was given by Mitford. He then raised his hand, paused, and dropped it, barking 'advance' at 11.[32] They moved at a walk to keep their ranks well-ordered towards the Lens-La Bassée road, taking some fire as

26 TNA, CAB 45/120, Major General Reginald Ford to Sir James Edmonds, 5 February 1926.

27 Edmonds, *Military Operations in France & Belgium, 1915, Vol. 2*, p.308.

28 It should be added that Mitford expected written orders and Sir William Kay believed them to be composed, but those orders did not reach his headquarters until much later in the day. TNA, CAB 45/121, Major General Reginal Ford to Sir James Edmonds, 5 February 1926.

29 TNA, CAB 45/121, Colonel Eden Vansittart to War Office, 7 October 1917. Vansittart, commander of the 8th Battalion, West Kents, indicated they walked quickly back to his battalion and only had seven minutes to get his men into formation before they attacked.

30 TNA, CAB 45/120, 'Information received from Officers interned in Holland', statement of Lieutenant L.G. Duke, 20 November 1918.

31 Edmonds, *Military Operations in France & Belgium, 1915, Vol. 2*, p.325. The timing here is a little off in the battalion war diaries, which all stress that the attack was to begin at 11:30 am. The maps in the official history offer an explanation – the battalions assembled and began their advance at 11 from Alley 4 trench. They then marched the 1,000 yards to the Lens-La Bassée road where their attack began in earnest against the second line at 11:30.

32 TNA, CAB 145/121, Colonel Eden Vansittart to War Office, 7 October 1917.

they crossed 1,000 yards of open ground before hitting the road. The West Kents began their attack 'at a marching pace in order to save the men's breath for the final charge and bayonet work.'[33] They looked as though they were on parade. Philip Warner writes, 'not since First Ypres had such dense masses of infantry deployed for an assault in full daylight over open ground.'[34]

As the lead battalions advanced, the four companies of the 8th Queen's formed in extended order behind them. Company and platoon commanders hurried their men into formation to follow the battalions to their front.[35] Peirs recalled that they 'went on as if on a field day' their ranks dressed and their subalterns at the front inspiring the men with their steadiness.[36] Lieutenant Duke indicated that his platoon in A Company had to scramble to get into line as they had so little time to prepare for their attack. Indeed, behind Duke in A Company, Major Fox of B Company had not even received his order to attack when Duke began assembling his platoon.[37] Ahead of them they could see the West Kents approaching the Lens-La Bassée road and beyond it the gentle forward slope of the slight ridge which held the German second line.

As the men moved neatly towards them, German observers saw a fertile field of targets. As the Queen's fell into their ranks and moved out, they began taking casualties. One of the first was Colonel Fairtlough, who fell mortally wounded, likely shot by a sniper targeting officers along the Lens-La Bassée road. He was a man with an imposing physique and easily recognisable as their CO; leading from the front he looked every inch the commander and was a prize target. The battalion moved forward past the wounded body of the man who had trained them and one of the few who had any military experience at all. Then others, too, began to fall from small arms fire and shelling as they advanced to the Lens-La Bassée road.[38] Ahead of them, just beyond the road, the West Kents began to take heavy fire from what

---

33 H.J. Wenyon and H.S. Brown, *The 8th Battalion The Queen's Own Royal West Kent Regiment*, p.19.

34 Warner, *The Battle of Loos*, p.45.

35 TNA, CAB 45/120, 'Information received from Officers interned in Holland,' statement of Lieutenant L.G. Duke, 20 November 1918.

36 Peirs to his father, 28 September 1915.

37 TNA, CAB 45/120, Written statement of Lieutenant L.G. Duke.

38 Peirs to his mother, 30 September 1915. Warner indicates that the Germans held their fire against the British first wave for about a quarter of an hour before then opening up on them. However, Peirs is clear that they took fire from the moment they emerged from their trenches. Lieutenant Duke's account (fn 33) confirms this, indicating 'From the first we came under rifle and artillery fire and men of my platoon were hit.' If they did hold their fire,

appeared to be their front, as well as on their flanks, as soon as they crossed the road and struggled in the second phase of their attack. Once the Queen's crossed the road, they too began taking fire from the village of Hulluch on their left. More men fell, but the battalion kept going.

The situation quickly turned nightmarish. As the 9th East Surreys pressed forward on the right of the brigade's advance, they were hit by machine gun fire coming from their front and enfilading fire on their right flank from Chalk Pit Wood and then Bois Hugo, which were supposed to be in British hands.[39] Their flank was entirely exposed and German IR 153 seized the opportunity to enfilade them, their machine guns firing in bursts as they traversed their lines. As the East Surreys moved to the right to meet the threat, the West Kents continued forward, taking their own flanking fire from Hulluch as the German IR 157 machine guns zeroed in on them and began enfilading their battalion's left flank. The fire from Hulluch was unexpected; the officers assumed the village was neutralised by the 3rd Brigade's attack that morning.[40] This was not the case and the West Kents and Queen's took heavy fire from their left. An artillery battery now opened up on them from the village, causing further carnage at first to their flank and then to their left rear as they struggled onwards.[41] German snipers were shooting officers, increasing confusion as subalterns began to fall at the heads of their platoons who kept pressing past their wounded or dying commanders.[42]

They kept going. As the West Kents and East Surreys took the brunt of the enemy's fire, the Queen's and the Buffs moved forward in support, the latter to fill a gap between the two assaulting battalions, and the Queen's to plug the gaps from the shredded platoons to their front. Now nearly officer-less, the remaining West Kents appeared to be stuck. As their regimental historians recalled grimly, 'What were the men to do? Turn to their officers

---

then the discrepancy is perhaps in the time it took the lead assault battalions to reach the road and the time it took the support battalions to form and march forward.

39 Their experience is expertly chronicled in Michael Lucas, *The Journey's End Battalion*, pp.16–18.

40 TNA, CAB 45/120, 'Information received from Officers interned in Holland,' statement of Lieutenant L.G. Duke, 20 November 1918. Duke indicates that he asked the CO of the West Kents if he could move his platoon on Hulluch, but that he was informed that another unit was responsible for doing this.

41 H.J. Wenyon and H.S. Brown, *The 8th Battalion The Queen's Own Royal West Kent Regiment*, p.20.

42 Michael Lucas, *The Journey's End Battalion*, p.16.

for orders? Out of twenty-five officers who had left our trench little more than an hour before, only one was not unhit?[43] Unable to advance, the men looked for cover and were lying down in the tall grass for shelter, scraping at the dirt in a vain attempt for protection from fire that seemed to come from everywhere.

The Queen's went forward over clumps of wounded and dead men from the West Kents, some of whom fell in their neat ranks as the machine guns fired across their lines. Compounding the carnage were the dead from the previous day's fighting, the tall grass now trampled, bloodied, and as the Germans famously remarked, full of corpses.[44] As the Queen's advanced, their numbers diminished; with each step they began taking heavier fire from their left and front, mostly small arms, but also from shrapnel shells. General Mitford recalled afterwards the sight he saw of his brigade advancing into heavy enemy fire, 'The advance of the 8/Queen's, 8/W. Kents, and 8/Buffs ... was a perfect line, as if a parade movement: true, the line thinned every few yards, owing to casualties.'[45] Though the fire on their left flank was more severe, the Queen's also began taking casualties from their right.[46] Like the West Kents before them, officer after officer went down; platoons surged forward in clumps under their NCOs as their lines thinned. As they advanced, they pressed on over the wounded, many of whom called out for aid. Still, they kept going on until they saw what had stopped the West Kents: a thicket of German barbed wire to the front of elements of IR 26 about 50 yards away, partially obscured by tall grass. Lieutenant Duke tried to get his platoon to overwhelm the enemy infantry to their front through bursts of frustrated rapid fire.[47] Groups of men rushed the wire, pitifully trying to break through, as more and more were hit. The fire was too severe; both of their flanks were up in the air and they were completely exposed.

The situation was hopeless; the wire was impenetrable. Half their officers were now dead or wounded. Fairtlough was far behind, presumed dead. In command, Major Peirs was pinned down with one of the platoons. Sporadic

---

43 H.J. Wenyon and H.S. Brown, *The 8ᵗʰ Battalion The Queen's Own Royal West Kent Regiment*, p.22.

44 'Leichenfeld von Loos'.

45 TNA, CAB 45/120, Major General Bertram Mitford to Sir James Edmonds, 23 January 1926.

46 Though, most of the fire from that flank would have been blunted by the East Surreys and Buffs to their right.

47 TNA, CAB 45/120, 'Information received from Officers interned in Holland,' statement of Lieutenant L.G. Duke, 20 November 1918.

shelling – now thought to be from their own guns – and small arms fire continued to menace the poor men who were now scratching out cover on the ground.[48] Scores of wounded now intermingled with them, adding an element of primal misery to the cacophony of industrial weaponry. Stuck in the killing space before the wire, the remnants of the brigade now formed one mass line of about one thousand or so survivors, pressed together along a 700-yard front. Unable to go forward, they held their ground; returning fire when they could, and some trying to tear down and push through the wire. At some point – we don't know when or who – one sensible officer ordered his men to retire.[49] The remnant of the brigade followed. Rather than being routed, the men withdrew their attack in good order 'in line and at a walk'.[50] Some of the German machine guns stopped firing, but others aimed at the retreating soldiers and targeted the wounded.[51] This was the experience for Peirs and his platoon as they were sniped at from the entire 700 yards back to the Lens-La Bassée road. They were the last men in the 8th Queen's to make it back to their assault trenches. Peirs did so at a walking pace with his stick in hand, certainly courting fire and tempting fate, a minor miracle that he made it through unscathed.[52]

All was chaos when they reached their trenches. The remnants of four battalions were now mixed and crowded together. Wounded men who could walk or be dragged into the trench cried out. Compounding their misery was German shelling, which continued for the next five hours, adding to their confusion and trauma as men took cover against the walls of the communication trench.[53] None of these men had been under severe shelling before and it had to have been excruciatingly disorienting. There were wounded all over the place on litters or sitting up against the trench walls. Medical officers and orderlies began their work of triaging and treating the men that they could during the bombardment.

The vast majority of the wounded had bullet wounds, which broke bones and tore ligaments and arteries apart as they worked through the body at a

---

48 Edmonds, *Military Operations in France & Belgium, 1915, Vol. 2*, p.330.
49 Lucas, *The Journey's End Battalion*, p.19.
50 SHC, Unofficial Regimental History, p.11.
51 TNA, CAB 45/120, 'Information received from Officers interned in Holland,' statement of Lieutenant L.G. Duke, 20 November 1918.
52 Peirs wondered at this too. See Peirs to his family, 28 September 1915.
53 TNA, CAB 45/121, Cosmo Stewart to Sir James Edmonds, 'Diary' p.8.

velocity of 800 metres per second. Some had shrapnel wounds, jagged and causing horrific trauma to tissue. Most of the wounded were in shock and overwhelmed by their pain. For those who were unscathed and had staggered back to their trenches, they also suffered a psychological state of adrenaline-induced confusion as they considered what had just happened. It would take days for men to recover their thoughts, to reassess and to cobble together a coherent narrative. Later in the day, it began to rain again as the German shells slowed and then stopped by 5:00 pm. The men lifted their heads to the rain and opened their mouths, as many had had no water all day.[54] The tension, anger, and disappointment was palpable. Surviving officers struggled to find their men and recover their platoons and companies.[55] By midnight, Major Peirs claimed to have only found seven men from his battalion among the survivors huddled in their trenches as the rain fell.[56] To their front, they heard the moans of the wounded, now being pulled from no man's land by brave stretcher-bearers willing to take the risk of saving lives. More and more men came back, further clogging their trench. By morning, each man awoke to find only a skeleton of the battalion they knew before.

Too Miserable for Words

For the survivors, the ordeal was incomprehensible. Their commanding officer was killed, as were other officers and NCOs. The battalion that had trained together for a year was completely shattered. Three weeks before they were a plucky tight-knit group of volunteers. Now they were in captured German communication trench, covered in mud, drenched with rain, and bearing the blood of their comrades on their uniforms, with their cries for help certainly on their minds. 'I am too miserable for words', Peirs wrote to his father in what was the most emotional beginning to the most emotional letter he wrote home to his family from France. 'I am quite all right, tho[ugh] why I wasn't touched I don't know', he continued. It is, in fact, a rare artifact of trauma from a man so composed, indicative of the moment when an otherwise extremely emotionally reserved officer expressed something as basic to humanity as profound grief.

---

54 TNA, CAB 45/121, Cosmo Stewart to Sir James Edmonds, 'Diary' p.10.
55 TNA, CAB 45/120, Major General Reginald Ford to Sir James Edmonds, 5 February 1926.
56 Peirs to his mother, 30 September 1915.

Peirs's letter home on 28 September 1915 is worth lingering upon.[57] It is disjointed as he struggles to create a narrative of his experience. He expresses loss and is clearly exhausted. It is important for him to complement his 'wonderful' men in a tepid justification for his sadness, yet he struggles and ultimately finds no solace in his duty. 'I should feel quite proud but I am simply heart broken now … I will write more when I feel more cheerful & will give you as full a description as I can.'[58] It is a difficult letter to read for what it says, but mostly, for the feelings that he fails to express that are obviously present. After the war, and with much more reflection, Peirs wrote to Sir James Edmonds of the toll Loos still took on him. 'Personally I must plead to considerable mental disturbance in my first action. I had never had a bullet or shell fired anywhere near me before, and in my view he is an exceptional man who can control himself, much more his men, in such a situation. Apply this to practically every man in the brigade and an additional reason for failure becomes apparent.'[59] If one considers that Peirs went on to become one of those 'exceptional men' then his words here are even more telling of the battalion's mass trauma after Loos.

Peirs's correspondence also demonstrates a man who also knew from the very beginning of his combat experience the significance of his first baptism by fire. Loos was not only a foundational moment in his own war experience, but it was for every officer and man who lived through it. Though he was friendly to many of his officers, Peirs seemed especially close to Captain Reginald 'Tommy' Thompson, who was wounded in his feet and hands in their attack. Both men had similar backgrounds; they were public school footballers who played for their university sides, Peirs for Oxford and Thompson as a full-back for Cambridge.[60] Six weeks after Loos, Thompson was at home recovering and about to be married. Peirs arranged for his father to send the 'rough & ready' footballer a new walking stick from Harrods with the inscription:

RGT

from

HJCP

---

57 It can be read in full at https://jackpeirs.org/letters/28-september-1915/.
58 Peirs to his family, 28 September 1915.
59 TNA, CAB 45/121, H.J.C. Peirs to Sir James Edmonds, 17 June 1926.
60 'School Master Wounded,' *The Thanet Advertiser*, 23 October 1915, p.5.

26.9.1915
16.11.1915[61]

The latter date was that of Thompson's wedding and the former, of course, when both men had fought at Loos and where Thompson was wounded. It was the date of their survival; the moment where each man passed the test to live another day and to be born again as combat veterans. The significance of Loos was deeply felt, but always with considerable pain due to the men lost in such an ultimately futile attack.

Published two years after the war, the battalion history of the 8th West Kents reflects Peirs's melancholy, though from the perspective of a sister unit. The authors recalled:

> the battalion was temporarily ruined, and what remained of one of the finest and most gallant battalions that ever left England required months of careful rebuilding before it was a semblance of its old self. To those who had seen the battalion grow from its infancy and who lived to look back on that day, there remained and will remain and everlasting regret that it should have been frittered away in two short hours on a hopeless task.[62]

Notably, their heroic language bears with it the genuine feelings of volunteer soldiers who were proud of their performance, but saw hopelessness in it too. Peirs reflected these sentiments; he too had lost friends and now was in command of a battalion in the place of his soldier-mentor Colonel Fairtlough.

In the immediate wake of the battle, the 8th Battalion suffered further miseries as the men attempted to comprehend what they had just been through. Rain began on the night of the 26th as they were sheltered in a captured German trench. Overnight, makeshift patrols went out into no man's land to drag back some of the hundreds of wounded men that cried out to their front, but many had been taken by the Germans, who now advanced back to the road.[63] The brigade was relieved the next day. It rained the whole time and the temperature dropped correspondingly. The men did not have their blankets or their

61 Peirs to his father, 9 November 1915.
62 H.J. Wenyon and H.S. Brown, *The 8th Battalion The Queen's Own Royal West Kent Regiment*, p.23.
63 Michael Lucas, *The Journey's End Battalion*, p.19.

overcoats, which had been left behind in the attack. Like the rest, Peirs was uncomfortable, having lost his Burberry. Wet, cold, and miserable they moved to Berguette and billeted on a farm. They were soaked when they arrived at their first proper shelter in a week. When Peirs wrote to his father about the battle on the 28th, he did so in a dirty uniform after days without rest.

In Berguette, the battalion licked its wounds. For the first time in days, they took off their puttees and boots. In front of them was hot food and a chance for some rest, at least for a few days. They were greeted by eighty-six new men fresh from England to replace the 400 they had lost at Loos, the battalion having been reduced from 904 officers and men on 26 September to 518 by the next day.[64] This began what would become a cycle of their service – significant losses, days of rest, drafts from England, and further training behind the lines – weeks ahead of decompression that followed and tested their powers of resiliency. For the new men it had to be harrowing to see what was left of the battalion: in front of them were hungry, dehydrated, and traumatised men. They had hollow eyes and some of them bore the blood of comrades on their uniforms. Some had lost equipment in the attack. They were certainly not the image from the parade ground at Blackdown, nor did they look like the polished Kitchener volunteers of newspaper reporting. They were veterans who now had to face their battalion's tragedy, their own memories, and the drafts of new men who were dumfounded by the sight of what they assumed was a full-strength Kitchener battalion.

The casualties were 419 men killed, wounded, or missing – 114 killed outright in the attack. There was also a serious decimation of the battalion's leadership: 10 out of 20 of their officers were killed or wounded after leading the attack from the front and bearing the burden of the sharpshooters' aim. Among the dead officers was Charles Howard Cressy, only 19, a young man who had volunteered straight from Marlborough College, where he played hockey. He was known to the Peirs family. Cressy's body remained on the field where he fell, never to be identified, a fate shared with most of the other men killed and left behind.

Among the fallen officers was Captain Cyril Annesley Cooke. Cooke was a 36-year-old Canadian landholder. He left behind his wife Georgina and their three children. Cooke wrote home an intimate letter to his wife just twelve days before he died, in which he closed with the words, 'I love you too much

---

64 TNA, WO 95/2193/1–034, 24th Division Fighting Strength, 25 September–2 October 1915.

to be able to think of anything else, heart of my heart. Light of my soul, love of my life.'[65]

As the battalion regrouped in the weeks after their attack, the War Office processed formal telegrams that would forever change the lives of their recipients. They made their way to the Baulk family of Kent, the Bone family of Sussex, the Harris family of Littlehampton, the widow of Arthur Lewis in Dalston, the parents of George Doe on High Street in Epping, etc. The first week of October proved one of eternal sadness for these families as they began their long struggle with uncertainty, and eventually for many, grief for loved ones who remained somewhere in no man's land along the fated compass bearing that directed the attack.

The officer casualties were reported by name in the war diary and in prominence in the local press, but they were only a small fraction of the men who were killed or missing at Loos. The vast majority were common soldiers, and many were young. The Caush brothers, Ernest and John, both lied about their age so that the younger brother, John, could join his elder brother in service despite only being 17 in 1914.

They were both domestic servants and former Boy Scouts.[66] Only 18 at Loos, John was killed in the attack near his brother. Ernest carried on the attack and then stuck with the battalion until he, too, met his death at the Somme a year later. Both brothers, united in their sacrifice, are now separated by 100 miles of foreign fields from their final resting places. John Caush was joined in death at Loos by a school chum, Raymond Everest, who was killed near him.[67] Indeed, of the seven men from their town who enlisted together in 1914, only three survived the war and two died at Loos.

The service of Lance Corporal Leonard Stovell offers a glimpse into the pre-war lives of so many of the civilians-turned-soldiers killed at Loos. Stovell was born in Croydon in 1887 and lived in Carshalton at the time of his enlistment. He grew up with six siblings and graduated from the Wallington Holy Trinity Boy's School and took courses in religious studies with the Diocese of Southwark, passing credibly an examination in religious studies in 1908. Stovell found employment in a stationery shop where he

---

65 Surrey History Centre, Cyril Cooke to his wife, 14 September 1915 from 'Surrey in the Great War', https://www.surreyinthegreatwar.org.uk/story/cyril-annesley-cooke/.

66 Surrey History Centre, 'Brothers in Arms', https://www.surreyinthegreatwar.org.uk/story/brothers-in-arms/.

67 Ibid.

worked before enlisting in October 1914. Educated and with a shop assistant's background, he was marked for promotion to lance corporal. His surviving photograph – with the lance-jack stripe on his arms – reveals a very young-looking 27-year-old man, looking off behind the camera with light coloured eyes and hair, whose facial expression invites empathy. He died at the head of his section at Loos and his body was never identified. He is one many missing men on the 8th Queen's panel on the Loos Memorial at Dud Corner.[68]

Stovell and dozens of others remained in no man's land, their bodies unable to be recovered due to the ongoing battle, their fates unknown to their families at home, who only received notice that they were 'missing'. The Ragless family of Elstead were among those desperate for information. Percy Ragless was a 6-foot-tall gardener who enlisted underage in 1914. After months of wondering what fate befell her son, his mother received a letter just before Christmas from Sergeant Harry Read of the Motor Machine Gun Corps, which included a notebook found on her son's body. The sergeant wrote, 'We were out on duty some days ago, and the men of my section paid their last respects to Pte. P. Ragless, of the 8th Queen's, on whose body we found the enclosed book. On behalf of my section and myself I extend to you our sincerest sympathy.'[69] The story here is an unusual, but not uncommon one; often for families of the officially missing, the search for information and closure was an exhausting and ultimately futile exercise. For the Ragless family, a random patrol was able to give them the closure that they needed. Sadly, this would not be their only loss in the war; Mrs Ragless had five sons in uniform, three of whom were killed in service.[70]

It was not only the families at home who mourned their loved ones. The men of the battalion also mourned in the months afterwards. They had grown to intimately know their messmates. They ate together, marched together, suffered sicknesses and discomforts together, slept together, bathed together, and in short, became comrades in a year of army life. For most, it was the most intimate experience they had with a group of men since they were schoolchildren, and they formed cohorts of friends based on shared history, affection, and necessity. Some – like the aforementioned Caush brothers and

68 Details from Ben Roy, https://jackpeirs.org/soldier-profiles/soldier-profile-lance-corporal-leonard-stovell/.

69 Quote and details of his service from '8th Queen's Man's Fate,' *Surrey Advertiser,* 13 December 1915.

70 'Three Sons Killed', *Surrey Advertiser,* 6 May 1918.

Raymond Everest – knew one another from home and/or previous employment, their attachments running deep into their civilian lives. Many others did not, but they formed deep bonds as they lived together. After a year of close unit training, all had someone to mourn after Loos.

Private Burchett's experience with grief is an example. He wrote to a friend's father – Job Ellis – of his deceased son. 'I am very sorry to say Frank was shot through the heart, and fell dead without uttering a word.' The quick death, no doubt, offered a small amount of comfort for the family before he continued. 'I have never missed anyone like I have missed Frank. We were all in the trenches together when we had the order to advance, and Frank was one of the first to meet his death.'[71] The intimacy of the battalion shows through the natural feelings of restraint that many have in writing to a grieving loved one of someone who died violently. A month after Loos, Burchett's grief was made public in the local paper. Joining Burchett in writing about the battle was Quartermaster Sergeant George Kerswell, who sent his own reflection on Loos to the *Surrey Advertiser*. He recalled bluntly, 'I shall never forget the day – never. Both my dear chums have been killed … It seems all very terrible. Lads you were talking to one hour were dead the next … One must not dwell on the sad results of these actions, of course, but naturally it is a little heartbreaking to think of many "gone west."'[72] These men shared their stories and mourned for families who were desperate for news from the men who served with their loved ones.

Some of the families continued their search for information on their own in the press. One such was the family of musician Thomas Bristow of Redhill, Surrey who died in the Hulluch Salient. Bristow was a former member of the Redhill Men's Own Band and ended up playing in the 8th Queen's regimental band as a drummer. After receiving notice that her son was missing, Mrs E.J. Bristow advertised for information related to his death in at least three local papers before the War Office informed her, a year later, that Thomas was presumed dead.[73] Her sense of desperation for news was, no doubt, compounded by the fact that her other son, Jesse, had been captured in April 1915 and she hoped for the same fate for Thomas. Sadly, Bristow would never again play for the Redhill Men's Own Band.

---

71 'Elstead Men in the 8th Queen's Private Frank Ellis Killed,' *Surrey Advertiser*, 25 October 1915.
72 'Stories of the Fighting. New Malden Man's Letter,' *Surrey Advertiser*, 11 October 1915.
73 'Missing Now Reported Dead,' *Surrey Mirror*, 3 November 1916.

At home in Carshalton, the Peirs family contacted several relatives to offer what comfort they could. The Cressy family was known to them. As was the Fairtlough family. Others reached out to Peirs for information and his family helped as they could. The sister of Captain Charles Waldie wrote to Peirs several times and called upon his family in Carshalton. She held out hope for good news of her brother, but as Peirs wrote to his sister in 1916, however, 'the chances are against him now.'[74] As a Canadian with a limited social network in Britain, having someone to write to within the battalion and a family in Surrey that offered kindness to her became a part of her coping with her brother's death.

Maud Fairtlough and her children joined the mourning of all these families. Her husband, Howard, the 'old man' of the battalion, lay in no man's land with his men. No one could say for certain where he was; his body was in contested and exposed ground, surrounded by those of his battalion and brigade that he had trained and had grown to know, now his comrades in death. On 2 October, the official telegram came to Surrey informing Maud that he had been killed. The telegram had an additional sentence that 'Lord Kitchener expresses his sympathy' for the man who had trained one of the battalions bearing his name.[75] A few days later, another telegram arrived from Buckingham Palace from King George V and Queen Mary, informing her that their majesties 'deeply regret the loss you and the army have sustained.'[76] Joining the official condolences were a host of other tributes in the press and a well-attended memorial service in Surrey.

The loss of her husband came with an excruciating ambiguity. Maud had very few details about the manner of his death and the location of his body. Like many other grieving widows and mothers, she longed to know more about her husband's final minutes. Peirs wrote to her on 30 September trying to fill in the details. As the battalion's new commanding officer, it fell to him to provide to her with what little information he had. Peirs sought comfort and consolation, writing 'from those who were near him at the time, I believe that his death was instantaneous.'[77] Though they had attempted to find his body, the area was now inaccessible. 'The regiment is heart broken

74 Peirs to Charlotte, 23 January 1916.
75 TNA, WO 339/20331, War Office telegram to Maud Fairtlough, 2 October 1915.
76 IWM, Doc 12610 Fairtlough Papers, Telegram from Buckingham Palace to Maud Fairtlough, p.492.
77 IWM, Doc 12610 Fairtlough Papers, Peirs to Maud Fairtlough, 30 September 1915, pp.477–8.

at his loss', he continued, 'as they ought to be as no man could have raised or trained a battalion better than he.' Of course, Peirs knew that such words could provide only small comfort to a woman who was searching for answers. Yet, he continued, 'you will have the satisfaction of knowing that he died like a gentleman at the head of his men and that the regiment adored him.'[78] Joining Peirs were condolences from their brigade commander General Mitford, as well as from common soldiers who adored their colonel.[79]

Though praise and condolences likely provided a small degree of comfort, nothing could assuage Maud Fairtlough's desire to know more about the circumstances of his death and where he was buried.[80] This lingered with her for the rest of the war and beyond. She had two children at home and three abroad serving their country, so her focus was on the living, as well as the memory of the dead. She was also faced with the financial burdens of her family alone. Her two children were her direct dependents: a son Leslie and a daughter Victoire. Her son was in public school and her daughter was living at home.[81] Of course, she had lost more than just a financial backer; she also lost a devoted spouse, and the children lost a loving father.[82] Nothing, though, could really replace his presence both at home and within a battalion. They clearly loved the man who had trained them for war and in tragic irony he had fallen within the first few moments they were in combat. The 'old man' was the one who formed them, trained them, led them, and was among the first to die with them.[83] The task fell to those remaining to cobble together what lessons they could from the debacle they had survived. For them, there would never be a day that passed without a faint recollection of Loos; it was the central collective trauma of their war experiences, the most poignant, bloody, and terrible day for the battalion.

---

78 Ibid.
79 IWM, Doc 12610 Fairtlough Papers, pp.499–514.
80 She continued to write to the Peirs family. See Maud Fairtlough to Peirs 30 March 1919.
81 For some details on her finances, see TNA, WO 339/20331, Maud Fairtlough to the War Office, received 29 April 1916.
82 Their correspondence indicates a degree of tenderness.
83 Like the others, Fairtlough is remembered on the Loos Memorial within eyesight of the battlefield.

Chapter 4

Hardening

On Sunday, 10 October 1915 the men formed into their ranks on parade outside of their camp near Reninghelst, Belgium. They were flanked by the other battalions in the 72nd Brigade, 24th Division. The sun beamed through the grey clouds of an autumnal northern European sky. Though the weather was fair compared to the recent rain, the men did not look or feel fine; their uniforms were damp from wet days and nearly all were dirty from their first training in trenches a few days before. In mind and spirit, they bore their tiredness; their faces worn and weathered from sun and exposure, eyes sunken despite the fact that they had rested.

It was not just the physical fatigue and the discomfort that burdened them; they were burdened by the obtrusive thoughts of men who now knew extreme danger and the depths of their own fears. It had been a matter of days since Loos and they were decompressing from their experience. Now they were starting, as a collective group, to attempt to put into a tidy narrative – one with a beginning, middle, and end – events that were disjointed in their telling and confusing in their chronology. They recalled the temporal details of their experiences through a thick filter of trauma, muddled and untrustworthy in their recollection, memories that might never be clear. The battalion's survivors echoed their commanding officer's 'considerable mental disturbance' from their failed attack at Hulluch.[1] Loos would follow its veterans for the rest of their lives.

It was now fully apparent what this disaster meant. They had left England six weeks before with a full complement: 1,000 fit and healthy men full of a careful balance of excitement and anxiety. Loos reduced them by half. Those on parade at Reninghelst were the survivors, now joined by few dozen replacements. The new men had come from England the week before. As the partially reconstituted 8th Queen's stood in church parade, they were flanked

---

1   TNA, CAB 45/121, H.J.C. Peirs to Sir James Edmonds, 17 June 1926.

by the other battalions who also knew their equal burden. The 8th West Kents, who took the brunt of the first volleys of machine gun fire in their attack and over whose wounded they walked towards the German wire, paraded with them. The 9th East Surreys, who had absorbed the machine gun bursts along their right flank (and whose men went down in droves), were there. The Buffs, who tried, as they did, to plug the gaps in their fragile and faltering assault, stood in ranks equally as thin as the others. The brigade in total lost 1,979 men.[2] Seventy-five officers were killed, wounded, or missing, many of the latter presumed dead.[3] The same shroud of sorrow draped each battalion as they gathered before the padre to pray. To say they stood as broken men is to patronise the many conflicted feelings of these newly initiated soldiers in earnest, for the first time under fire.

It was not just the number of casualties inflicted upon them. It was also the quality of the men they lost. For a year, they had built bonds of comradeship and had had confidence in their officers. Only a week before, the 8th Queen's were led by a commanding officer whom they trusted implicitly. Colonel Frederick Howard Fairtlough was the very image of British martiality. A week before, too, they had junior officers whom they had come to know and respect through a year spent on the parade ground. These officers were all of the old public-school type; plucky, well-heeled, and with a certain football-pitch enthusiasm for their training. Joining them were their NCOs, men appointed because of their ability to command respect, who had grown into their authority and learned to keep order; men who knew their soldiers intimately after training them and living amongst their ranks for a year. Now, as they stood at church parade, their colonel was dead and half their officers and NCOs were killed or wounded. We know little about how these soldiers grieved their comrades at the front, but we can assume that all lost messmates and chums for whom they mourned dearly.

There they stood in their reduced platoons and companies under a new commanding officer, 29-year-old solicitor, whose major's crowns were only sewn on his uniform sleeves a few months before their embarkation. Yet, their civilian CO had the bearing of a man who had been raised with a sense of entitlement and authority, but also one who had demonstrated coolness

---

2 TNA, WO 95 2193–1_033, 24th Division Casualties Battle of Loos 25–28 September (approximate).

3 Edmonds, *Military Operations in France & Belgium, 1915, Vol. 2*, p.342.

under fire. His uniform might be tailored, but it was worn from a week's marching and sleeping and it bore the stains and strain of their burden too. Before Loos the men knew Peirs as their colonel's right-hand man, the one Fairtlough relied on and trusted to oil the machine of the battalion. A former militia officer, Peirs knew how to pose on the parade ground, and at Loos he had proven himself in battle. They saw him advance calmly under fire, command the battalion after Fairtlough fell, and then withdraw in good order; they saw him cross 700 yards of open terrain untouched by machine gun or sniper fire. They saw him search for his men that night in the rain and darkness, looking after the survivors. If they had no confidence in his ability to command before, Peirs had earned it in the shadow of Hulluch as he walked back across a field of wounded and dead, one of the last men of the last platoon of a decimated battalion to make it back from the German second line.

Thus, the remnant of the old 8ᵗʰ Queen's stood before the padre at attention in their reduced companies. The brigade chaplain held in his hands two pages of field notebook paper. Copied upon it was a message he had received from General Bertram Mitford, their brigade commander, who was ill and unable to address the men himself. He began reading it slowly out loud:

> 72nd Infantry Brigade. Last Sunday the Brigade went into <u>action</u> for the first time only a year after they came forward at their <u>country's call</u>. The way the Brigade advanced under very heavy machine gun fire from flanks and rear has evoked the approbation of the Divisional and Corps Commanders. You were an example in steadiness and determination to carry out your task not only to the <u>New Armies</u> but to seasoned troops who could not have done better than you did.[4]

No doubt, Peirs kept his focus on the words of the chaplain, who was reading with the deliberate clarity of the clergy. He certainly agreed with the sentiments Mitford expressed and he had written nearly the same praise of his men to his family in the aftermath of the battle. Yet, perhaps his mind wandered; perhaps he found the task difficult, however necessary, to listen to

---

4   TNA, WO 95/2214/1, 8ᵗʰ Queen's War Diary, 10 October 1915.

such glowing terms of what had been a disaster. Theirs was an unsupported attack by a green brigade against a heavily entrenched enemy. Hindsight made stark the predictable failure of their task.

Surely, Mitford's sentiment was undoubtedly sincere, not to mention correct in his praise of their bravery. But many of the men, equally surely, did not feel brave. Peirs knew that much, and he knew that they knew it too. Perhaps now with a week of sodden uniforms and sore feet, they were too weary to feel deeply; some were probably numb in their fatigue. Some were likely anxious and worried about both what they had been through and what they would go through. Some were deep in mourning, unable to stop thinking about their comrades left behind. All probably felt severely the loss and a pang of guilt for leaving so many men dead and wounded on the field. Even someone as stoic as Peirs thought about his fellow officers, Fairtlough and Charlie Cressy, whose corpses now lay in no man's land. The padre continued:

> As I say you carried out your task but you had to retire. Yet do not think it was a failure for it was not, as you caused 16 of the enemy's battalions of reserve to be brought up into our area and taken away from the French just south of us thereby enabling the French to make an appreciable advance.[5]

This was a bitter consolation. The purpose of their attack was not to tie down German soldiers, but to break through the German second line and to turn the tide of the battle. Most of the other ranks did not know that was the intention of their advance, but no one could have found great comfort in knowing their pals died to tie down sixteen German battalions. He continued:

> I should like all of you who know the relatives of those who are not with us to make known to them how gallantly they fought and how nobly they served their country in whose service they fell and what prestige they brought to the names of the regiments to which they belonged. Men of the Queens, Buffs, East Surreys, and West Kents you have added glory to the ancient regiments of which you are the children. You have made the 72nd Infantry Brigade a

---

5   Ibid.

name which none of you can be other than proud of and which
I know in the future you will never allow to diminish. I feel it a
great honour to have had the chance of commanding such troops
on service and I shall never forget the ground about HULLUCH
village.[6]

Children of storied regiments with esteemed histories only get one so far.
For all their confidence a week before, they had additional feelings of failure,
guilt, and hindsight's scorn for naivete.

The attack at Hulluch was a brutal initiation. The men had on their minds
the hundreds of men who now lay before the German wire. Mitford was a
good and sympathetic commander and one cannot fault him for trying to
assuage his men's sadness, while also trying to save face for himself and the
brigade staff. Hindsight proved him right – the brigade did all that it could
with the information it had and the orders it was given – but at the time
both his brigade and the whole division's conduct was subject to stigma for
their failure.

Peirs and his remaining officers knew this as they stood on command.
Yet, they now had their talking points from their brigadier and knew how
to frame the story of their attack. The great task now facing the officers and
NCOs was to take these dirty and demoralised men and make them into
effective fighters. They had to lick their wounds, to learn from Loos, and
to reconstitute an effective fighting battalion. The Queen's had a temporary
commanding officer who proved resilient, but also one who understood that
his men were not regular soldiers and had to be treated with additional care
and respect. Peirs understood something fundamental, but essential; his
battalion was a collection of civilians bearing arms. Loos proved to him that
they had courage. His task was now to make sure that they could meet their
next trial with skill.

Church parade finished and the brigade was dismissed. Peirs went back
to his billet to copy General Mitford's message for his commanding officer's
widow, Maud Fairtlough. The next day, the battalion turned out on parade
to meet their new divisional commanding officer, Major General John
Capper. Their new commander was a monocled iron-jawed career army
officer whose tone was distinctly different than Mitford. He 'he bade us not

---

6 Ibid.

to be disheartened by our recent losses but rather to be urged by them to a greater fury towards the enemy who caused them.'[7] Capper's own brother had been killed at Loos. The question now was how to muster their collective sense of fury.

Recovery

Loos was a disaster for the battalion, the brigade, and the division. The War Office required a report to learn what exactly went wrong. Though the reasons for failure were complex, the exhausted state of the men and the inexperience of the officers in the division were a part of the narrative developing from the attack. The emerging verdict was that the 24th Division was too exhausted to carry out a proper assault on the German second line because of 'poor march discipline' that wore out the men.[8] To those who survived, this conclusion seemed unfair. Despite their fatigue, they performed as well as any brigade could under the same circumstances. Though their fatigue was palpable, so too was a failure in staff planning in their march into theatre, a failure to understand and accommodate for the complicated defensive position they were charged with attacking, and unrealistic expectations for taking their objectives given the materials at hand, especially in artillery preparation and protection of their flanks.

This sense of utter sadness was deeply psychological for the men who survived. Regimental Quartermaster Sergeant George Kerswell reflected mournfully in an otherwise chipper letter to the *Surrey Advertiser* in December 1915 about what they had been through. He wrote:

> Of course, the battalion is not the same as before Loos. Before that terrible Sunday, I believe I knew every officer, N.C.O. and man in the battalion, but the loss of so many dear good friends and the advent of new drafts has altered the regiment altogether. I have no doubt that the new additions are every bit as good as the men whose gaps they fill, but one has lost that personal touch. Perhaps I am more sentimental than a soldier should be, but when you have

---

7   SHC, Unpublished Battalion History, p.14.
8   The Loos report is found in the National Archives WO 158/261. Though Capper's report is more complicated than this simple verdict, it is a point emphasised in section 34 (p.20). For a detailed critique of the 'myths' surrounding the general reserve's deployment at Loos, see Nigel Atter, *In the Shadow of Bois Hugo*, pp.12–13, 31–4, 68–71.

slept, marched, dined, and played with lads for a whole year, and lost them in one afternoon, it cannot pass unnoticed.[9]

It should be emphasised that Kerswell wrote this with several months of distance from Loos, where he had time to decompress and think about the experience. Like the other survivors, he was contextualising his experiences, taking fragments of his own memories and those of his chums and forming them into a story, a story to be told over and over again. Kerswell's reflection is a rare public admission of mourning. All men knew the risks of death and maiming were part of the soldier's life; none expected so many without another word heard from again.

Though utterly tragic, the 72nd Brigade's debut moment on the battlefield serves as a benchmark for understanding their conduct for the rest of the war. From Loos onwards, the 8th Queen's and its sister battalions needed to learn how to fight on the Western Front to prove that they were not ill-disciplined amateurs. It became the task of Peirs and the survivors to revive the battered battalion and to turn them into a resilient, effective, and adaptable unit.

The process of training the battalion into effective soldiers developed over the winter of 1915/16. Though they had been under fire, the men had not developed the routine or physical/emotional hardening necessary for trench warfare. The process of conditioning and acclimating them to the front began in earnest after Loos. Pragmatically, with half their officers killed or wounded, the battalion had to both reconstitute its ranks but also train new officers and NCOs on the job. And rather than being given a period of rest after their ordeal, the brigade immediately began rotating in and out of trenches to relieve other units and to gain experience in the line. The survivors had no significant time to rest; they had to put their boots back on and get back to work.

The days after their attack were physically difficult. Leaving the Loos battlefield on 27 September, they had three days of rest at Berguette before then making their way to Houtkerque, a French village near the Belgian border. It was a hard 12-mile march; their boots sank inches into thick mud and the pace was slow. The nights were cold and the mornings came with frost. They marched a further 18 miles to rotate into the line in support of

---

9 'The 8th Queen's. Cheery letter from Q.M.S. Kerswell,' *Surrey Advertiser,* 13 December 1915, p.2.

the 27th Brigade, the distance arduous, with unforgiving muddy roads.[10] To compound their discomfort, their billets were terrible and they found the locals 'boorish'.[11] The battalion war diary, in an unusual editorial aside, wrote that there was 'great difficulty in finding billets as people not very friendly.'[12]

Yet, the brief rest after Loos and the march away from the front seemed to have a restorative effect. Peirs wrote to his mother more cheerfully on 2 October, 'One thing is that it is a land of good drink as the white wine is A1 and the beer very pleasant and we only have to go 2 miles to buy cigars without paying duty i.e. into Belgium.'[13] Three days after arriving at Houtkerque, the battalion went back to work rotating companies into nearby trenches for instruction. This began their trench education. For the next eight months they rotated in and out of trenches before being transferred to the Somme the following summer.

It should be emphasised that they entered trench training only nine days after Loos. In those nine days they had only three days of decent rest, the remainder spent marching, reorganising, and training. As the battalion gained experience, they demonstrated a trait identified by Alexander Watson that service 'actually strengthened men's will, if not their ability, to endure.'[14] Rest was an important part of this equation, one written about by Lord Moran, who likened courage to a bank account and noted that men's courage was spent through exposure, battle, monotony, and beyond anything else, shelling.[15] When Moran joined the 24th Division just after Loos as a battalion medical officer in early October 1915, what he saw of the Kitchener volunteers did not impress him. He found the men ill-disciplined and still strongly civilian. His servant observed that they appeared almost broken by battle, asking 'where 'ave these blokes come out of? They're scared pink.'[16]

Even with Moran's uncharitable critique of his new division, it is interesting to see how quickly Peirs and the battalion got back to work after their ordeal. There was no widespread malingering or even any indication within the written records of the men being demoralised. In his letters to his family

---

10 TNA, WO 95/2214/1, 8th Queen's War Diary, 5 October 1915.

11 Peirs to his family, 2 October 1915.

12 Peirs to his family, 2 October 1915; TNA, WO 95/2214/1, 8th Queen's War Diary, 2 October 1915.

13 Peirs to his family, 2 October 1915.

14 Alexander Watson, *Enduring the Great War*, p.72.

15 Lord Moran, *Anatomy of Courage* (New York: Carroll & Graf Publishers, 2007), pp.xxii–xxiii.

16 Ibid., p.83.

in early October, Peirs seems his old self; his focus was on food, drink, and tobacco and he fretted about replacing his lost Burberry with a better rain-coat (an Aquascutum). Emotional recovery was a fairly ordinary trait of men on the Western Front. Work, no doubt, helped the men focus on something other than lost comrades; the battalion's war diary's subtext in early October 1915 shows both the physical and emotional stamina of men who had no sus-tained time to rest or grieve. Rather than their busyness being a detriment, putting their bodies back to the task at hand, with minimal risks, might have kept their minds off what they had just been through.

The question became what was the army to do with this diminished battalion, brigade, and division? First, it reformed each of these entities and did so with fresh drafts from England to complement the survivors. Second, their new divisional commanding officer, Major General John Capper, was talented career army engineer with a penchant for innovative technology. He was a no-nonsense commander and he had a personal reason for being out for vengeance with the loss of his brother, Major General Sir Thompson Capper. It fell to Capper to strike the right tone with the division and to see that it got back to fighting strength. The day after he took command, the division was moved into V Corps in the British Second Army in Belgium.[17] There they began on-the-job training in trench warfare.

The Salient
The battalion did not take part in any significant action from October 1915 until August 1916; however, they were nearly constantly busy manning trenches, training, and conducting small scale operations. To some degree, the period from Loos to the Somme marks the most important period for the development of the unit. Here they learned how to survive in the attritional struggle that lay before them for the next three years. In Belgian trenches, the battalion became hardened by service.

The Queen's took to trenches near Ypres. This small bit of western Belgium held the rump of the Belgian army and the British Second Army, who manned the muddy ramparts stretching from the North Sea to the French border. Ypres was a costly place, one that developed deep cultural meaning for the British beyond its strategic importance of protecting the

---

17 TNA, WO 95/2210/2, 72nd Brigade War Diary, 6 October 1915.

channel ports.[18] The market town held deep psychological value to the men who had defended it with their lives since October 1914. The Belgians and the British were determined to hold onto this sliver of the otherwise occupied nation.

One could scarcely imagine a worse place to fight. Mostly flat and with a high water table, trench warfare in Flanders was waterlogged and miserable. The Germans occupied the high ground to the east – a series of low-lying ridges – and were able to observe and harass the British with little recourse. It was a particularly dismal place for infantry manning trenches; outside of the major offensives, battalions mostly held the line. The fighting consisted of strafing with mortars, artillery, and active snipers. This low-intensity conflict caused daily casualties, as did the cold and the filthy conditions of Flanders. To serve at Ypres was mostly to endure Ypres. It was, however, a place where men could be conditioned to the western front.

The 24th Division moved northwards from France and into trenches in the salient. As Michael Lucas wrote in his battalion history of the 9th East Surreys, 'Following its bloody initiation at Loos, the 24th Division's losses needed to be made good and other perceived deficiencies addressed. It had to take its place in the trenches, to hold the line over the winter period when active operations were likely to be reduced.'[19] Those deficiencies were mostly inexperience between what they had learned at home compared to the realities of combat at the front. To address them, the division went into rotation for trench duty, and when they were behind the lines, rigorous training in developing fighting techniques.

In mid-October, the 8th Queen's began its first tour of trenches. Understrength with only 440 men, the battalion entered wet and collapsing trenches that they attempted to improve at night within observation of German snipers. It was a difficult and physically laborious business. The communication trenches were in rough shape and the men had to attempt to improve them so that they could get up and down the line safely, which they could only do under darkness.[20] Once relieved, they faced a 10-mile march back to billets. Complicating this was the occasional sniper or whizz bang shell. They took ten casualties during their first three days of rotation. At the

---

18 See Mark Connelly and Stefan Goebel's book on the cultural meaning of Ypres. Mark Connelly and Stefan Goebel, *Ypres* (Oxford: Oxford University Press, 2018).

19 Michael Lucas, *The Journey's End Battalion*, p.25.

20 Peirs to Cecily, 8 November 1915.

end of the month they repeated their rotation, only with fewer casualties. After a week of training, they again repeated their tenure in the trenches in November, moving back and forth between their camp at Dickebusch and trenches for most of the month.

Notably, they did so under new leadership. Though Major Peirs had hoped to command the battalion and had been given some indication by General Mitford that this would be the case, the division thought it more prudent to replace killed or invalided COs with men who had more experience. The battalion came under the command of Lieutenant Colonel Archibald Tringham, DSO, a spry 46-year-old officer with vast experience in imperial service in India, Malta, and the Boer War.[21] Though Peirs was initially apprehensive of their new commander for being too much a regular army martinet for volunteer soldiers, their partnership proved to be a good one.

In their first exposure to trench warfare the battalion learned how to function in a static environment. They identified and improved weak spots in field fortifications, they organised wiring parties, and they patrolled no man's land. They learned how to mess together in terrible conditions; how to keep warm despite the damp and cold; they learned how to cope with dirty bodies and uniforms; and they learned how to gain fleeting amounts of rest during the quiet hours of the day. They learned, in short, trench routine and the physical and emotional adjustment to a straining environment. They also learned the universal soldier's balance of time between monotony and terror. They could pick out the sounds of enemy mortars and shells and how to avoid risk from snipers, the latter very active in their section of the line. Learning the logic of the front was something that they could gain only from experience.

When the men left their trenches in early December they were badly in need of a rest. Their last rotation had been for eight long days in a particularly grim section of the line. Despite their attention to hygiene, the men's feet were sore and swollen, particularly after marching on French pavé (cobblestones) to their rest area.[22] In Nordausques they trained and rested for the next month. There they dug mock German trenches and attacked them. For the first time they trained extensively with bombs and the men had courses of instruction in close-order fighting, skills developed for trench raiding.

---

21 SHC, QRWS/30/TRIN, p.1.
22 SHC, Unpublished Battalion History, p.16.

Officers and NCOs had specialty courses where they learned scouting and sniping. The battalion also participated in football matches and foot races to raise morale. Two of the Queen's subalterns, lieutenants Lane-Nichols and Payne, finished in first place in running before then being disqualified for wearing shoes.[23] The brigade arranged weekly cinema and evening concerts. At the end of the month, the men had Christmas dinner together with their companies. At New Year, every man was a refreshed and a more informed fighter. Beyond this, they were rejuvenated and ready to go back into the line:

> A month's rest had greatly improved the morale, had enabled us to assimilate the very large reinforcements received since Loos and had given officers and men a chance of knowing and working with each other. But above all it had given us time to digest the lessons we had already learnt by experience [...] when we returned to the line, we felt far more self-confident and knowledgeable.[24]

Rested and ready, they went back to the salient. The men were physically fitter than they had been since their arrival in France. Along with the rest of the brigade, they began again their next trench rotation.

Though the battalion war diary records winter 1916 largely in terms of the matter-of-fact daily life of siege warfare at Ypres, there are indications that the battalion adapted their fighting methods. When the men began their January trench tour, they marched through Ypres to the ruined asylum, where they changed their ammunition boots for hip waders before marching out along the Menin Road to take their position in the Hooge sector.[25] The battalion now had Lewis guns, snipers, and men trained and specifically designated as bombers.[26] They grew more sophisticated in their use of new weapons as they trained in new tactics. This was reflected at the brigade level where there was increased emphasis on rotating officers and NCOs into training schemes.

When the men were in the line, their duty was largely to repair trenches and to go on patrol. Patrols became a nightly occurrence. Working parties

---

23 TNA, WO/95/2210/2, 72nd Brigade War Diary, December 1915.
24 SHC, Unpublished Battalion History, p.18.
25 TNA, WO 95/2214/1, 8th Queen's War Diary, 12 January 1916.
26 TNA, WO 95/2214/1, 8th Queen's War Diary, 12 January 1916; SHC, Unpublished Battalion History, p.18.

laboured to keep trenches intact and as dry as possible. There were daily casualties from shelling, sniping, and from German machine gun strafing, which all indicates that they faced an opponent who was not comfortable with 'live and let live'. The brigade retaliated in kind and British snipers were equally active. Their aggressiveness displayed a sense of confidence in the new environment.

Another aspect of learning came through anticipating the enemy's movement through observation and intelligence. Though their field of view was limited, the battalion paid attention to what was happening to their front and were at times on high alert. For example, in January 1916 there was concern that the Germans were planning a gas attack. While positioned in trenches to the north of the Menin Road, the enemy placed a flag to their front to taunt the British. A private of the 8th Buffs attempted to retrieve the flag at dusk. He was wounded in the attempt and left stranded in no man's land. Private Homer of the Queen's went out after him and, under heavy fire, completed the recue and brought him back to safety.[27]

The next day, after nightfall, Lieutenant C.P. Burnley went on patrol alone and retrieved the flag.[28] On one side of the flag was an imperial eagle; on the other, a series of inscriptions:

> 'What is King Albert doing'
> 'Thick (Bulging) Bertha from Essen'[29]
> 'Follow the example of Servia and Montenegro whom you courageously betrayed.'
> 'Kaiser's birthday 27.1.16'[30]

The last sentence caused particular disturbance as it was interpreted as a threat of an attack on the Kaiser's birthday, or at least, of a significant bombardment which did not happen. Their war diaries indicate that both the brigade and division remained skittish about a possible German attack for

---

27 Homer earned the DCM for his bravery. *Surrey Advertiser*, 20 March 1916, 1; See also SHC, Unpublished Battalion History, p.18. Homer sadly died of wounds on 30 April 1916.
28 This act of bravery was not his only confrontation with the enemy that spring. Burnley was captured in March while on patrol.
29 Nickname for a 42-centimetre cannon.
30 TNA, WO/95 2210/2, 72nd Brigade War Diary, 25 January 1916.

the next three months. In particular, staff were afraid of a gas attack; daily the brigade war diary recorded the direction and force of the wind.

Despite this small drama, most of the early year was spent in trenches trying to make them inhabitable with frequent rotations. Peirs indicated some irritability with the constant back and forth between the lines:

> These constant reliefs are an awful nuisance, but we find that the men cannot stand too much as they have little or no shelter & many of them very little sleep. Those actually in the front line are better off than those in the support lines, as the latter have to find all the fatigues & it is no joke lugging up rations over broken ground & muddy trenches in the dark. We have to bring all our water up & engineer stoves, so you can imagine that there is a lot to carry.[31]

Peirs felt the perennial frustration of battalion officers that the brass hats were unaware of the conditions in the line. When General Capper toured his trenches, Peirs believed that he was 'humbled' by the conditions in which these men had to endure.[32]

Though living in terrible conditions for most of the winter, the battalion earned a rest in March when they went into training for half the month. Now clad in steel helmets, they trained in gas defence, sniping, and more bomb throwing. When they went back into the line at the end of the month, it was noted that the brigade's 'ascendency over the enemy's snipers has become more marked.'[33] When April came, they continued actively patrolling in no man's land, exerting dominance over their front and keeping the enemy harassed. Of course, the enemy replied in kind, and the brigade took casualties nearly every day. Most worrying was the threat of gas. At the end of April, a British bombardment exploded gas cylinders in the enemy's trenches. Intelligence from enemy deserters confirmed that a gas attack was imminent. Staff officers minded the wind and the battalion remained on high alert.

---

31 Peirs Papers, 26 January 1916.
32 Peirs Papers, 29 January 1916.
33 TNA, WO 95/2210/2, 72nd Brigade War Diary, 18 March 1916.

Wulverghem

In April 1916, the 24th Division moved south of Ypres to Wulverghem. British forces were active in maintaining their trenches and in mining towards the German lines to the east along Messines Ridge. In places the trench lines were close; some areas were only 40 or 50 yards apart. On 26 April 1916, the 8th Queen's moved up the line to relieve the 8th Royal West Kents.

The battalion knew gas cylinders were in the German trenches and anticipated a German raid. While Lieutenant Colonel Tringham was on leave in England, Peirs took command and made sure that the battalion's Lewis guns were ready, that the wire was thick and strong to their front, and that there was ample supply of bombs to break up an attack. They had clear orders: 'In the event of attack, the front line will be maintained with determination and should the enemy gain a footing in a portion of this line, a counter-attack will be launched by the Commander on the spot, with the object of clearing the trenches and limiting the enemy's sphere of operations.'[34] Months of training had prepared them to repulse a raid; yet, the men had never been exposed to a gas attack and did not have full confidence in their gas helmets. More worrisome, the helmets themselves had eyepieces that made it difficult to see through clearly. Especially during a nighttime engagement, clear visibility was the difference in recognising friend from foe, and thus could be the difference between life and death.

Aside from a few Lewis gunners who were issued with the new Small Box Respirator, the men of the 24th Division were all issued with the Phenate Hexamine (PH) gas helmet as their defensive countermeasure to chlorine gas. The PH helmet was not a hard helmet, as the name would suggest, but was a cloth bag soaked in chemicals that could neutralise gas.[35] The front of the helmet had eyeholes and a protruding mouthpiece that gave soldiers a cone-shaped beak when wearing it. It was an ugly and awkward bag that irritated the skin, but it was also an effective countermeasure if it was placed on the head quickly before exposure to gas and if worn correctly, with the bottom of the bag tucked into the soldier's tunic so that gas could not get

---

34 TNA, WO 95/2210/2, 72nd Brigade War Diary, 'Action in Case of Attack,' April 1916.
35 Australian War Memorial, 'PH Helmet respirator: British Army', https://www.awm.gov.au/collection/C164321.

underneath.[36] The men of the Queen's had trained with their helmets, but had notably never fought with them on.

The German units opposite were the 209th and 212th regiments of the 45th Reserve Division made up of men from Prussia, Pomerania, and Hamburg. The division had fought in the Second Battle of Ypres, where poison gas was used for the first time, and had been in Belgium for well over a year. In April, they positioned nearly 5,000 gas cylinders in their trenches for use in an extensive raid in force; its purpose to destroy the British mines opposite.

The 24th Division had ample warning. They knew gas cylinders were in the German front lines. Gas was dangerous and volatile, particularly within a region with active artillery, and the cylinders would not be forward unless they were going to be used. The division also had warning from a number of captured deserters who came across no man's land and reported that an attack was imminent. This information not only made it to GHQ, but also made it to each battalion commander in the line. So, the men were ready for an attack, but they could not predict when it would take place. For that, they had to mind the wind. A shift to a westerly wind was a telltale sign that an attack was possible, if not probable.

On 29 April, the wind shifted and the brigade went on gas alert. The wind was a strong 12 miles per hour, enough to certainly carry enemy gas well beyond their front-line trenches and affect rear areas. As evening turned to night the men waited on their firesteps. At 12:30 am, the German front line came alive with rifle and machine gun fire strafing the front of their trenches. They stood alert by the parapet. This sudden covering outburst of machine gun fire could have been a demonstration of force, or it could have been cover for a raid. They simply did not know.

A few minutes later, the men's nostrils and throats became irritated. Some began choking. As they took panicky deep breaths, they felt their throats tighten and their airways burning. The call of gas went out and the battalion fired verey lights above to illuminate both their own position and no man's land. What they saw was a battlefield blanketed with a thick gas cloud 6 feet high. Filling their trench was a toxic mixture of chlorine and phosgene gas. The men hastened to put on their PH helmets, some succeeding in time to

---

36 These are the points emphasised in the after action report in the gas attack. See TNA, WO 95/2210/2, 72nd Brigade War Diary, 29–30 April, 'Gas Attack – Summary of Reports'.

man their guns and wait for an attack. Others had already succumbed and were choking as they strained to get their helmets on.

While chlorine gas had been used on the Western Front over a year previously, phosgene was a relatively new agent and was used as a choking gas. Indeed, in large doses, it has greater lethality than chlorine. Both gases cause burning and choking; phosgene, though, causes extensive lung damage that can be either immediate or manifest itself within days of the exposure. As their position was close to the German lines, this meant that the Queen's received the brunt of the concentration of gas before it moved on and dissipated towards the rear areas. The men also had their gas helmets in their bags and not on top of their heads, which meant some fumbled to get them on in time. All of the men in the battalion had been exposed to gas to varying degrees, as soon as it was smelt within their trenches. Some who could not reach their helmets lay dying, while their comrades looked on helplessly. Others who had taken deep breaths of it, while still getting their helmets on, now choked and gasped for breath under their chemical hoods, each man wondering if his next breath would be his last. All were certainly under varying degrees of heightened adrenaline that for some was surely panic; their eyes blurry and their nostrils and throats irritated.

Yet, they stood firm and held their position. The gas was heavy at first, but then the strong wind blew it mostly out of their trenches. Now with their helmets on, they stayed put with their wounded comrades and waited for the attack that would surely come. Officers and NCOs maintained order; no one panicked and ran. Most stood at the parapet and watched for silhouettes coming from the east towards them. Then mortar rounds and shrapnel began landing to their rear, deliberate shelling of their support lines to break up their communications and to prevent reinforcement in the event they were overrun. Certainly, this meant an attack. They had to stay where they were; to their front were the Germans, in their trench was gas, and in their rear was fierce shelling. They had no choice but to hold the line.

The Lewis guns were the first to fire. They began sweeping the enemy's parapet at the first sign of an attack. German soldiers who had already crawled out into no man's land began their rush towards their wire. The men on the firestep levelled their rifles and sought targets in no man's land, likely without much success due to the difficulty in seeing through their masks. Still, the men held their nerve and stopped the German raid to their front. Once they saw that the Germans were attacking without masks, the men tested the air and removed their PH helmets, before finding their targets with their rifles. To their left, the 1st Staffords had a harder time, their line penetrated by a raiding party. Some of the men of the Queen's came to their aid and ejected the Germans by bombing up the trench, a hazardous business. By 3:00 am the show was over and the men, now out of their masks and exhausted, began counting their casualties and cleaning up.[37]

When daybreak came, they were astonished by what they saw in no man's land. The grass had turned brown and their trenches were full of dead rats, a reminder of the lethality of the concentrated gas. Peirs wrote to his mother that afternoon that the 'gas simply burns up all the vegetation where it is strongest & the whole of No Mans [*sic*] Land where it came over is now absolutely withered.'[38] They had high casualties – 110 men were exposed to gas and evacuated – about a fourth of their trench strength.[39] Considering that they had virtually no warning until the gas was in their trenches, the situation could have been worse. It could have been better, however, had they worn their gas helmets on top of their heads instead of keeping them within their protective bag. The wind changed in a few days and they were no longer under direct threat of another gas attack, which had the men relieved. Peirs wrote again to his mother to assuage her worry with a lighthearted observation of the attack:

> It would make you scream with laughter to watch a party of men in their gas helmets. They look exactly like so many ducks & they waddle in the same way, as it is very difficult to see out of one, & when you speak to a man you see a whole row of heads turning round & peering up at you, as you can only look straight in front of your face. Each helmet has a tube sticking out from the mouth which looks exactly like a beak – the men call it a goblin parade when they have to wear them.[40]

---

37 Details from the raid above are drawn from the brigade and battalion war diaries as well as both the official and unofficial histories. The facts of the raid are relatively consistent throughout the accounts.
38 Peirs to his mother, 30 April 1916.
39 TNA, WO 95/2214/1, 8th Queen's War Diary, 30 April 1916.
40 Peirs to his mother, 30 April 1916.

The attack was terrifying and the men were uncomfortable and likely scared in their PH helmets. Knowing that his mother would learn of the gas attack from the papers, Peirs tried to soothe her worry with humour, a common coping mechanism for fear.[41] Within Peirs's gallows humour was an important fact; the battalion had become hardened soldiers. They had adjusted to both the routine and the terror of trench life.[42]

The Raid

The 72nd Brigade did not let the German gas attack go unchecked. They began planning their own raids, both a punitive measure and to gather intelligence. The rationale for aggressiveness was to keep the enemy on their toes and to instill effective combat experience and confidence among soldiers. In particular, New Army units were 'met by an incessant demand for raids and actions d'eclat which could show that it had been "bloodied" and was unafraid of the storm of steel.'[43] Raids became a way to acclimate soldiers to violence before they went into major operations. As Paddy Griffith writes, 'Green formations had to be given their battle inoculation gradually, otherwise they would be too fragile when it comes to a really severe test.'[44] In 1916, the most severe test would take place to the south at the Somme. It was therefore important for units to have some degree of small unit tactical experience before facing a more arduous test of their abilities.

For the Queen's that test was two-fold. The first aspect was their ability to hold the line and defend themselves, which they demonstrated in the gas attack at Wulverghem. The second was in their ability to close with the enemy and exhibit offensive tactical skill. The changing character of combat in the First World War necessitated training that emphasized more specialised roles and the combined combat arms of infantry and artillery. Failed attacks – usually – were those where the men did not have clear and realistic objectives and/or were unsupported with tools to help them close with the enemy. When the 8th Queen's was ordered to raid the enemy's trenches in

41 For more on humour as coping mechanism, see Alexander Watson, *Enduring the Great War*, p.92.
42 For their gallantry during the attack, the commander of Second Army, General Herbert Plumer awarded Captain Griffith the Military Cross, Sergeant A.L. Trott the Distinguished Conduct Medal, and five men received the Military Medal.
43 Paddy Griffith, *Battle Tactics of the Western Front* (New Haven: Yale University Press, 1994), p.61.
44 Ibid.

June 1916, it was the most extensively planned and prepared for operation they had yet conducted in the war.

The purpose of the raid was to gain intelligence on enemy positions by identifying their strength and to ascertain the likelihood of their attacking again with gas. After the gas attack in April, the British were on almost continuous alert to changes in the winds, especially as they knew the enemy had gas cylinders in their trenches.[45] The threat was more than just paranoia: the Germans released another cloud of chlorine and phosgene gas on 17 June. Though this was just a chemical attack unsupported by enemy infantry, both the gas and the accompanying bombardment caused 83 casualties out of a total trench strength of 623.[46] Five officers fell: two company commanders and one subaltern were wounded and two officers, second lieutenants A.F.M. Grant and H.M.N. Chatterton, died.[47] Two major gas attacks with substantial casualties in the matter of six weeks meant that the men were ready to take the fight to the enemy. The 72nd Brigade assigned the task to the 8th Queen's.

Peirs commanded the raiding party which was divided up into four groups, each under the command of a capable lieutenant. Three of the groups were to advance across no man's land and assault the enemy's position. Once they broke into the enemy's trenches, one group was to move left, one up the centre of the enemy's supporting communication trench, and one unit to the right. A fourth group was to carry extra equipment and provide logistical support for the main three assault groups. The men began training the week of 10 June. They trained in nighttime movement, grenade throwing, and close-order fighting.[48] By 20 June, all preparations were made. The men moved up into trenches at the end of the month and at 11:00 pm on 28 June, awaited at the firestep of their trench to go over the top. They stood among dozens of gas cylinders that had been brought up to cover their attack.

At 11:31 pm, divisional artillery opened up on the trenches opposite. To not give away their position, they had a 'dummy' bombardment further up the line. Soldiers released gas from their trenches, which drifted over to the

---

45 Some had been exploded by their artillery.
46 TNA, WO 95/2214/1, 8th Queen's War Diary, 17 June 1916. The unofficial war diary indicates that many of these casualties came from the support company behind the lines, who took the brunt of the bombardment.
47 Ibid. The battalion now had few of its original officers.
48 TNA, WO 95/2210/2, 72nd Brigade War Diary, 'Report on Raid Made on the Enemy Trenches West of Messines', p.1.

enemy under cover of the bombardment. Released with the gas was a thick cloud of smoke to further obscure and confuse the enemy. The gas ceased at 11:40, the smoke continuing to cover the raiding party as it advanced. Once the gas stopped, Group D (logistics) moved forward to clear the way for the assault parties. They were then followed by the main assault groups A, B, and C, who discovered the enemy wire cut and a clear path into the enemy trenches. As they were shielded by smoke, the men did not take any casualties as they approached the German trench. In all, their artillery dropped 633 shells on the trenches opposite in an hour, the fire so concentrated and accurate that it cut the enemy's wire before rolling back towards the German second line to prevent a counter-attack.[49]

The assault parties were a mixture of bayonet-men and bombers who carried trench clubs. The men blackened their faces with cork and had dozens of Mills bombs, more than they could use in the raid.[50] They did not wear gas masks but had them around their necks in case the gas was still in their trenches. They moved quickly and within just a few minutes they slid down into the German RIR 212 front line trench and began bombing their way up, killing the enemy in their trenches and dug outs with bayonets and grenades. Their objective was to take as many prisoners as they could for identification and interrogation, to capture an enemy gas cylinder (if possible), and to kill and harass the enemy opposite.

Lieutenant F.D. Reynolds's Group A moved to the left and bombed up the trench about 20 yards from their starting point. They encountered an enemy soldier who surrendered quickly before two others emerged from the darkness, Lieutenant Reynolds killing them with his pistol. They moved up the line and blew up a German dugout, killing four or five soldiers within. Group A took four casualties from either enemy bomb fragments or friendly fragments that were thrown from the parapet too close to the assault parties. Group B, under the command of D.W. Lane-Nichols, moved to the right and began working its way up the enemy trench. Encountering an enemy dug out, they threw bombs into it before Lane-Nichols then went in with his pistol. Struck by a German soldier, Lane-Nichols turned and shot him.

---

49 Master of Belhaven, *The War Diary of the Master of Belhaven* (London: John Murray, 1919), p.209. Notably, this was the battalion's first experience with a barrage that rolled at timed increments.

50 TNA, WO 95/2210/2, 72nd Brigade War Diary, Appendix, 'Lessons Learnt' in Report on Raid Made on the Enemy Trenches West of Messines, p.6.

He personally took three other prisoners, one of whom he dragged out from under a bench by his hair. He pushed the four prisoners out into the trench 'by dint of jamming his revolver into their ribs.'[51] Before either Group A or B could move further up the trench, the order to withdraw was given, and the three assault groups brought back their six German prisoners by 12:10 am. At least twenty-four enemy soldiers were killed at a cost of seven wounded.

As soon as the raiding party returned, the division's artillery bombarded the German lines again to prevent retaliation and released a second cloud of gas towards the enemy.[52] Peirs watched from the parapet until one of his men threw a German prisoner into the trench, knocking him over.[53] He then met with his officers and NCOs and reported back to brigade. The brigade, division, and corps all sent their congratulations.[54] In turn, Peirs put forward lieutenants Lane-Nichols and Reynolds for Military Crosses, which they received, as well as Sergeant Barnard, Sergeant Kerslake, and privates Baker and Lee who received military medals.[55] The raid was a well-planned and well-executed success. Beyond that, it was also a morale boost for the officers and men that they could meet the enemy in their own trenches and get the better of them. Their careful training, planning, and the skillful use of many different tools at their disposal paid off.

The Somme

As Peirs and his men took note of their success, to the south in Picardy the British Army was about to begin the largest campaign yet fought in France. On 1 July 1916, the British Fourth Army attacked to the north of the River Somme, a day which has been remembered tragically ever since by the high casualties and failure to achieve anything close to the army's objectives. Over 19,000 men died on the first day of the battle, over 57,000 total BEF casualties. This marked the grim start of what would become a four-month-long attritional campaign.

The Somme is a symbolic hallmark for the industrialised suffering and futility of First World War battles. Yet, it was a complicated campaign that brought together the material might of the contestant nations as they sought

---

51 Peirs to his mother, 1 July 1916.
52 TNA, WO 95/2214/1, 8th Queen's War Diary, June 1916, Appendix VII.
53 Peirs to his mother, 1 July 1916.
54 TNA, WO 95/2214/1, 8th Queen's War Diary, 28 June 1916.
55 TNA, WO 95/2214/1, 8th Queen's War Diary, 15 July 1916.

advantage over the enemy. As William Philpott writes, 'The centerpiece of this industrial war was an industrial battle in which population, economy, industry and imagination all strained to sustain battle longer and more intense than any fought before.'[56] Destined to play a small part in a much larger battle involving three imperial powers was the 8th Queen's.

A pastoral and quiet front before the battle uprooted it, the Somme's landscape was quickly ruined by the battle. After the initial failed attack on 1 July, the British Fourth Army staff gradually realised that a decisive breakthrough was illusory, the Germans opposite not only strident but elastic in their deep defenses and their ability to counter-attack. By mid-July, the high command favoured more limited attacks, ones which could achieve tactical results and wear down the enemy. In those first two weeks of July, the officers and men of the Queen's followed the 'Great Battle' to the south with optimism and hope that the Germans would be stretched so thin that the war would end in 1916.[57] Then they were ordered to do their bit.

The 618 remaining men of the battalion left their trenches in Belgium on 20 July 1916 and went by bus, train, and then foot back into France. They arrived at Fourdrinoy five days later. There they trained with Lewis guns and digging for five days before then moving to Morlancourt, just south of Albert. They could hear the great guns hammering away at the front. At the beginning of August, they marched to Sandpit Camp, just to the west of the front lines. As they came up, it was hot and dusty, the soil chalky and the weather dry, a stark contrast to what they had left in Belgium.[58] The occasional German airplane flew overhead, sometimes dropping an odd bomb near their position, to no avail. Their brigade artillery officer, the Honorable Ralph Hamilton, recalled how the terrain changed as they continued their march onto newly captured battleground.

> We passed through the remains of our wire and were in 'No Man's Land,' which is about eighty yards wide here. Then we crossed the German front line, and found ourselves in a maze of trenches and shell-homes. One could see what a terrific bombardment there had been, as the whole place was one mass of shell-holes, large and

---

56 William Philpott, *Three Armies on the Somme* (New York: Knopf, 2009), p.4.
57 Peirs mentions this in his letters home and there is no reason to believe that it was hyperbole or false-optimism on his part.
58 Master of Belhaven, *War Diary of the Master of Belhaven*, pp.219–21.

small. In fact, it was most exhausting work walking about, as one was climbing in and out of the holes every step. In many places the trenches had ceased to exist, and at no place could one see a single yard of the original ground surface.[59]

This purgatorial space was their section of the line; the names of their objectives are now iconic – Guillemont and Delville Wood.

It should be acknowledged that though their division was there to fight, it had limited involvement in the overall Somme campaign. They were replacements brought in after some of the initial assault divisions had taken heavy casualties; indeed, the unit that relieved them at Ypres was the 36th Ulster Division. Still, they had a part to play, though it would prove ultimately fairly futile in the broader scheme of the battle. The division was unlucky to arrive on the Somme at a time in which divisions were getting chewed up in failed attacks.[60] In turn, the 8th Queen's endured high casualties for very little gain, a refrain that could apply to so many other units in August 1916.

The battalion moved up the line on 10 August to relieve 1/5th King's Own, who were in trenches to the southwest of Guillemont. As a grim indicator of what was expected, the battalion only fielded part of its strength – 381 men out of more than 600 – the rump staying behind to constitute a reserve from which they could rebuild the battalion if they took high casualties.[61] This proved justified; in their first three-day tour at Guillemont they took eighty-six casualties from shelling, and a level of intensity of bombardment that they had not yet witnessed in the war.[62] Among those mortally wounded was Private C. Cox, aged 23. His commanding officer Captain D.W. Lane-Nichols's wrote a kind letter to his mother.

> He gave his life in looking after the comfort of a dying officer, Lieut. J.E. Stopgood, the second in command of my company. I am not given to flattery, but nevertheless I feel you should know that your son lived a clean, honest life, and met with a gallant death … You and your husband are to be congratulated on having such a son. Your loss, believe me, is our loss. Such men are not so common,

---

59 Ibid., p.221.
60 Robin Prior and Trevor Wilson, *The Somme* (New Haven, CT: Yale University Press), 162–7.
61 SHC, Unofficial Battalion History, p.25.
62 Ibid.

and when they meet their death they are missed by many in addition to their parents and relatives. We may rest assured that he will reap his just reward, for we are we not told that greater love hath no man than that he will lay down his life for a friend.[63]

Lane-Nichols was a young, veteran officer, who had risen from a subaltern to a company commander in one year of service. Though his letter certainly reads as the comforting words to a grieving mother, it is notable that he distinguishes Cox's character and expressed being moved by the man's loyalty to one of Lane-Nichols's officers in his time of death. The reality was that such uncommon men were often deeply mourned because their comrades looked up to them as an example of soldierly virtue. And with each time the Queen's were under fire, more men were lost.

After a brief rest the battalion moved back up the line to the craters south of Guillemont. It was here that they faced their most significant challenge on the Somme, one shared by many other battalions. Guillemont was a fortified and fiercely defended village that proved harder to capture than assumed. The 24th Division was ordered to initiate a series of attacks to advance upon the village. The Queen's, at first, were in reserve; they supported a failed attack by the 9th East Surreys on the village on the 16th. On the 18th the 24th Division attacked again with somewhat better results.[64] Guillemont remained in enemy hands, however. The 8th Queen's chance came only a few days later when they were ordered to attack in conjunction with the 17th Brigade on their left.

The area in which they were to fight was a broken up and miserably confusing collection of captured German trenches, old communication trenches, half dug British trenches, and large shell holes. Always one to comment on the landscape, Ralph Hamilton wrote, 'there is not a single acre for miles that has not got trenches in it. Another feature of the landscape is the miles and miles of tangled barbed wire everywhere.'[65] Second Lieutenant Leonard Smallwood was shocked at the sights and smells of their position. He recalled, 'Our position was simply a number of shell holes roughly linked up by a quarry, ground and parapets filled with dead both German and

63 'Reigate Lad Dies of Wounds,' *Dorking and Leatherhead Advertiser*, 2 September 1916, p.5.
64 Prior and Wilson, *The Somme*, pp.166–7.
65 Hamilton, *War Diary*, p.235.

English, chiefly German. I felt sick.'[66] The battalion was to attack an enemy strongpoint – the quarry mentioned above – where the Germans were not only well appointed to resist, but had a supreme advantage of defense. Any attacker had to contend with both crossing the landscape as well as the enemy's murderous fire. Previous British attempts at Guillemont had ended in both failure and high casualties for the attacking battalions.

Orders in hand, the Queen's came up the line to a strongpoint known as the Quarry. In anticipation of an attack the next day, Peirs sent B Company out on patrol to feel its way forward and establish advance posts. They were not to engage with the enemy; they were to quietly move forward and occupy shell holes in advance of their attack the next day. As they set out, their company commander D.W. Lane-Nichols was killed by a sniper. Lane-Nichols had only just had his captain's stars sewn on his tunic earlier in the month, along with his Military Cross ribbon on his breast. He died in the pockmarked ground to the front of Guillemont six days after he wrote to Private Cox's mother mourning her son's death. As Lane-Nichols fell, B Company came under immediate enemy resistance and was not able to gain a significant foothold. One platoon under Sergeant Shepherd dug in and held their position in the face of resistance until the following day.

The German defences were strong. Guillemont had a formidable trench network of fortified approaches to the village. In addition to this, there were pockets of resistance in the shell holes in no man's land.[67] Any assaulting force had to bomb their way forward, hole to hole, before then arriving at the enemy's main defensive line. At 4:30 pm on 21 August, the 8th Queen's attacked in conjunction with the 17th Brigade on their left. Though the 17th Brigade made some progress, the Queen's ran into significant trouble from the outset. Second Lieutenant Smallwood recalled, 'the ground was simply covered with the flashes of German rifles, instead of a few there were hundreds of Huns.'[68] Their left flank advanced and linked up to the 1st Royal Fusiliers. Their right flank got held up and encountered stiff resistance. A severe bomb fight commenced. Their progress stalled and the battalion had to withdraw to its original position by nightfall. By 8:00 pm, after nearly four hours of fighting, the situation grew worse. The brigade war diary records a desperate

---

66 SHC, ESR/25/Small/1/6, Diary of Leonard Smallwood, p.1. Used by permission of the Surrey History Centre. Copyright of the Surrey History Centre.

67 TNA, WO 95 2210–2, 72nd Brigade War Diary, 21 August 1916.

68 SHC, ESR/25/Small/1/6, Diary of Leonard Smallwood, p.1.

situation: 'Casualties very heavy. Trenches are being shelled very severely and men are being constantly buried.'[69]

The attack at Guillemont proved to be an exceptionally costly and ultimately futile demonstration against an enemy objective that was incredibly well fortified and held by a determined force. Summed up neatly by Robin Prior and Trevor Wilson, the scale of the attack as well as the artillery support for it were insufficient to do the job.[70] Over four hours of small arms and bomb fighting, the battalion lost eighty-nine men and seven officers killed or wounded. Among those were A Company Commander C.H. Woollatt, B Company Commander D.W. Lane-Nichols, and Lieutenant J.E. Tollemache. Woollatt had been with the battalion since its inception and both Lane-Nichols and Tollemache had also proven themselves in battle. The wounded included F.D. Higham, another company commander, and Major Peirs, who was not severely hurt in the action. Still, three out of four company commanders were killed or wounded, leaving a serious gap in the senior leadership of the battalion.

Limping, the battalion came out of the line on the 22nd and then had a few days' rest behind where they took on a draft of replacements. Lord Moran of 17th Brigade recalled the fatigue wearing on the of the men of the division who had just been to Guillemont. 'All around me are faces sleep might not have visited for a week, they have dark shadows under eyes that are older, more serious ... The sap has gone out of them, they are dried up.'[71] Peirs wrote to his mother a bit more cheerfully on the 23rd that he had 'no news I can tell you' except that he 'got hit by a bit of shell the other day on my right forearm, but it only bruised my arm ... I may appear in the list a wounded hero, so don't worry if you see my name.'[72] He enclosed a cheque for footballs that his father ordered for the men. Two days later, the footballs arrived and the surviving men were playing behind the lines. Later they attended an open-air concert which was accompanied by a 9.2-inch cannon firing behind the players.[73] The respite, even for a few days, was restorative. Peirs wrote to his sister that though they were not out of danger, he was very much relieved, 'the usual strafe continues though we are now behind instead of in it which

69 TNA, WO 95 2210–2, 72nd Brigade War Diary, 21 August 1916.
70 Prior and Wilson, *The Somme*, p.167.
71 Moran, *Anatomy of Courage*, p.134.
72 Peirs to his mother, 23 August 1916.
73 Peirs to Odd, 25 August 1916.

makes a lot of difference.'[74] In addition to the footballs, Peirs also managed to get the battalion some beer, which he remarked was 'extraordinarily popular.'[75]

After eight days sleeping under canvas in reserve, the battalion got its orders back to the front, this time to march past the ruined Mametz Wood, which had been cleared of Germans at great cost by the Welsh Division the previous month. Their destination was near Longueval. There they relieved the 6th Somersets in support of the rest of the brigade who had taken up a defensive position in the contested, deforested, and utterly destroyed charnel house of Delville Wood.

The previous month, the South African brigade attacked Delville Wood and spent six days being reduced to a shell of their former existence before then being rotated out. For the next month, the British held their position, but under constant bombardment and counter-attacks by the Germans. By the time the Queen's came up the line, the wood no longer existed – it was a shredded remnant – and the landscape one of shell holes, trenches, broken trees, detritus, and bodies. Ypres, with its wetness and purgatorial flat plains of mud and misery, would be the worst place they would fight; Delville Wood, with its shattered former beauty had to have come a close second in terms of its hopelessness. Thankfully, their tour was short, but once again at great cost due to the fact that the German 35th Fusiliers launched a counter-attack right after the 24th Division rotated into the wood.[76] Supporting their attack was a fierce artillery bombardment on British trenches.

The 8th West Kents drew the short end and were the first up the line to the Inner Trench. There they took substantial casualties from shelling. The 8th Queen's rotated in to relieve them under heavy fire on 1 September, taking sixteen casualties in the relief. Near them were the 9th East Surreys, who were facing not only shelling but also an epidemic of diarrhea in their battalion.[77] The shelling had churned up the ground so badly that the Queen's seemed to have difficulty in finding their position at all, which they did, but then had to re-dig trenches that had been destroyed. Second Lieutenant Smallwood recalled, 'no trench maps were of any use. All the communication trenches were smashed to hell – trenches were wiped out and there was no sign of a

---

74 Ibid.
75 Peirs to his mother, 26 August 1916.
76 Edmonds, *Military Operations in France & Belgium, 1916, Vol. 2*, p.205.
77 TNA, WO 95/2210/2, 72nd Brigade War Diary, 2 September 1916.

trench left. Dead bodies were everywhere – it was a repulsive sight.'[78] The next three days they sat on their position and were shelled constantly. The heavy shelling made it difficult to get water to the battalion and some resorted to drinking rain out of their macs, or worse.[79] The 9th East Surreys bore the brunt of it and their situation got so bad that their medical officer believed they could not hold.[80] The Queen's fared a little better, but by the end of their four day tour, their position no longer resembled trenches but instead a connection of shell holes reinforced as strongpoints. In just holding their small stretch of Delville Wood, they took 142 casualties (26 KIA, 104 WIA and 13 MIA).[81] The brigade as a whole lost 33 officers killed or wounded and a staggering 740 other ranks, 153 killed in action and 51 missing, many of whom were presumed dead.[82] At the Somme, both action as well as inaction – or better phrased, just holding a miserable section of line – was deadly.

Back to Where they Started

The battalion – along with the brigade as a whole – suffered immensely at the Somme in two relatively minor engagements that ultimately had little military consequence. As has been argued since, the BEF gained valuable fighting experience in the four months of the Somme campaign,[83] yet it is hard, when one considers the record of the Queen's, what that experience was worth in practical terms. They were able to test their abilities at reconnoitering and bombing at Guillemont, but at a high cost. Similarly, at Delville Wood they held a section of line effectively, but essentially were placeholders suffering near-constant bombardment before emerging a somewhat wrecked battalion. If anything, their training in 1916 was what made them better soldiers, and their combat experience at the Somme – such as it was – hardened them by testing their ability to endure. But that ability was not subject to question after the ordeal in which they had gone through.

After being pulled out of Delville Wood, the battalion took to training and rest behind the lines. Everyone needed a break. Officers rotated out on

78 SHC, ESR/25/Small/1/6, Diary of Leonard Smallwood, p.2.
79 Ibid.
80 TNA, WO 95/2210/2, 72nd Brigade War Diary, 4 September 1916.
81 TNA, WO 95/2214/1, 8th Queen's War Diary, 6 September 1916.
82 TNA, WO 95/2210/2, 72nd Brigade War Diary, 6 September 1916.
83 Gary Sheffield, *Forgotten Victory*, pp.187–9.

forty-eight hour passes to Paris for R and R.[84] Three officers and 150 men were sent to the seaside town of Ault for rest. As his men rested, Lieutenant Colonel Archibald Tringham took leave to England, where his wife had a serious, but undisclosed, illness.[85] His wife Mary was the daughter of the landscape painter Benjamin Leader and she had a brother in service, also a painter and Charterhouse graduate, Captain Benjamin Eastlake Leader. Tringham left one extremely stressful situation where his battalion had sustained high casualties and entered another as his wife battled her illness. Tringham returned and then took temporary command of 17th Infantry Brigade before being called home in late October, his wife having a relapse of her illness after the death of her brother on active service.[86] The CO bounced back and forth from his battalion, to his home, back to battalion, to brigade command, and then back to his home to look after his sick wife, who was no doubt careworn from grieving and worry.

After a period of rest, the battalion rotated into trenches near Hulluch in October. They knew this terrain well: situated in the Loos Salient, their current stretch of line was the one in which they had traversed a year previous in their attack on the German second line. Returning to Hulluch was a grim homecoming. Veteran officers were conscious that somewhere in the ground were the bodies of Charlie Cressy and Colonel Fairtlough. For the veteran rankers, they were conscious, too, that somewhere nearby were dozens of their chums. The Queen's took their position at Lone Tree redoubt and settled in for three months of German Minenwerfer strafing, occasional enemy raids, aerial darts thrown down on their position, and coordinated and sustained harassment of their lines. It was not a cushy duty.

On Christmas Eve 1916, the 600 officers and men of the battalion went up the line to relieve the 9th East Surreys. Three companies went to the front, the fourth and the headquarters in reserve. Their trenches were in bad condition from the rain and daily shelling. Major Peirs took with him a book and some cigars sent by his family for Christmas, the cakes and other edibles accompanying his Christmas presents had been already eaten.[87] The nights were cold with frost and the days were short, wet, and grey. It was

84 TNA, WO 95/2214/1, 8th Queen's War Diary, 8–18 September.
85 Peirs to his father, 14 September 1916.
86 Peirs to his mother, 21 October 1916.
87 Peirs to his family, 20 December 1916.

a dismal time to be away from home in the bleak industrial heartland of northern France.

Christmas Day came violently with Minenwerfers. The men of the battalion took shelter until their own artillery could reply in kind. The previous year at Christmas they dined together, drank beer, and sang festive songs. This year they were under bombardment in partly collapsing trenches. Though there is no record of it, the men were likely reflective upon their ordeal, the holiday compounding the misery of their situation and amplifying it as the shells came over. Normally in his dugout during routine tours of the trenches, Peirs would write home. But this Christmas he did not. We have only the war diary's cold assessment: 'Xmas Day … The trenches are in terrible condition owing to the rain.'[88] The men were too.

---

88 TNA, WO 95/2214/1, 8th Queen's War Diary, 25 December 1916.

Chapter 5

Life and Death

In the Imperial War Museum there is a small leatherette notebook that was carried in the tunic pocket of Private D.O. Lee. It is one of the few surviving manuscript documents of a common soldier of the 8th Queen's found in an archive. On first glance, the most noticeable thing about it is a postcard of his sweetheart taped to the back cover. It is inscribed with a brief dedication, 'Dave, Daisy with Love xxxxx'. Near it is Daisy's address, presumably so that Lee could easily access it to write to her. Turning the notebook over, on the back cover there is an oval hole cut out from the cardboard and leatherette with a postcard portrait of Daisy. In the bottom left corner, also cut out, is a heart-shaped portrait of her that was taken from a tintype. Daisy has an unmemorable expression on her face; her hair is short and dark.[1]

It is clear that Lee cared for Daisy and that this notebook was a prized possession. There are three photographs of her in it, which indicates that she was often on his mind, a person whose memory he cherished, a face of both hope and longing for him as he served. Her presence in the notebook – her face in particular – reminds us that the lives of those at the front and on the home front were intertwined and linked together. In his hand Lee held not only the practical gift of a soldier's notebook, but he also held a bit of home. As John Bourne writes, 'Men who fought on the Western Front were never entirely severed from civilian society.'[2] Lee carried his civilian identity with him and was certainly still very much immersed in the society he came from. However, his notebook also stood as a reminder in his tunic pocket of just how different his world was now in France from what he left behind. No doubt he was different too; no man who survived the Western Front would ever be quite the same person that left his sweetheart behind.

1   IWM, Doc. 15123, Papers of D.O. Lee, Notebook.
2   John Bourne, 'The British Working Man in Arms', in Hugh Cecil and Peter Liddle (eds.), *Facing Armageddon* (London: Leo Cooper, 1996), p.339.

Inside the notebook are the fragmented memories of a man we know little about. D.O. Lee, or Dave as we can now call him, recorded an odd assortment of memories. There are drawings, notes, and short reminiscences. Though the drawings are quite elaborate, the notes are a random assortment. His notebook was more a space for creative amusement than a journal or a diary. Most notably, he drew cartoons in the Bairnsfather style, of humorous encounters with the enemy, of men trying to court women, and the petty discomforts of the poor bloody infantry at the front. The notes are pragmatic; detailed instructions for operating a Lewis gun, a Mills bomb, a rifle grenade, and for putting on one's gas helmet – all skills developed in theatre as the Queen's learned how to fight in 1915–16. There are also some song lyrics and common French phrases. There is a short, incomplete, anecdote of going on a drinking spree with his chums, imbibing rum and smoking cigars after he got out of base hospital. He repeats over and over again that it was a 'bon' time.

Lee's notebook reveals a small glimpse of the day-to-day life of a common soldier in the Queen's. He is conscious of his duty and methodical in the ways in which he writes instructions on weapons. He has a sense of humour about the war and about the officers over him. He is confident and committed: one drawing, copied from a cartoon, has the British Army depicted as a fist punching the Kaiser in the face. When one looks closely, both the face and the fist are imposed on a map of France, the outline of the Kaiser's face is the German front line trenches. The fist hitting him square in the nose is the BEF on the broad Somme front. Lee drew it after surviving Loos, enduring the trenches of Belgium, and when he was then deployed south to meet the enemy again on the Somme. In the summer of 1916, Lee clearly believed that the offensive was a serious blow to the Germans.

His notebook carries little by the way of revelatory substance, but much in terms of its meaning and its humanity. For years he kept it in his tunic. He turned to his art as a way to divert his attention from the trenches. Though not formally forbidden from keeping a diary, he decided not to journal about his experiences, but instead he took to drawing in his pocket notebook to understand and contextualise army life.[3] He also illustrated for amusement and pleasure. One such portrait is of a woman in a ballgown, a society beauty

---

3 For detailed analysis on soldier diaries, see Jessica Meyer, *Men of War* (London: Palgrave, 2009), Chapter 2.

possibly seen in a magazine. Her softness and unquestionably accentuated femininity was something so foreign from his day-to-day existence at the front, where he was surrounded by men who reeked of body odour, mud, and sour wet wool; men who belched and farted and stunk of stale strong tobacco. His world was one of fried bacon and a brew up of petrol-tasting strong tea and certainly not the champagne and silks of his starlet. For a man who saw around him only varying shades of khaki, the penciled vibrancy of the colours in his notebook stands in stark contrast to both the homosocial environment in which he was immersed, but also both the brutality and banality of life at the front. There is hopefulness in his notebook that someday he would leave the Lewis guns and Mills bombs aside and return home to his Daisy.

Daisy's photographs reveal a great deal, but not much about her. They are too faded to get a real impression of her looks and too staged to understand what she was like, if that is even possible from an image. Yet, we can assume that she helped to give him a purpose within the masculine role he understood before the war – that as a fighter doing the men's work at the front she could not – but also as a protector of the nation, of home, of the life he hoped to make with her possibly in peacetime. If he survived.

His world at the front was a lot of things. It was fun, sometimes. It was funny too. It was joyful when men sang and mirthfully got up to no good behind the lines. It was sporting and competitive when they had games and gambled. Of course, it was also violent and destructive, both on a macro and micro scale. Lee lost friends. He saw men mutilated. He saw some going through exceptional agony. He saw men frightened, grief-stricken, and angry. He learned to live with not only the presence of death, but his own role in dealing it out. His mind and body adjusted to army life and he became desensitised from the physical and emotional discomfort of the trenches. It is no wonder he wanted to hold her face close, to remind him just of how otherworldly the existence he was living now was. The war was certainly an aberration from his civilian existence, but it was also a horrific and utter distortion of what life was supposed to be. Life was meant to be lived; however hard it might be. Humans were meant to love one another, so said the creeds. This is what he had been brought up to believe. And this juxtaposition between the basic morality of the civilian and the duty of a soldier were bound up in his tiny notebook in the Imperial War Museum where he expressed his agency through drawing as both an escape from the war as well as a reminder of a more peaceful life at home.

Not every man in the battalion had his artistic skill. Not everyone had a sweetheart. Not every man was devoted. Not every man was both whimsical and dutiful. Not everyone kept a notebook. Yet, in Dave Lee we see a glimpse of what we do not know, just as much as what we do. For every Dave Lee and Jack Peirs there were hundreds whose stories of service in the 8th Queen's have evaporated. Hundreds were killed, their stories now remembered on headstones. Hundreds more wounded, their stories lingering afterwards in scars and, for many, lasting disability. Some saw long service in the battalion; some saw very brief service before sickness, transfer, or a bit of flying metal saw it end. Most of their stories are forgotten or lost. What has made it to the archives, though, are the very incomplete fragments of the men who fought, bled, and died in this battalion and what they thought of the war that they were fighting.

So far, this book has pursued a basic task: to show the transformation of a battalion of civilians into soldiers through a battalion's experience at the front. At all levels up and down the command structure of the 8th Queen's, men became accustomed to army life, adjusted physically and mentally to the front, and became skilled in the execution of their duties. This is not to say that every man in the battalion could deal with the strain; many did not and many also, we should assume, pined dearly for their homes and families. Yet, most of the research into the morale of the BEF indicates that a majority of soldiers were able to adapt and perform their duties despite the difficulties of service.[4] Over time, soldiers formed bonds of comradeship, developed thicker skin towards the discomfort of the trenches, and developed trust in their battalion and company officers. Those who were the best off were those in units that were well led and looked after the welfare of their soldiers. Frequent periods of rest functioned as an antidote to exhaustion. Family support, too, kept men sane and gave them a sense of purpose, as well as a reminder of something to return to when the war would inevitably end.[5] All of these factors made for more effective soldiers. Effective soldiers made for an effective fighting force; despite the high casualties inflicted upon it, the Queen's became a better battalion through their acclimation and experience.

---

4   For studies on morale and leadership, see J.G. Fuller, *Troop Morale and Popular Culture in the British and Dominion Armies* (Oxford: Clarendon, 1991). Gary Sheffield, *Leadership in the Trenches* (London: Palgrave Macmillan, 2000). Alexander Watson, *Enduring the Great War*.
5   See Michael Roper, *The Secret Battle*, Chapter 2.

By 1917, they were a competent, albeit unexceptional unit. Like most of the BEF, they adapted with the changing character of war on the western front.

We know the most about the day-to-day life of the battalion and its esprit de corps through the letters of Peirs. Yet, to see the war through his eyes is to only see the image he wanted to project to his family – the plucky, sarcastic, public-school officer doing his duty. This is not to say that he was not this person; I have every belief that he was what he represented and portrayed, but also that he was careful in curating his persona through what he wrote home so as to not worry his family or to dwell too much on the emotional toll the war was taking.[6] There is no evidence that he was deeply traumatised by his experience; quite the opposite, in fact, as he became a better officer and commander as the war kept going. But he certainly felt the strain at times. He was a real person who felt fear, tiredness, anger, sadness, grief, and anxiety. Like many men of his generation, he was conditioned to not express these things. He certainly was not going to write to his family and express more than very base level of emotions. It is telling that only once, in nearly 300 letters, does he express despair.[7]

What was day-to-day life like for men of the battalion? How did men like Dave Lee and Jack Peirs fare at the front? What was their daily routine like when they went up the line and back down it again? What about the men whose stories were cut short? What remains of them beyond their names on memorial markers and gravesites? This chapter will focus on the intimate life of the battalion as it came off the Somme front and then moved up northwards to Ypres again in 1917. The year 1916 proved to be a fraught and fragile one for the battalion. They began the year with restored confidence and replenished numbers. By the time they came off the Somme, their numbers had dwindled and the battalion was badly bruised. Moreover, the men killed at Guillemont and Delville Wood constituted some of the last of the battalion's original cohort of volunteers. Their deaths came at a time of transformation for the Queen's as well as the entire BEF, who were learning to fight attritional battles, and to live with the losses so attained through the brutal slog of 1916. The men who survived to tell their tales of the Somme were those who would never look at the war the same way again.

---

6   For potential motivations for Peirs's pluck, see Meyer, *Men at War*, Chapter 1.
7   Peirs to his father, 28 September 1915.

Life in the Line

The day-to-day duties of an infantry battalion on the Western Front consisted of trench rotation, fatigues, training, and active fighting.[8] Of the four components, fighting was the rarest. From September 1915 until January 1917 the 8th Queen's fought in only two significant engagements at Loos and Guillemont. Of minor engagements, the battalion defended itself in one concentrated gas attack and trench raid by the Germans at the end of April 1916. In June, a small part of the battalion participated in their own successful raid against the enemy. The battalion also fought defensively at Delville Wood, but that consisted mostly of holding the line and taking casualties under a terrible multi-day bombardment. Of battalion-level attacks, only Loos and Guillemont were significant actions, and both ended ultimately in failure and high casualties. It should be emphasised that both of these engagements took place in a matter of hours and each consisting of only one day's worth of concentrated fighting. As a whole, the battalion had just two of the stereotypical 'over the top' attacks in their first year at the front.

Yet, by January 1917, hundreds of their number had been killed and wounded in service. Loos and the Somme brought the largest concentration of casualties, of course. But the battalion gradually lost men killed and wounded throughout their service and often through routine trench duty. Their service in the line was typical for infantry in the BEF. At the front, battalions developed a routine of rotating between three positions: serving in a front line trench, serving in close support, and serving in reserve. After a period of trench rotation, brigades and divisions were pulled out and put into reserve where they rested and trained. J.G. Fuller estimated that that three-fifths of the time an infantryman spent at the front was in relative safety in rest areas.[9] Being in any of the three forward positions was a matter of being exposed to risk, the closer one got to the front lines, the more that risk was amplified. Indeed, although the average soldier spent more time in rest than in trench duty, they still approached tours with trepidation. Going up the line was a precarious business – German artillery often had British communication trenches zeroed and actively bombarded them when they believed reliefs were coming up in concentration. Once in the line, men were

---

8   This is broadly consistent with Andy Arnold's analysis of the 1st Queen's and their war experiences. See https://ww1geek.com/2021/05/22/analysis-of-a-war-diary/.

9   J.G. Fuller, *Troop Morale*, p.58.

subjected to mortar and artillery attacks, strafing from the enemy planes, and active snipers looking for targets along their parapet. To read the battalion war diary is an exercise in counting the handfuls of men who were lost gradually with every tour in and out of the trenches.

Being in a trench on passive routine duty, however, was far better than being exposed above ground in an attack. Though trench life was certainly exhausting and uncomfortable, it was also mundane and relatively safe for most men, most of the time. Soldiers grew accustomed to living in close quarters behind the parapet. There they prepared meals and ate them together. They complained about their poor quality and insufficiency.[10] They brewed tea together in the mornings and looked forward to each subsequent brew up throughout the day to keep warm both in body and soul. They also scratched out a bit of comfort in an environment that seemed devoid of it; smoking was a ubiquitous stimulant; pipes and cigarettes helped men to make it through long, dull days. Men laughed and groused together and developed a particular hybrid civilian-military patter that many would carry back to their civilian lives after the war. Some of the keys to survival in the trenches were humour, faith in one's battalion-level leadership, religion for some, acceptance of one's lot, self-deception and luck.[11]

The daily routine was discombobulating and topsy turvy. Days were spent largely resting or doing routine maintenance underground. Nights were spent in working parties improving their trench, or more precariously, in no man's land strengthening defenses. Over time, patrols became a frequent occurrence, particularly in areas where no man's land was expansive. While on patrol there was an opportunity to gain intelligence on the enemy or assert dominance over no man's land. For junior officers and NCOs, patrols were also an opportunity for notice and possibly decoration, which was not altogether unwanted, especially in units that had a reputation to uphold. Though Lieutenant Colonel Tringham and Major Peirs were both pragmatic officers who understood the fundamentally civilian character of their men, they also

---

10 Both Fuller and Richard Holmes fixate on food through their research because of its profound importance to the morale of men serving. See Fuller, *Troop Morale*, 59–61 and Holmes, *Tommy*, pp.317–26.

11 See Alexander Watson, 'Self-Deception and Survival: Mental Coping Strategies on the Western Front, 1914–1918', *Journal of Contemporary History*, Vol. 41, No. 2, April 2006, pp.247–68.

were distinctly martial in their demeanor and conscious of their regiment's tradition and reputation.

Trench life was both dispiriting and tiring. It took a toll on men's minds and bodies. This is not to say that all men became disillusioned with the war; but all felt exhaustion and some felt a sense of despair or fatalism. It is not hard to understand why. Soldiers were often lice-infested, their food was sufficient but of poor nutritional quality, and their bodies were in a near constant state of discomfort no matter the season. When soldiers complained about the war to loved ones it was nearly always about the conditions of the front. The small petty discomforts added up and became amplified by their frequency and monotony. To serve for long periods was to become dispirited and certainly disenchanted with army life.[12] For many, fighting seemed preferable than passively holding the line, which was not only a boring duty but it robbed men of their sense of agency.[13] They literally had nowhere to go and no control over their fate when stuck in a trench. This is partly why officers strove to keep men busy working, why they took them on patrol, and actively planned raids. The men of the 8th Queen's signed up to fight and not to endure passively the punishment of punitive artillery strikes. That being written, the British Army did an admirable job comparatively of rotating men between periods of high risk, lower risk, and rest. Officers learned the limits of men's ability to endure trench life relatively quickly and that rest was essential to the upkeep of morale. Of course, this does not mean that men were cheerful to go into the line, but only to say that they knew in a matter of days that they would feel better if they kept their head down and were among the lucky majority to make it out of their tours unscathed.

Still the war punished men in body and mind in ways in which they could not have expected. Ultimately, attrition took its toll. Michael Roper argues that the geography of the trenches increased the strain. 'The environment and routines of the trenches contributed to deep anxieties of this kind. Trench warfare disoriented perception.'[14] Men felt the insecurity of the unknown

---

12 The term is used here in its most basic sense: that the romantic enchantment of going to war wore thinner with every night spent in the trenches.

13 Jessica Meyer's excellent essay on masculinity, action, and inaction hammers home this point. See Meyer, 'Gladder to Be Going Out Than Afraid': Shellshock and Heroic Masculinity in Britain, 1914–1919', in *Uncovered Fields: Perspectives in First World War Studies*, editors Jenny Macleod and Pierre Purseigle (Brill: 2004).

14 Michael Roper, *The Secret Battle*, p.260.

keenly. By itself, stress is exhausting and men's bodies in the line were both strained and sleepless. Their bodies eventually broke down. Every man got sick. Many, if not most, suffered some kind of wound. Some men emotionally broke down from the strain. Others suffered terrible mutilation from shell or gunshot, their bodies permanently damaged, their lot with the fraternity of millions of disabled servicemen in Europe after the war. As Joanna Bourke writes, in the BEF men's bodies were meant to be put into danger and used knowingly of their destruction. 'The most important point to be made about the male body during the Great War is that it was intended to be mutilated.'[15] Some were also marked for death. The battalion's trench strength bears out this harsh reality. In the first two years of the battalion's existence, it fluctuated between 400 and 800 effective soldiers, with an average trench strength of just over 600 men, 350 fewer than what made for a full battalion at home in 1915. Over and over again, new men were brought into the ranks of depleted companies and veterans who had recovered from wounds or illness rejoined their chums after rest. The most common story of a fighting battalion is of its reconstitution after brief periods of heavier losses.

The realities of attrition meant that the battalion was also continuously adapting. When not in the line and at 'rest', men trained for their next rotation or their next attack. High officer casualties meant that just as replacement soldiers were learning how to fight, their junior officers fresh from southern England were also learning how to lead. In the ranks it was the same thing; there were both long-term veterans as well as men who had just come from the regimental depot. This is why the battalion spent nearly all their time training when they were out of the line. At any given time, there was a maddening mixture of men's experience. Both Peirs and Tringham knew that training and drill was also essential to keeping the spirit of the battalion up. It was important to keep the men moving, their bodies and minds occupied, their skills sharpening.

None of this is to say that they did not have moments of enjoyment behind the lines. Officers knew that one of the keys to effective morale was to keep men busy with both military and non-military tasks. Officers arranged field days, team sports like soccer and cricket, leg races, and boxing matches. Sport had less to do with preparing the men for war and more to do with

---

15 Joanna Bourke, *Dismembering the Male*, p.31.

building confidence and improving their spirits.[16] The men had sporadic access to field cinemas as well as touring shows. They sometimes improvised by creating their own musical or theatrical entertainment. Notably, their officers secured for them beer, the British soldier seeing a pint or two at rest as a right and a comforting ritual from home.[17] Their officers, too, lived it up when not in the line; they had elaborate messes with cakes and tinned food sent from home to supplement what foodstuffs they could procure from the locals. Unlike their men, they dined with whisky and wines, the officer's mess a part of their regimental tradition, even in a service battalion made up of officers on temporary commissions. Many of the officers early in the war were used to formal dining from their schools or universities and military messes, even with their fussy traditions, were not too stark a difference from civilian life. The essential point is that behind the lines the men learned to cope and to preserve small bits of their civilian identities while still in uniform. It was important for them to do so given that the next tour, or the next attack, could be their last.

Life and Death

Service tested men emotionally and physically as they came to grips with the strain and emotional hurdle to merely live on the Western Front. Though most of the men who served would survive the war, hundreds who donned the paschal lamb cap badge of the Queen's were killed in service. By January 1917, over 300 men of the battalion had been killed.[18] Each left behind at least someone who knew them, who mourned, who remembered a life that was lost for reasons that became ever so complicated as the casualty lists lengthened. The battalion was not one of the 'pals' battalions, so death was not concentrated in one particular community. Yet, losses spread throughout the south-east of England as attrition simply ground down the list of effective men on the regimental roll.

Men were killed in service either through the normal course of their duty – in what we might call 'passive' conditions – or in battle. The distinction between the two is one of intensity of risk. For men moving up the line into the trenches, there was always a risk of being wounded or killed in

---

16 Gary Sheffield, *Leadership in the Trenches*, p.46.
17 Peirs fretted over procuring beer for the men. See Peirs to his father, 3 June 1917.
18 This number is arrived at through the battalion war diary and the Commonwealth War Graves Commission database: https://www.cwgc.org.

serving within their particular part of the line and doing the routine work as an active-duty soldier. German artillery, particularly mortars, inflicted routine casualties that often were random in their selection. The enemy might bombard their lines in retaliation, to thwart what they thought might be an attack or raid, or to keep soldiers on guard and uncomfortable. German planes, as well, strafed British trenches with bombs and darts. Worse were snipers who hunted their targets. Men could be killed seemingly randomly, whether they were careful or not. For many, there was an element of luck to survival, and over the course of their duty men would turn to coping mechanisms like fatalism and superstition to explain and justify why they survived and why one of their chums did not.[19]

If one category is the everyday attrition of a unit being slowly ground down through routine service, the other is pitched battle, which inflicted a far higher concentration of casualties on an infantry battalion because of the increased risk of attacking without adequate shelter from machine guns and shells. Because of an entrenched enemy, First World War assaults were often disproportionately costly on the attacker. An attack could be 'successful' if an objective was met and captured, but that success could mean that the unit suffered terrible casualties. Proportionately, it was not uncommon for units to lose a quarter or more of their number in an attack. Junior officers faced a higher chance of becoming casualties because of their exposure to enemy fire and the social and military expectation that they lead from the front.[20] Officers came from a class and generation that valued heroism, but heroes could be particularly unlucky on the Western Front. The experience of the 8th Queen's bears out this morbid calculation: in each attack they lost men in numbers that to modern eyes seem staggering, particularly of their experienced officers. Death on the Western Front was brutal, industrial, and more often than not, random in its selection. Heroism became expressed through endurance and emotional survival rather than strutting the parapet with one's cane in hand or charging the enemy with a bayonet.[21]

---

19 Watson, *Enduring*, Chapter 3.
20 Gary Sheffield, *Leadership in the Trenches*, pp.47–50. Jay Winter, *The Great War and the British People*, pp.86–92.
21 The parapet image comes from Frederic Manning's *Her Privates We*, p.22. The point here is not to dismiss exceptional heroism but to indicate that survival became a more democratic and accepted form of heroism by men at the front.

Official records – like war diaries and after-action reports – do not really get at the heart of understanding the lives of men killed and the last minutes of their lives. In the battalion war diary, officers killed are listed briefly by name, but the bulk of the casualties inflicted were other ranks, who were unnamed and only counted by number. 'Four men killed', '86 men wounded', or '105 men missing' tells us little except that the battalion's life was slowly being bled out during offensives like the Somme. Again and again in its service, the 8ᵗʰ Queen's was mauled and then reconstituted and reformed. One gets the impression of a battalion lurching forward to the next campaign that would wear them down further before then being rebuilt. Whether it was Loos, the Ypres Salient, or the Somme, they left behind young men in scores. By January 1917, they were almost a different unit entirely.

Some of the men's fates were unknown, their bodies unrecovered. The most senior of the missing was Colonel Howard Fairtlough, whose wife and children never knew the exact fate or final resting place of their distinguished husband and father. Only his name remained inscribed on the Loos Memorial at Dud Corner. Of a very different social background, but joining Colonel Fairtlough on the memorial, is James Bate. A 19-year-old collier from the industrial region of Wigan, James joined the battalion in April 1915. After training that spring and summer with the Queen's, he arrived in France on 8 September 1915. He immediately got into trouble for an unrecorded infraction and was given four days of Field Punishment Number 2. Upon finishing his sentence, he marched with the rest of the battalion to Loos where he was killed in the assault on Hulluch. James was left behind on the field as the rest of the men retreated back to their trenches. The cause of death is unknown, but presumably was a gunshot wound as the majority of casualties inflicted were by small arms. Bate's father received his plaque and scroll from the King, but never knew the exact fate of his lost boy.[22]

Near Bate was John Alfred Caush from Dormansland, Surrey. John was 17 when he enlisted in October 1915, but had claimed to be 19 so he could serve. At the time of his enlistment, he lived with his mother and two siblings in the neighbourhood of Oak View. He trained with the battalion and served with good conduct. Like Fairtlough and Bate, he went to his death assaulting the German second line. All that remains of his memory is his name on two memorials – one at Loos and the other at St John's church in his village. His

22 TNA, WO 363/8310.

mother Jane lived with speculation about his fate for the rest of her life; her tragedy compounded by the death of another one of her sons, Ernest, who was killed at the Somme in 1916. Jane joined Maud Fairtlough and thousands of other women who lost their brothers, fathers, and husbands in the first two years of the war but were left without even the barest details of their fate beyond the impersonal words scribbled across their service records – 'Missing Presumed Dead.'[23]

Of course, not all men were killed in action, but some such as William Castleton succumbed to exposure and disease. William was a 20-year-old house servant from Banstead, Surrey when he enlisted in February 1915. Like James Bate, he almost immediately got into trouble when he arrived in France with the battalion in September 1915 and received three days of Field Punishment No 2. He fought at Loos and survived the attack. In the weeks afterwards, he was promoted to corporal. Prolonged service broke down his health. In March 1916, he was admitted to hospital for a bad case of scabies. The condition is brought on by a mite that burrows under the skin and causes an intense itching rash. It was a common in the trenches where men lived in crowded quarters and did not have opportunities for regular washing. His condition had to have been severe because he was in the hospital for nearly two weeks before he acquired a far deadlier disease, pneumonia. This was possibly misdiagnosed because he was shortly afterwards transferred to an isolation hospital where he was diagnosed with Cerebro-spinal fever (meningococcal meningitis) and then died within days. His last weeks were ones of utter misery in hospital – first for the rash all over his body – and then a hacking cough, shortness of breath, fever, muscle and head pain. Though he could have died of this condition at home, the rigours of service no doubt contributed to the rapid and grueling decline of an otherwise healthy young man.[24]

Bate, Caush, and Castleton were men whose lives were cut short in their prime by service, all in ways in which they could not have envisioned when they first put on their khaki tunics. Indeed, part of the tragedy of the First World War – really of all wars – is in the timeless story of young men facing not only the brutality of battle, but the slow deterioration that happens to

---

23 TNA, WO 363/4399; See also his entry in 'Surrey in the Great War', https://www.surrey-inthegreatwar.org.uk/person/118978 and the IWM, Lives of the First World War, https://livesofthefirstworldwar.iwm.org.uk/lifestory/753742.
24 TNA WO 363/623.

their bodies at the front with its exposure, poor quality food, and stress. Though soldiers after a few months became acclimated to the risks of their new environment and surely understood the risks of being killed or dying of disease, their families often had trouble conceptualising what they were going through at the front. For every dead man or boy there were countless questions asked by families who were fixated on the 'what ifs' of those in mourning.

For the nearly 300 families affected by the loss of a Queen's soldier, by 1917 these questions remained largely unanswered – or answered insufficiently – as they joined thousands of others in bereavement. Indeed, mourning had become bureaucratised with official correspondence and ephemera that eventually coalesced in rituals of remembrance. Every known family of men who died in service received first a telegram. Eventually, they also received a commemorative plaque and scroll from the king to display in their homes. Often, they received a letter from a service friend or the commanding officer of their relation. Sometimes they were sent the last belongings that could be recovered from the body, if it could be recovered. And later, the families were given the medals their relation was entitled to receive. Many families still hold on to these items as relics. As easy as it is to see these as mere tokens meant to assuage the grief of the masses, they were also a means of closure and a way to codify remembrance.

Of course, patriotic symbols did not put food on the table. For the family of George Breeden this was all too apparent. Breeden was unlike most of the men in the battalion. He was a bit older than the average soldier, being in his thirties when he volunteered in April 1915. He had a wife and four children at home in Southwark, London. When he donned his khaki uniform, all his children were under the age of 16. His wife Catherine had to care and provide for them at home. Breeden missed the battalion's initial embarkation, but arrived in France as a replacement after Loos. He survived the winter at Ypres and the spring gas attack at Wulverghem. When the battalion went up the line at the Somme, he was wounded during a bombardment, one of more than eighty men hurt by the deadly accuracy of the German guns. He was treated at the South African Military Hospital, and died there a week later. His wife and children received his personal effects: some letters and photographs, scissors, a crucifix, and a broken watch, possibly shattered at the time of his wounding. Catherine received first the telegram of his death, then his effects, and eventually, a pension for 20/6 for herself and her three

Christmas illustration from General Mitford and 72nd Brigade Headquarters saved by Major Peirs. The illustration is by Private Edward Cole of the 9th East Surrey Regiment. (*MS – 250: The First World War Letters of H.J.C. Peirs, Special Collections and College Archives, Musselman Library, Gettysburg College*)

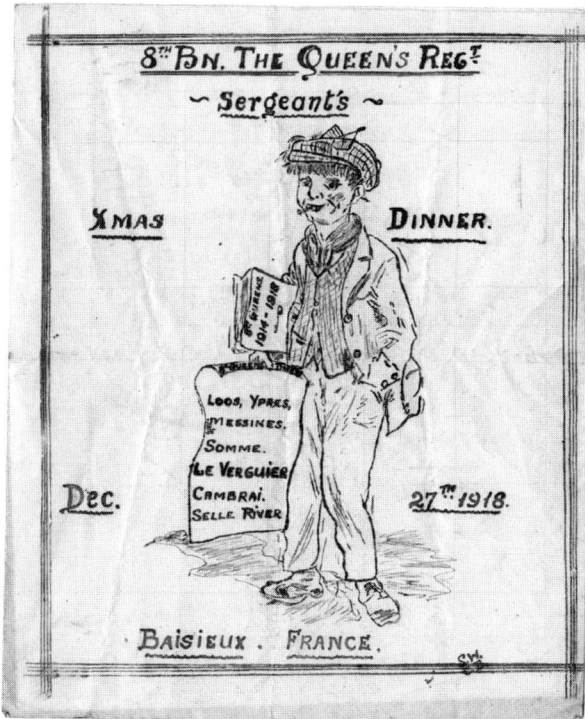

Sergeant's Christmas Dinner 1918 held in Baisieux, France bearing an illustration of a civilian with a battalion history of the 8th Queen's under his arm and a poster of the battalion's battles in his hand. (*MS – 250: The First World War Letters of H.J.C. Peirs, Special Collections and College Archives, Musselman Library, Gettysburg College*)

MENU

17th Infantry Brigade

December 30th.
1918.

PROGRAMME of MUSICAL
EVENTS.

30th DECEMBER 1918.

MARCH........Entry of the
Boyards.

VALSE........Tom Jones.

FANTAISIE...Carmen.

SONG.........Fairy Dreams.

SELECTION...Shanghai.

THREE DANCES..The Con-
queror.

SELECTION...Scotch Airs.

MENU du DINER
30e Décembre 1918.

Hors d'Oeuvres Variés.

Consommé à l'encouragement.

Plie frite Montecourt.

Dindon Rôti Le Verguier.
Choux de Bruxelles Bassier Vert.
Pommes St.Pierre.

Pouding de Noël.
Sce au Rhum.

Bécasse aux
eclaireurs de Lovat.

Dessert. Café, Liqueurs.

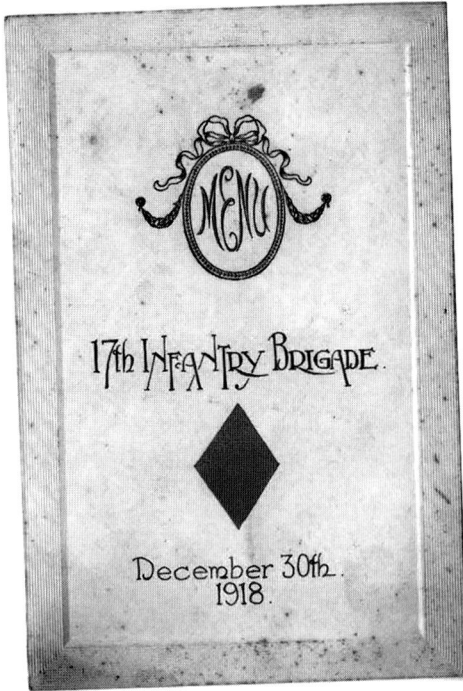

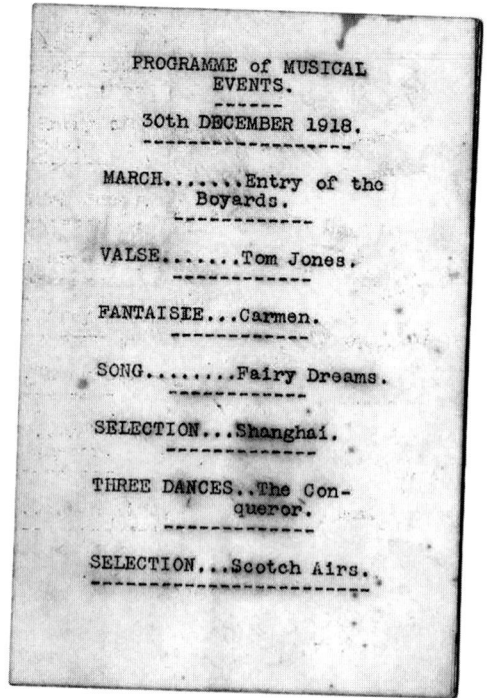

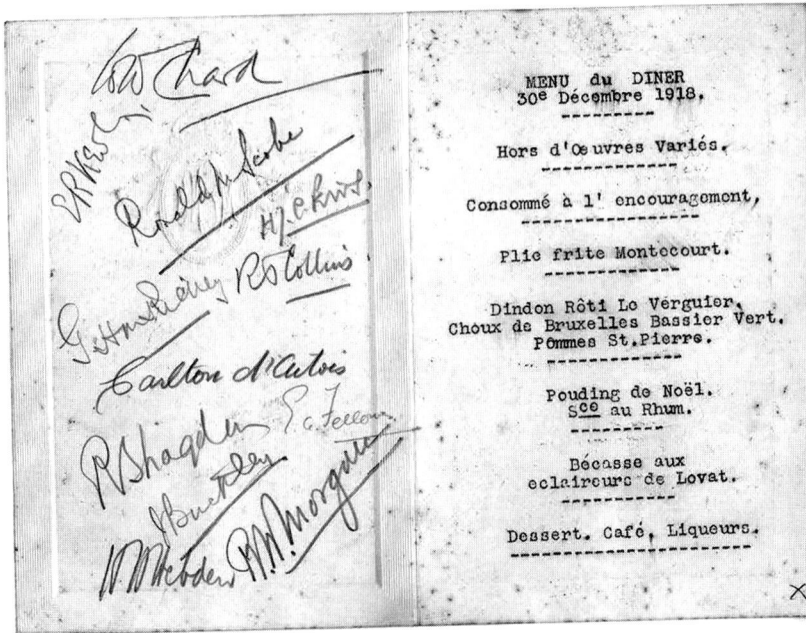

17th Infantry Brigade dinner menu and program of musical entertainment from 30 December 1918. Inside are signatures, including those of 8th Queen's officers. (*MS – 250: The First World War Letters of H.J.C. Peirs, Special Collections and College Archives, Musselman Library, Gettysburg College*)

Message by Brigadier General Bertram Mitford to soldiers of the 72nd Infantry Brigade after their failed attack at Loos. Peirs copied Mitford's message for his records. (*MS – 250: The First World War Letters of H.J.C. Peirs, Special Collections and College Archives, Musselman Library, Gettysburg College*)

The first letter of peace after four years of war. Peirs to his father on 11 November 1918 beginning with the words, 'So that's that.' (*MS – 250: The First World War Letters of H.J.C. Peirs, Special Collections and College Archives, Musselman Library, Gettysburg College*)

War Office telegram to the Peirs family in Carshalton informing them that their son was 'wounded slightly August 21st but remains at duty.' Peirs's arm was hit by a bomb fragment at Guillemont. He wrote his mother two days later to reassure her: 'However I may appear in the list as a wounded hero, so don't worry if you see my name.' (*MS – 250: The First World War Letters of H.J.C. Peirs, Special Collections and College Archives, Musselman Library, Gettysburg College*)

Notice of the armistice circulated to commanding officers of the 17th Infantry Brigade informing them that hostilities would cease at 11 am. At the time, the 8th Queen's was out of combat and billeted in Bavai, France. (*MS – 250: The First World War Letters of H.J.C. Peirs, Special Collections and College Archives, Musselman Library, Gettysburg College*)

Major Peirs casually standing with his pipe next to Colonel Frederick Howard Fairtlough in August 1915. The partnership between them proved foundational to the battalion's early training of officers and men. After Fairtlough's death at Loos, Peirs wrote his wife Maud, 'you will have the satisfaction of knowing that he died like a gentleman at the head of his men and that the regiment adored him.' (*MS – 250: The First World War Letters of H.J.C. Peirs, Special Collections and College Archives, Musselman Library, Gettysburg College*)

Summer 1918 photo of non-commissioned officers of the 8th Queen's with their three senior officers seated center, from left to right, R.H. Rowland, H.J.C. Peirs, and E.A. Fellowes. All except for Rowland are wearing their distinctive shorts. (*MS – 250: The First World War Letters of H.J.C. Peirs, Special Collections and College Archives, Musselman Library, Gettysburg College*)

Memorial plaque commemorating the belfry in Le Verguier offered by members of the 24th Division in honor of their comrades killed in the war. Dedicated on 3 October 1926. (*Photo by R.C. Miessler*)

Le Verguier town memorial with the church in the background. The belfry and bells are in honor of the 24th Division. Photo taken on the 100th anniversary of the 8th Queen's stand in the village on 21–22 March 2018. (*Photo by Meghan O'Donnell*)

The solicitor-officer. Major Peirs in 1915 before his deployment to France. Photo by LaFayette, New Bond Street, London. (*MS – 250: The First World War Letters of H.J.C. Peirs, Special Collections and College Archives, Musselman Library, Gettysburg College*)

Photograph from the ceremony dedicating the Le Verguier belfry on 3 October 1926. The caption on the back reads 'Sir John Capper & the English Guard of Honour' describing the general reviewing veterans of the 24th Division at the site of their holding action on 21-22 March 1918. Photo by Central Press Photograph 119 Fleet Street, London. (*MS – 250: The First World War Letters of H.J.C. Peirs, Special Collections and College Archives, Musselman Library, Gettysburg College*)

On 3 October 1926 veterans of the 24th Division dedicated a new belfry and memorial tablet in Le Verguier, France. Colonel Duggan (left) and General Sir John Capper (right) laid the memorial wreath at the village war memorial. Photo by Central Press Photograph 119 Fleet Street, London. (*MS – 250: The First World War Letters of H.J.C. Peirs, Special Collections and College Archives, Musselman Library, Gettysburg College*)

The officer on leave. Major Peirs in the home garden of the Peirs family home, Queen's Well, Carshalton. Note the Distinguished Service Order ribbon on his tunic. (*MS – 250: The First World War Letters of H.J.C. Peirs, Special Collections and College Archives, Musselman Library, Gettysburg College*)

French and British crowd in Le Verguier for the dedication of the village belfry and memorial tablet. Notably, the Guard of Honor consists of demobilized citizens returning to where they fought joined in this photo by General Sir John Capper and the mayor of the village, Charles Severin. Photo by Central Press Photograph 119 Fleet Street, London. (*MS – 250: The First World War Letters of H.J.C. Peirs, Special Collections and College Archives, Musselman Library, Gettysburg College*)

The 8th Queen's original officers. The photograph was taken in Blackdown before their embarkation in 1915. Colonel Frederick Howard Fairtlough, CMG, is seated in the center with his senior officers, Major H.J.C. Peirs to his left and Major George Fox to his right. (*MS – 250: The First World War Letters of H.J.C. Peirs, Special Collections and College Archives, Musselman Library, Gettysburg College*)

The sunken road at Le Verguier where the 8th Queen's made their final stand before withdrawing on 22 March 1918. The battalion headquarters was located in a dug out cut into the side of the road. It was along this road that the survivors of the battle withdrew on 22 March 1918. The photo was taken in Le Verguier 1919 and sent to Peirs by Mayor Severin. (*MS – 250: The First World War Letters of H.J.C. Peirs, Special Collections and College Archives, Musselman Library, Gettysburg College*)

Survivors. Post-Armistice photo of the battalion's officers. Front row (left to right) Major R.H. Rowland, DSO, Lt Colonel H.J.C. Peirs, DSO, and Captain E.A. Fellowes, MC. Back row (left to right) Unidentified officer and Captain W.R.G. Bye, MC. (*MS – 250: The First World War Letters of H.J.C. Peirs, Special Collections and College Archives, Musselman Library, Gettysburg College*)

underage children. His body was interned in Abbeville with those of hundreds of others whose stories were equally tragic for those they left behind.[25]

Breeden was one of the battalion's many casualties in 1916, a year that was particularly hard on the battalion's seasoned officers. For a battalion to function at peak performance, it needed experienced officers who knew their duties as well as the capabilities of the men under their command. This took training, experience, and time. In the winter of 1915–16, the junior officers of the 8th Queen's gained competence and were functioning at peak performance before being deployed to the Somme. Over the summer, attrition took its toll particularly on the young men in command of the platoons and companies in the battalion. Some of these officers had been with the battalion since the beginning and had as much experience as any New Army subalterns to wear stars on their sleeves.

One such officer was Frank Daniel Reynolds. Born in 1894, he arrived in France as one of the cadre of replacements after Loos. In the spring of 1916, he was chosen as one of the group leaders in the battalion's raid against the German trenches at Wulverghem. In that action he killed an enemy soldier, took prisoners, and was wounded by a bomb fragment to his left arm. Peirs nominated him for the Military Cross, which he received while in hospital. His recovery, however, became complicated. Soon after he went into treatment for his fragment wound, he began to display additional symptoms that compounded his treatment. He was vomiting, dizzy, had painful headaches, and was so out of sorts that his medical record indicated a 'loss of confidence'. His condition worsened and his doctors began to believe he had a brain abscess, possibly related to his bomb wound that had caused blood poisoning. He was sent to a specialised hospital in London. His condition continued to worsen, and the abscess did not heal. He died a year later from a brain infection, a long and slow decline for a brave young man. At his bedside were his family who watched the 23-year-old officer slowly lose strength in front of them and suffer a sad and brutal death.[26]

When the battalion made its way from Ypres to the Somme in the summer of 1916, the officers and men surely expected more casualties. The ensuing campaign, though, proved to be transitional for the battalion's

25 TNA, WO 363/8167.
26 TNA, WO 339/17695.

existing leadership as attrition wore down their cohort of junior officers. The first was John Lambert Hopgood, recently promoted to company command when he was mortally wounded as the battalion came out of its first tour in the trenches at the Somme. Hopgood was 21 years old. He joined the battalion in 1914 and his commission endorsed by none other than Colonel Fairtlough, who saw promise in the young public-school-educated man. In his obituary, it is noted that John rushed home from holiday with his mother in Switzerland to volunteer in August 1914. He arrived in theatre in October 1915. As the battalion came out of the trenches near Talus Boisee on 16 August 1916, a shell exploded by Hopgood, a fragment mortally wounding him. He died the following day. His commanding officer, Lieutenant Colonel Tringham, wrote, 'We all miss your son greatly as a comrade and, as his commanding officer, I miss him also as one of my best officers.' Another officer wrote home to his mother of the young man's courage, 'the men loved and admired him for his pluck for which he was always conspicuous.'[27] His mother, Ethel, was sent his effects, which included his identity disk, two pipes, a tie bar, and his pocket book; the relics of the 21-year-old man, who for her would always remain a boy, sent to war.[28]

The man who took over B Company from Hopgood was also killed at the Somme. He was another one of the raid leaders at Wulverghem and was well-regarded for his bravery. Lieutenant Douglas Lane-Nichols joined the 8th Queen's from the Inns of Court Officers' Training School in September 1914. While the battalion trained in England, he married a woman named Gladys who bore him a son, Derek, within the year. Lane-Nichols deployed with the original cohort of the battalion's officers in September 1915 and fought at Loos. He survived. In June 1916, he led one of the assault parties in the Wulverghem raid. He captured several German soldiers by blunt force and earned a Military Cross for his gallantry.[29] In the desperate attack at Guillemont, Lane-Nichols and B Company were caught in a bombing exchange where he was killed by a sniper. His wife received his Military

---

27 Both quotes are from IWM, HU 115890, Bond of Sacrifice, https://www.iwm.org.uk/collections/item/object/205301522.

28 TNA, WO 339/1473.

29 TNA, WO 95/2214/1, 8th Battalion, War Diary, July 1916.

Cross in a posthumous ceremony, no doubt a small comfort, as she had to carry on raising their infant son who would have no memory of his father.[30]

Killed in the same engagement was Captain Claud Humpston Woollatt. He was 29 years old and one of the original cohort of officers within the battalion. He was well-educated and fluent in Russian.[31] He joined up on 7 September 1914 through the Inns of Court OTC. By the time of the Somme he was a company commander and one of the most experienced and trusted men in the battalion. It was in that capacity he was killed in the fighting on 21 August near Guillemont. Sadly, Woollatt had a 21-year-old brother, Philip, who was killed five weeks before him on 13 July at the Somme.[32] Philip was in the 7th Battalion of the Queen's and died near Trones Wood. In fact, when Claud came up the line to attack Guillemont, he passed the trenches where his brother had been killed. Both brothers, killed within 1 kilometer of one another, are now fittingly listed together on the Thiepval Memorial.

Captain Woollatt's story after his death took a particularly callous turn. The War Office charged him posthumously for taking his company's public money into the trenches where it was not recovered after he was killed. Rather than letting the matter rest, his estate was docked 52 pounds. His grieving father of two dead sons had to deal with the paperwork of a War Office auditor.[33] At the time of his death at Guillemont, Claud Woollatt had certainly learned of his brother's death nearby and was under the strain of active command. The absentmindedness with funds can be understood. Yet, bureaucracies are unfeeling, especially when it comes to money, and the last thing his father surely had to deal with was a war office bill to his son's estate.

Though Lane-Nichols and Woollatt were the most senior officers killed at Guillemont and represented two out of the four company commanders lost, two other veteran officers were killed nearby. Lieutenant John Eadred Tollemache was a Cambridge-educated son of a baronet who applied for a commission to the Queen's in August 1914. Originally serving in the 6th Battalion, Tollemache was transferred to the 8th, where he took up regular platoon duties. In 1916, he suffered two bouts of sickness: jaundice in January and then trench fever in July. He bounced back relatively quickly from these

---

30 TNA, WO 339/1701.
31 TNA, WO 339/1071, 'Application for Appointment to a Temporary Commission'.
32 SHC, QRWS/17, 7th Queen's War Diary, July 1916.
33 WO 339/1071.

painful conditions, but in April 1916, his service was somewhat marred by an incident when he disobeyed the order of a superior and was court martialed. He was reprimanded, a light sentence for a serious infraction which might imply that was likely justified, in part, for his conduct. The court martial did not impede his career with the battalion; shortly after the incident, in June 1916, he was one of the officers chosen to lead the raid against the enemy at Wulverghem. In July, he was promoted to lieutenant a month before being killed at Guillemont.[34]

Killed near him was a man from a different background who also earned distinction in his service. Alban Powell was a 24-year-old clerk who enlisted with the Queen's in 1914 and was made a sergeant before the battalion deployed to France. He was awarded a Distinguished Conduct Medal for his conduct at Loos, before then being recommended for a commission as a second lieutenant. He was personally interviewed by 72nd Brigade's commanding officer, General Bertram Mitford, who forwarded his recommendation and specifically asked that he be commissioned in the 8th Queen's as per the wishes of the battalion's commanding officer, Archibald Tringham. Often, ranker officers were not sent back to their original units for fear that they would have a rough adjustment with the men that they were now commanding; that he was not only promoted from the ranks but also resumed service in his unit spoke of the respect that his men and fellow officers had for him and the cohesiveness of the Queen's.[35] He joined Tollemache in death at Guillemont, his father the Reverend Arthur Wentworth Powell receiving the notice and his mother Alice being named the sole executor of his estate and war annuity. His parents received letters, a tobacco pouch, his trench whistle, some books of poems, and five religious emblems as part of his personal items.[36]

The officers and men lost at the Somme represent a tragedy, surely. Their loss also tells us something about British battalions in the First World War. It was impossible to make up for the experience of men like Woollatt, Lane-Nichols, and Powell – their deaths left a void that took months to fill. Others, such as George Fox and W.R.G. 'Peter' Bye were recognised for their administrative talents and left for brigade staff appointments. Yet, the battalion continued to function, in part because their command structure

---

34 TNA, WO 339/12281 as well as https://petershamremembers.wordpress.com/2013/09/01/john-eadred-tollemache/
35 Sheffield, *Leadership in the Trenches*, pp.112–13.
36 TNA, WO 339/60259.

remained intact and the battalion was one in which senior officers were able to set a good example.[37] They received replacement officers and men and then turned them into the next cohort of effective soldiers. These men learned their jobs as their predecessors did in the trenches. They went through extensive training. They filled the big boots left behind by the first cohort of officers and NCOs, Peirs being the most obvious example after Loos, but all the way down the chain of command men were learning how to lead. From the Somme forward, the simple arithmetic of attrition guaranteed that there were few of the original officers and men from the original cohort at Blackdown from 1915 still serving in the line by 1917.

1916 going on 1917

One of the best-known British memoirists of the First World War was Charles Carrington. Throughout his life, Carrington contended that his service on the Western Front was a sacred and personally transformative moment. He was an ardent voice against the idea of soldier disillusionment and an aggressive defender of the BEF's combat performance. One of Carrington's contentions in his book *A Subaltern's War* was that the Somme made the BEF better fighters. He wrote:

> The Somme battle raised the morale of the British Army. Although we did not win a decisive victory, there was what matters most, a definite and growing sense of superiority over the enemy, man to man. The attacks in mid-July were more successful and better managed than those of July 1st. In August and September things were better still.[38]

Though there is much merit to what Carrington writes here, it is hard to see how this could have been the case with the 8th Queen's, who lost most of their experienced officers through attrition in 1916 and were starting afresh in 1917. Indeed, there was nothing 'better still' for the battalion as they slogged through the Somme.

To get through, the battalion relied on its senior leadership. There is no doubt that Tringham and Peirs were the central figures in reconstituting the

---

37 For more on this point, see Sheffield, *Leadership in the Trenches*, p.161.
38 Charles Edmonds, *A Subaltern's War* (London: Peter Davies, 1929), p.114.

battalion after their dreadful experiences at Guillemont and Delville Wood. In fact, to contrast Carrington more, the Somme was a low point for the battalion. At first, they lost nearly ninety men before they even saw action. Then they attacked and failed to take their position at Guillemont. From Guillemont they lost dozens of men holding the line at Delville Wood. When they moved north, they began trench duty in waterlogged and filthy trenches that required continuous maintenance as they were literally collapsing by the moment from water and poor construction. The only thing the average soldier knew as 1916 drew to a close was that the war would go on and that whatever expectations they had for victory in the summer had been shattered alongside the shattered trees of Delville Wood. Thus, they limped back north to Flanders and began afresh training new drafts of officers and men.

Attrition meant that the battalion was different in its composition than when it started. Rather than being made up of entirely volunteers and plucky public-school officers, the new men were a mixture of those who chose to be there and those who were conscripted as part of the Military Service Act of 1916. Officers were also of a different sort. Some were of the old ilk of public-school boys. Many, though, came up through the ranks or were of lower middle-class origins. It was up to the battalion's senior leadership to set the right tone and to train the new officers and men. Both Tringham and Peirs were adept at this task and remained stalwart reminders of the 'old' battalion before it had been bruised and bled at the Somme.

The above two points deserve to be underscored. The scholarship on the BEF's progress during the war follows largely Carrington's lead and has advocated a process of learning and adaptation at the front.[39] This is an entirely valid and convincing way to see the army (or individual armies) as a whole. It is, however, harder to see this sense of learning and progress at the much lower level of a volunteer battalion that kept getting wrecked in battle. The 8th Queen's was surely becoming more sophisticated as a fighting force and tactically more proficient, but the Somme took what was a battalion functioning at a high point of competence and reduced it by half. For the battalion's soldiers, it was hard to see that sense of learning when they were

---

39 Some of the best works on this point: John Terraine, *White Heat* and *To Win a War*; Gary Sheffield, *Forgotten Victory*; Jonathan Boff, *Winning and Losing on the Western Front*. To understand the complexity of learning, see Aimee Fox, *Learning to Fight*.

scraping at their shell holes in Delville Wood, desperately trying to keep their heads down.

As with Loos, after the Somme the battalion recovered. They went back to the routine of trench service in the winter of 1917 and their ranks gradually swelled in number as drafts came over from England to replace their losses. After three months of gradual increase in strength, the battalion stood at 29 officers and 717 other ranks by March, 'an unusually high' number of men in a battalion with an average trench strength in the 600s.[40] These men were immediately put into trench rotation. Over the winter the trenches were cold and wet, nights were largely miserable, and the mornings were frosty. Tours up the line were followed by periods of rest and training, the new men learning the dull routine that their predecessors endured the previous winter. All over again the men became conditioned to service.

The new men looked different than the old. In January 1916, the men had yet to be issued steel helmets and carried their PH helmets to protect them from gas. Few knew the tactics and mechanics of bomb throwing and rifle grenades – or they were learning them – and the battalion had only been through one action, which was unusually brutal and for which they were ill-prepared and had scant trench service. They had only just been issued with Lewis guns and their new teams of machine gunners were going through extensive training to figure out their use in battle. The men were also still relatively new to France, having only been in the country for five months, and only in trench duty for two. One year later, in January 1917, they had helmets and small box respirators. Those who had survived the Somme were hardened in mind and body. After a year's experience of army life, they were accustomed to the sound of shells and sniper fire, as well as the cruel ironies of survival at the front. The veterans became the backbone of the 'new' battalion of men who needed to learn the lessons of their predecessors through active service.

The Somme also exposed an emotional change for the battalion as it trudged forward. Since September 1915, they had been through the ringer, gradually losing their optimism about the course and conduct of the war. This is not to say that the battalion was demoralised, for which there is no evidence, but that the gossamer of optimism had run thin. Loos had exposed their naivete and the limitations of infantry in an artillery and machine gun

---

40 SHC, Unofficial Battalion History, p.28.

dominated battlefield. The Somme had shown that extensive training and good leadership mattered for sure, but it was hard to see the payoff if the objectives were unrealistic and the enemy determined to hold their ground. Though officers like Peirs firmly believed they were getting the better of the German army, by the dawn of the new year optimism was in shorter supply, the war seemingly would go on indefinitely. The Somme had not been so much a failure as a grave disappointment, a place where men died and their hopes for the ending of the war with them.

If we return to Private D.O. Lee's notebook, we see clear evidence of that optimism. He believed that at the Somme the BEF was giving the Kaiser a bloody nose. He wanted to do his job in the big push and to make Daisy proud of her soldier. He also wanted the war to end and to go home as part of the winning side. His notebook remains what it was as he illustrated in it – a snapshot of a New Army soldier who believed his training and conditioning would make him part of a great victory, one victory to break the Germans and end the war. Instead of a bloody nose, Lee saw his own battalion bloodied at Guillemont and Delville Wood. In January 1917, there was nothing to do but to endure it. There was nothing for men like him to do but to carry on doing the best of what they surely knew to be a bad job. As he and the other survivors kept warm around their braziers at Hulluch in February 1917, they waited with anticipation for what would come of the New Year. Would there be another offensive? Would the Germans take the war to them for a change? Or would it be more trenches, fear, and failed attacks? They had no idea what the year would bring, but it is hard to imagine they confronted the unknown with the optimism they had the year before. For Dave Lee, we will never know the answer. He died at Ypres in July as the battalion prepared to fight another offensive.

Chapter 6

Attrition

At the Somme, a newly reconstituted and trench-hardened battalion had been shook to its core with the brutal reality of what the war had become. The wearing-down of the Queen's at Guillemont and Delville Wood reflected the character of the war in 1916. As summer moved into early autumn, hopes for a decisive battle at the Somme dissolved. The weather turned grim, the offensive stopped, and there was a feeling by October that the war would go on into 1917 and beyond. Firepower undoubtedly was the most important thing on the battlefield. For the common soldier, the year 1916 proved frustrating, but not without value. On the one hand, soldiers in the BEF were gaining confidence and developing competency. On the other, whether successful or not, each attack came with a deeply personal cost for men who lived together, messed together, hoped for peace together, and died together. Indeed, the war was now both a material as well as an emotional struggle of endurance. To survive the Western Front was to endure the Western Front. This simple fact applied to both individuals as well as their battalions.

Of course, on New Year's Day 1917 nobody knew what the year would hold. To show something of the fickleness of prediction, we can look backwards a bit and examine how the men felt earlier the previous year. In May 1916, when the battalion was manning its trenches in Wulverghem, Peirs wrote home to his family in response to a rumour, presumably from a newspaper, that the war was going to end. 'I am glad to hear the war is to finish in the autumn, as it is a good thing to have it decided!' he wrote sarcastically. 'I have guessed at February [1917] as a likely moment for some time now.'[1] Tellingly of the ironic humour cultivated by his fellow officers, he then added that at the brigade they 'keep a book of guesses & have kept it now for some time. They have had to scratch off a lot of people already who guessed a date before this. The earliest guess they had I think was last Xmas [1916] & they have

---

1   Peirs to his mother, 31 May 1916.

nothing over Xmas 1917.'² Now that the battalion was through the Somme and into the New Year, presumably, the brigade's officers had to recast their bets on whether the war would end in 1917. That is if they lived to see the war's ending, of course; the sad reality was that many who jovially bet on the war's ending did not see the year through with their men.

As the previous chapter emphasised, like so many other units drawn from the original drafts of Kitchener's volunteers, the 8ᵗʰ Queen's no longer resembled its former self. Too many men had been lost since 1915. Those veterans who remained of the original cohort were all changed by their experiences. The brutal reality of the war meant that line infantry battalions went through a cycle of replacing and recycling men killed and wounded over and over again. From 1917 onwards, the 8ᵗʰ Queen's was a cog in the strategic wheel of exhaustion turned by GHQ as they adapted their warfighting and grasped with the war as it was unfolding in front of their map-weary eyes. However, there was a vast difference between the war seen and waged at the battalion level and the war plotted at GHQ. The men called upon to fight bore in their bodies the difficulties of doing so; like all soldiers, they recognised the growing dissonance between what commanders expected and what they could accomplish.

If he is any gauge of how the battalion officer saw the staff, then Major Peirs was skeptical at what he called the 'court' and their unrealistic expectations for men in the line. Sitting in a drippy dugout in November 1916, he wrote to his sister Olive of a recent tour by the staff of his squalid section of trench. The battalion was up the line in Hulluch, near where they had fought at Loos. The weather was vile, their trenches collapsing, and the Germans actively strafing their lines with aerial darts. He wrote:

> We had a whole bevy, Corps Divisional & Brigade staff all round together & they eventually decided some rotten little point, & I can't carry out their decision because I have other things for the men to do & consequently carry on as before. In fact I don't really know what they do want & I'm quite certain they don't, as they know nothing of the conditions & I've no doubt they went home & had a 7 course dinner thinking they'd done a good day's work, while we shammock about this beastly muck-heap & keep

---

2 Ibid.

the Bosch out of their blessed cook-house. Really I do get a trifle annoyed with them at times.[3]

Peirs was a quintessential team player of the old sort; he was not one to display disloyalty or let the side down. Indeed, after the war he chastised one of his former officers for wielding a blade too keenly against fellow officers on the staff: 'I admit they [the staff] were bloody, but that is no reason why you should put it down in cold type.'[4] Yet, Peirs's cynicism towards the staff and brass hats was not uncommon; the men who do the fighting, whether in today's wars or theirs, often see those in the comfortable rear areas as lacking in a basic understanding of the plight of men in the line. Though Peirs was unwavering in his moral determination, he never lost his civilian's intolerance for military bureaucracy. And though it is easy to question and dismiss the regimental officer's lamentations within the broader scheme of the war, it does not invalidate them. Officers like Peirs had to write home letters to the families of lost soldiers justifying their deaths; they were the ones who had to live with how the war was fought in the trenches.

Though he had little say in the conduct of the war, what Peirs could control was the day-to-day business of the battalion and the war fought in front of his face. Working in tandem with his commanding officer, Lieutenant Colonel Archibald Tringham, the two men laboured after the Somme to rebuild the battalion and to get their new drafts into shape. The two most senior officers had grown to trust one another. Though Peirs was initially skeptical of Tringham when he arrived with the battalion in October 1915, it was clear that the man knew his business and was an efficient leader.[5] Like most other battalions, they had learned lessons from the Somme, but these were hard-fought and not easily recognised for a brigade and division that seemed to take the war's brunt on the chin. Though their combat record by 1917 was not exceptional, the 24th Division had grown in competence after two years on active service. In 1917, the division would again show that it was able to adapt to the changing conditions and methods of fighting on the Western Front. And like in 1916, these lessons came at a formidable cost.

---

3   Peirs to his Olive, 7 November 1916.
4   IWM, Doc 11129. Box 66/304/1, Papers of Captain Charles Lodge Patch MC,. Peirs to C.J. Lodge Patch, 10 December 1919.
5   Peirs to his father, 5 November 1915.

Recovery: January–April 1917

The battalion came out of the line in intervals between 1–4 January 1917. They had been in the trenches for a miserable spell over Christmas and ate their celebratory dinners, served by company, as they came out of the line. As Tringham was off in temporary brigade command, Peirs was left to fret over the men's comfort and whether they would have beer, plum pudding, and fresh meat for their Christmas dinners.[6] Much more restorative than an army feast, the men had down time and relaxed by watching concerts and attending a cinema close to where they were billeted.[7] They were significantly under-strength; between the Somme and their stint of trench duty under fire in the early winter, they had only 506 men.

At half strength the battalion, as it was, went back up the line on 5 January. They did not lose time asserting dominance over no man's land. Forty-five men and two officers carried out a successful raid against the enemy on 9 January that resulted in one prisoner and three German dugouts being bombed. The raid was well-executed: divisional artillery cut a gap in the enemy's wire and the raiding party got across and into German trenches through a smokescreen. They remained in German lines for seventeen minutes and returned before the enemy's retaliatory barrage. Remarkably, they took no casualties.[8] The weather now was cold and frosty, and the men were certainly happy to leave their trenches two days later, though the enemy gave them a good sending off with a harassing bombardment as they went into rest.[9] In early February, the battalion took on more soldiers and went back up the line. Days before their relief by the 37th Division, the battalion was cheered by the officers of the 13th Royal Fusiliers, who were on tour of their new home and found the men there holding it worthy of such praise.[10] Unfortunately, the memoirist Guy Chapman was on staff duty and was not one of the fusiliers cheering them.[11] The battalion was thus in good spirits when they went into rest, having put in their time of winter trench duty.

---

6   Peirs to his family, 2 January 1917.
7   Peirs to his mother, 6 January 1917.
8   TNA, WO 95/2214/3, 8th Queen's War Diary, 9 January 1917.
9   SHC, Unofficial Battalion History, p.28.
10   Ibid.
11   Chapman was the author of *A Passionate Prodigality* (1933) as well as *A Kind of Survivor* (1975).

The battalion then moved to Allouagne, to the west of Bethune, where their officers took instruction in a new training regimen for their platoons. In the intellectual wake of the Somme, the British Army began reassessing its tactics with an eye for innovation. The most significant lesson learned after two years of fighting is neatly summed up by the quip that 'the artillery conquers, the infantry occupy.'[12] The most successful infantry attacks came through careful artillery preparation, where men advanced behind a curtain of fire, or a creeping barrage that temporarily stunned the enemy and offered fire-protection for exposed infantrymen. Moreover, the British infantryman now had tools at his disposal that could aid in the success of assaulting teams by providing firepower support that they did not have at the start of the war. Infantry companies had Lewis machine guns, infantrymen were trained and experienced with bombing and with the use of rifle grenades, and they were instructed in small unit assault tactics.

In early 1917, a new training scheme reorganized infantry platoons according to tactical specialty.[13] Each platoon was split into sections of men trained to fight together with a particular tactical tool: a Lewis gun team, bombers, rifle-grenadiers, and rifleman. In theory, the new system was tactically evolutionary and meant that each platoon could fight their way forward and reduce an enemy position with enhanced mutually supporting firepower. In practice, specialisations became subject to the laws of attrition, where whole sections could be wiped out by bomb blast or machine gun burst. Though innovative, over time the officers of the 8th Queen's believed this reorganisation was too clunky and unsustainable when checked by reality.[14] Still, the battalion reorganised and trained their sections according to the new method in February 1917.

The month of March found the battalion back in trench rotation at Calonne, territory that they knew relatively well. Peirs went on leave and attended an investiture ceremony at Buckingham Palace for his DSO earned the previous year. While he was away, Captain R.H. Rowland, one of the remaining officers from 1914, took over his duties. Tringham was once again

---

12 For artillery problems and evolution at the Somme, see The Long, Long Trail 'British Artillery Bombardment Before the Infantry Attach on the Somme', https://www.longlongtrail.co.uk/battles/battles-of-the-western-front-in-france-and-flanders/the-battles-of-the-somme-1916/british-artillery-bombardment-before-the-infantry-attack-on-the-somme/.

13 Paddy Griffith, *Battle Tactics of the Western Front*, p.77–8.

14 SHC, Unofficial Battalion History, p.28.

pulled away to command the 17th Brigade, leaving Rowland and then Peirs in charge upon his return from England. Their tour in the trenches was relatively routine, except for a number of significant bombardments of their lines, several of which also came with the added terror of aerial darts.

Adapting and Learning: April–July

The evening of 4 April came with a somewhat delayed spring thaw. For days there had been lingering snow, the last breaths of winter. Major Peirs returned to his headquarters dugout after sending a patrol into no man's land in an attempt to collar an enemy soldier for intelligence and regimental identification. As he waited for the patrol to return, he lit his pipe, and began writing to his sister Gladys. The enemy, he wrote, was largely inactive in his sector, but the increased British activity meant that they were shelled with frequency.

> Unfortunately he [the enemy] seems to know exactly where our mess is & where my own little bed is hidden & drops whizz bangs nearby in a most disconcerting manner. Luckily I don't mind how many whizz bangs he puts over as my roof is impregnable to whizz bangs & I am only praying that the whizz bang man doesn't go & dine with anyone connected with the 5.9s or they may like to have a go & we shall have to emigrate.[15]

As he complained, a kitten jumped up on his table and began playing with the whiskey bottle cork in front of him, swatting and batting at it as he attempted to write to his sister, conscious of the bottle of ink precariously within reach of the its paw. The patrol returning, he left the cat in command of the dugout and set out to meet it.

April 1917 was an important month for the BEF on the Western Front. Months in the making, the opening attack of the Battle of Arras was a success and the formidable German position at Vimy Ridge taken. The French had tried and failed to capture the ridge repeatedly, leaving in their wake thousands of dead to little avail. The difference between their attempts in 1915 and the BEF's successful attack of 1917 came from years of trial and error. Though it is debatable how steeply the BEF's learning curve can be measured, what is impossible to ignore is the achievement of the Canadian

---

15 Peirs to Glad, 4 April 1917.

Corps and the British 5th Division in taking the position on 9 April after a thorough and concentrated bombardment and behind a creeping barrage. Just to the north and in support of their assault was the 24th Division, who witnessed their success and lauded their compatriots to the south. The 9th East Surreys mocked the Germans opposite their trenches by erecting a billboard saying 'We have captured over 10,000 prisoners and 100 guns at Vimy. Will you surrender too?'[16]

Though Arras and Vimy occupied the BEF's attention, the 8th Queen's were out of the line taking baths on 8 April. The following day they were on church parade for Easter when the offensive began. They were within sound of the guns of Vimy coming to their east and were not entirely out of danger as a random shell fell in their midst, killing Captain George Penrose and wounding Lieutenant G.S.G. Hamilton. Penrose was one of original officers of the battalion and had served at Loos and through the Somme. A company commander by 1916, Penrose was known to the playwright R.C. Sherriff in the 9th East Surreys, who he took under his wing the first time the writer was in the trenches in 1916. Sherriff described the captain as an 'elegant, courtly young man' who knew his business and was respected by the men under his command.[17] The men buried Penrose on the 10th and sent his remaining effects to his widow.[18]

As the Arras offensive continued, the battalion trained behind the lines for a few days until they received a sudden order to move within twenty minutes' notice on 13 April. The enemy appeared to have withdrawn from some of their positions near Lens. Brigade intelligence reported overnight that there was activity behind German lines that included the loading of trucks and demolition explosions and smoke all behind their lines, evidence of a scorched-earth withdrawal.[19] This did not mean that the Germans were in retreat; it did, however, mean that they were straightening their lines and falling back upon prepared positions. The battalion had a frantic few days as they advanced from Maroc Camp to the outskirts of Lens, where Peirs established their forward battalion headquarters at the Lens-Grenay railway station.

---

16 Lucas, *The Journeys End Battalion*, p.90.
17 Roland Wales, 'Captain George Penrose, a Mentor to R.C. Sherriff', https://www.surreyinthegreatwar.org.uk/story/captain-george-penrose-a-mentor-to-rc-sherriff/.
18 TNA, WO 339/30771.
19 TNA WO 95/2211/2, 72nd Brigade War Diary, Intelligence Summary, 12 April 1917, Appendix 17.

The battalion moved carefully, not knowing what to expect as they crept through villages that had been reduced to rubble. Junior officers sent patrols to feel out for resistance and then moved their companies from one tactical position to the next in bounds after the area to their front was reconnoitered.[20] The ground ahead was heavily entrenched; German positions at Cité St Pierre had anywhere from six to twelve distinctive defensive positions, with a continuous and interlocking system of communications trenches that created a web of positions that each had to be checked for pockets of resistance. As they moved forward, patrols took casualties from German snipers harassing the advancing platoons. On 16 April, patrols again probed their way forward, this time under cover of an artillery barrage.[21] As they moved slowly from position to position, the battalion took forty-one casualties. Once secure in their new positions, they rotated into reserve, having been on the move for four days. Safely out of the line, Peirs wrote to his sister from the comfort of a ruined country house that was now his headquarters:

I don't quite know why, but everyone seems very pleased with the Division. Our Brigade certainly had some hard fighting and did very well, but we hadn't much to do except chase the retreating Bosch and simply advanced as far as he let us. I think we were on his heels much earlier than he expected, and consequently got a good deal more ground than he intended us to have. One Brigade got all sorts of stores which the Bosch would never have left it he could help it.[22]

Modesty aside, both the battalion and the brigade were able to move at quick notice and pursue an enemy that was actively withdrawing through careful small unit tactical initiative. Though a planned and strategic withdrawal by the enemy, it was the most the front in the Loos/Lens Salient had moved in years. By the end of the month, they were out of the line and training in the French countryside and 'in the depths of bucolicism & almost out of hearing of guns.'[23]

---

20 TNA, WO 95/2214/3, 8th Queen's War Diary, 72nd Brigade Operational Order 132, 14 April 1917.
21 TNA, WO 95/2211/2, 72nd Brigade War Diary, Operational Order 134, 16 April 1916, Appendix 20.
22 Peirs to Glad, 21 April 1917.
23 Peirs to his father, 26 April 1917.

Waiting

As the battalion continued its tour of the trenches during the months of May and June, the British Army on the Western Front began planning a major offensive at Ypres. Coming off the success of Vimy Ridge, Field Marshal Haig and his staff, in conjunction with the French, began planning for joint summer offensives. When elements of the French army fell into mutiny after the Nivelle Offensive in May, the burden of continuing the pressure on the Germans on the Western Front fell to the BEF.[24]

Haig and his staff identified Ypres as the area that made the most strategic sense for an offensive. The field marshal believed, optimistically, that his army could break through German lines and free the northern ports of Osted and Zebrugge, which were being used as U-boat bases.[25] He understood that a general defeat of the Germans in Belgium could turn the tide of the war. Initially, Haig's optimism even included a joint land and amphibious landing, the latter of which was abandoned. With his attention fixated on Ypres, Haig's staff began the process of envisioning a victory there.

Their plan consisted of two separate set piece battles. The first was an attempt to take Messines Ridge to the south of Ypres by Second Army, under the command of Herbert Plumer. Long a thorn in the side of the BEF, Messines Ridge was a key position for German observation and artillery dominance to the south of Ypres. Haig entrusted Plumer's Second Army with the task of taking the ridge, which they did on 7 June after detonating nineteen mines that collapsed German trenches. Second Army's rapid success on the day indicated the value in careful preparation, concentration of artillery, and mines. Plumer had a difficult but limited objective attack with a clear obtainable goal. If capitalised upon immediately, Messines could have possibly led to further success north along the Gheluvelt Plateau and Pilckem Ridge. Plumer's immediate success further reinforced to Haig and his staff the rightness of their plan for a northern operation.

The 8th Queen's was nearby but did little in the opening phase of the Messines battle. Though the 73rd and 17th brigades in their division fought and successfully took their objectives, the 72nd Brigade remained in reserve.[26] The 8th Queen's went forward to man front-line trenches to the north at

24 Neiberg, *Fighting the Great War*, p.254.
25 Nick Lloyd, *Passchendaele* (New York: Basic Books, 2017), p.39.
26 TNA, WO 95/2194/2, 24th Division War Diary, 7 June 1917.

Observatory Ridge to the east of Zillebeke, as Second Army consolidated their lines. They remained in captured German trenches there from 13–18 June, in what proved to be a more harrowing time than anticipated, as German artillery concentrated on their lines and the battalion came under bombardment for three days. Compounding the misery were low-flying German planes strafing their trenches with machine gun fire. The battalion took forty-two casualties (thirteen killed and twenty-nine wounded) in a short spell in the trenches.

Afterwards, they received a brief respite and then went back to the trenches near Klein Zillebeke, where they were again heavily shelled in a 'continuous' bombardment of their lines.[27] On 25 June, the Germans attempted a demonstration against their position, but it was beaten off successfully. Peirs recalled to his mother that their dugouts were cramped and uncomfortable:

> When in the line we lived in an old Bosch dug-out made of solid concrete and about 9 ft by 16 ft by 6 ft high inside & most uncomfortable. 3 of us & a signaler crowd into this & most unfortunately the Bosch knows exactly where it is & the thinnest side & doorway is towards him, but it would stand a good deal & the only damage he did was to smash up most of our mess plate (otherwise some enameled plates & mugs). However it was distinctly uncomfortable at the times when he was shooting at it.[28]

A technocrat, Peirs marvelled at the Germans' ability to build concrete bunkers as the enemy 'seems to have concrete galore.' By the end of the month, the battalion was relieved to be safely ensconced at Coloumby, a place full of 'strawberries and cream.'[29]

Installed in their training camp and tempted by summer fruits, the 8th Queen's began training again for what would come next. The BEF had fought two major and somewhat successful offensives in the spring of 1917.[30] At Arras and at Messines, the 24th Division had been present, but the 72nd

27 TNA, WO 95/2214/3, 8th Queen's War Diary, 25–25 June 1917.
28 Peirs to his mother, 28 June 1917.
29 Ibid.
30 Both Vimy and Messines were successful, but did not achieve a major strategic change to the western front.

Brigade had been in support and had got off relatively lightly. Though they had certainly taken casualties, the battalion had not fought a major planned engagement since August 1916 at Guillemont. As they settled into their company and platoon training at the end of June 1917, there was a sense that their good luck would change. Their period of waiting for what would come next was about to end.

Planning

After Messines, Haig turned the planning for his next offensive over to his two most experienced generals; Sir Herbert Plumer and Sir Henry Rawlinson. Plumer advocated a set-piece attack that envisioned taking the high ground of Messines in the south and Pilckem Ridge in the north. After these objectives were taken, another attack could then be assessed and planned. Rawlinson, having come north and observed the landscape, drew up his own plan: an attack along a broad front using 42 divisions and 5,000 artillery pieces to take Pilckem Ridge and Messines. Then a series of set-piece bite and hold battles creeping east – essentially a sequel to the Somme. Haig hoped for something more aggressive. [31] Wary of the conservativism of Plumer and Rawlinson, he turned to Fifth Army commander General Hubert Gough, who he believed had the dash to implement an offensive stretching from Pickelm Ridge to the north down to the Gheluvelt Plateau.[32]

Gough was a former cavalryman whose career on the Western Front was known by 1917 for his rapid ascent to army command, despite not having any significant successes to his credit. Moreover, Gough was a polarising figure who could 'be witty and charming or petty and vindictive.'[33] Gough's plan at Ypres was ambitious: a major assault along a broad front under a creeping artillery barrage that would penetrate enemy lines as far as 4,000–5,000 yards deep.[34] This was more than twice the distance than Plumer and Rawlinson believed possible in one shot. Moreover, the terrain was not uniform; some positions were easier to fight on, while others, such as the Gheluvelt Plateau to the south, were wooded and boggy, making any advance substantially more time-consuming and difficult. It was that position to the south that the

---

31 Lloyd, *Passchendaele*, p.41.
32 Robin Prior and Trevor Wilson, *Passchendaele: The Untold Story* (New Haven, CT: Yale University Press, 1996), p.46.
33 Lloyd, *Passchendaele*, p.65.
34 Prior and Wilson, *Passchendaele*, p.74.

24th Division found itself leading one of the attacks alongside the 8th and 30th divisions. At the spearhead of the 24th Division was the 72nd Brigade, who had not seen major combat since Delville Wood at the Somme. At the very tip of that spear was the 1st North Staffordshires and the 8th Queen's.

Training

As June turned into July, the 8th Battalion arrived in Coulomby Camp for a period of six days' rest after their recent tour of the trenches. After taking drafts in June, the battalion swelled in strength to 34 officers and 868 other ranks. Up to strength, the battalion rested in the good weather, and with their brigade, conducted a series of sports competitions to keep the men active. The most entertaining appeared to be the transportation show where men and mules competed for prizes. Evidently, the mule race with its five jumps was the best one of the events; the Queen's did well in overall prizes against the other battalions.[35] For men that had lived with stress, the opportunity to relax and be playful was an opportunity to rejuvenate a sense of their humanity; to laugh and shout and carry-on just beyond the reach of the war.

The war's reach, though, was only as short as the roads leading from Haig's staff to corps commanders, from corps to division, and from division to brigade. And after four days of rest, the 72nd Brigade received Operation Order 159 detailing their attack to be carried out at the end of the month. Lieutenant Colonel Tringham and Major Peirs designed an attack plan for their battalion and submitted it to brigade for approval. Then they began a training regimen for their men to accomplish their objectives.

Compared to the attacks at Loos and Guillemont, Operation Order 159 reveals significant tactical sophistication and is reflective of the growth of staff work and detailed planning within the BEF on the Western Front. What stands out is the careful attention paid to artillery preparation. The infantry attack was to be preceded by a barrage of enemy positions. This was to be followed by a creeping barrage in which each of the advancing battalions would follow. There was particular emphasis on communications and control; attacking companies had multiple ways to contact their battalion and brigade headquarters, including runners, kite balloons, wireless, and pigeons. Once their objectives were reached, contact aeroplanes were to fly

---

35 Peirs to his mother, 8 July 1917.

overhead to spot flares indicating their position and the extent of the advance. Each of the attacking battalions had artillery support at the ready; stokes mortars and extra machine guns were to be deployed forward to provide immediate fire support in the event of an enemy counter-attack. To the man, orders included specifics as to the amount of equipment each soldier was to carry, the availability of getting water and supplies to their positions under fire, and the ability to both evacuate the wounded as well as replace officers and NCOs who were wounded and killed. It would be the most sophisticated set-piece attack that the battalion fought in the entire war.[36]

Having their orders, Peirs and Tringham began work on their plan. The 1st Staffordshires were to advance on their left and were responsible for taking positions in the remnants of Shrewsbury Forest. The 8th Queen's were to skirt the lower edge of the wood on their right. They were responsible for taking two enemy strongpoints known as Jehovah and Jordan trenches. With his divisional and brigade general outline for the attack – along with its detailed artillery plan for a creeping barrage – Peirs drew up the battalion's orders.

Essentially, Peirs planned the battalion to attack with two companies forward, D Company to the left, under Captain William Yandell, and A Company to the right, under Captain Frank Sidney Rider. Both company commanders were former rankers with experience in command.[37] In support, was C Company, under Second Lieutenant L.G. Stedman, and B Company, under Captain Fellowes, in reserve. The assault companies were divided into waves and each platoon was further divided into mutually supporting weapons sections of riflemen, bombers, rifle grenadiers, and Lewis gun teams. Of the latter, both A and D companies had four Lewis guns each, totaling eight in the attack. The first wave was to be conducted by their riflemen and bombers with their Lewis guns in the second line on the flanks to provide support in case the advancing infantry got bogged down.

Training was key to implementing such a sophisticated attack. Tringham and Peirs reconnoitered their position well in advance and the 24th Division's staff created mock attacking ground for the battalion to train behind the lines. The men began special weapons training first, with rifle grenades and their Lewis guns. They then spent six days training for their attack, three of which were along the flagged mock attack area. The battalion then moved

---

36 TNA, WO 95/2211/3, 72nd Brigade Operational Order 159, 5 July 1917.
37 TNA, WO 339/41659; WO 339/40711.

closer to the front, arriving at Micmac Camp on 26 July, where they rested. Three days later, they went up the line and into the maze of trenches near Hill 60. In the process of moving up, they lost one officer and twenty-eight men. On 30 July, the battalion was in its assault position at the division's front. The men rested as well as they could as stores of ammunition, bombs, food and water came up in support of their upcoming attack.

In Action

The sun set behind Peirs as he made his way up the communication trench. He carried his map case and cloth tape as he moved up ahead of the battalion. The rest of the men followed him once it was dark and safe to do so. When the major arrived at the frontline trench, it was already dark and he looked out over the parapet with his binoculars at the shell-holed field in front of him; this was what the men would have to attack through the next morning.

Peirs went forward to a listening post jutting out from the front lines and then climbed into no man's land, which was a reasonably safe distance from the enemy, especially at night. He walked to the left parallel to the front-line trench and then stopped at the intersection between his battalion's front and that of the 1st Staffordshires, where he saw an NCO marking the boundary. There a roll of tape was tied to a stake and pushed into the soft ground. They unrolled it moving south, the white tape clearly visible on the ground in the faint light of the night sky. Peirs looked around constantly for motion or movement. He looked also to the sky, where he saw billowing clouds, a sign of coming rain. He felt the rising humidity and the nerves of being exposed as he personally marked the position for his battalion's attack. It was as if he was marking the starting line of a field day race.

When he finished, the men were already on their way up the line. It took them some time as the enemy shelled their communication trenches. In the early hours of the morning, the first two companies of the battalion crawled out of their assault trench and moved as silently as possible to the tapeline directly facing the enemy. They were shielded by darkness and a bombardment to their front that reached its crescendo as the men found their positions. It was 3:30 am and the day had not begun to break. The men of A and D companies assembled at the tapeline just as they rehearsed. They clustered in their assault groups broken down by platoon and then divided by section into Lewis gun teams, rifle grenadiers, bombers, and riflemen, the latter with their bayonets fixed ready to do the brutal close-order work of seizing and mopping up an enemy strongpoint.

All had trained for this moment, but many of the men had not yet been in an attack. The anticipation bred worry and some men shook with anxiety. All felt fear, but all expressed it differently. Their NCOs tried to both calm and steel their charges with last-minute pats on the back and whispers to keep down. The veterans of the Somme knew that many would be wounded and some killed by shelling, bullets, or grenades that came from the unseen foes to their front. For the uninitiated, they wondered whether they had the courage to fight, to kill, and to survive. For veterans, they knew that survival was not something that could be gamed but was predicated by that fickle thing: fortune. All hoped that they would not fail, that their training and officers were leading them to success, and that their luck had not run out just yet. So far, their attacking history had not warranted optimism, but perhaps by 1917 their thorough training would pay off.

At the tapeline, the battalion's headquarters officers moved back and forth putting men into their positions. The familiar outline of Peirs was known to all; in addition to laying out their lines he had planned all the details of the attack and was now overseeing their formation with his stick in hand and his uniform already bearing Belgian mud. Near him was Lieutenant Guy Hamilton, his adjutant, who had been involved in the meticulous planning and training over the previous month. The two of them saw to it that the men were in their right places, and it was up to them to see the attack through. Their commanding officer, Lieutenant Colonel Tringham, was held back in case the other senior officers were killed. As Peirs and Hamilton moved along the tapeline, the bombardment to their front increased and the enemy positions were highlighted by the explosions for brief seconds after each shell found its home. Silhouetted to their front was the distant outline of an enemy strong point, as well as the felled trees of Shrewsbury Forest that had been harvested by their own guns. The assault teams waited for the cacophony of calibres to reach its crescendo and for their officers' whistles to blow.[38]

Suddenly, they came under bombardment. For many, this was their first experience being shelled in the open without the cover of their trenches. Their officers instructed them to hold firm at the tapeline as they counted down the time until zero hour. As they waited, time seemed to stand still.

---

38 TNA, WO 95/2214/4, 8th Queen's War Diary, 31 July 1917.

Men began to breath the heavy, quick breaths of the anxious and no doubt some began to panic as the time ticked down painfully slowly to zero hour. Then at 3:50, as their officers held their whistles to their lips, their eyes on their watches, their men looked to their front where 'our own barrage began, and the enemy artillery soon answered to the imperious summons of the stream of coloured lights that mingling with the bursts of shrapnel, and the dark clouds of high explosive combine to render a modern battle a magnificent spectacle, if looked on from afar.'[39] The men were not looking upon the barrage from afar, though. They were underneath the weight of German 77 millimeter and 4.2-inch howitzer shells that were hitting the tapeline as their stunned officers waited for the signal to jump off and advance behind their creeping barrage. Some now groaned with wounds and the call went out for stretcher bearers. Then at 3:54 am, their officers blew their whistles, the noise resonating above the sounds of shells and wounded men shouting for aid.

Their first objective was Job's Post: a concrete dugout flanked by entrenched shell holes designed as a forward position to delay or breakup an assault. 'After a stiff little fight'. the post fell to Captain Yandell's D Company.[40] Reconfiguring their assault teams, the advance companies kept going to their first major objective, Jehovah Trench. The two companies kept up their advance, conscious of their strict timetable and to not lose the protection of the barrage. To their front the bombardment raged around Jehovah Trench. They crept up to it under the curtain of fire and took the trench fifty-six minutes after jumping off the tapeline. There they found the German dugouts in bad shape and the defenders stunned and in no shape to resist. The assault companies paused to wait for their moppers-up and then formed again for their next objective, Jordan Trench. Again, moving behind their own barrage, D and A company advanced on either side of the German communications trench Alarm Weg, which linked Jehovah and Jordan Trench. They took their final position with little resistance and began consolidating in anticipation of an expected enemy counter-attack. The attack took two hours. By 6:00 am, just as their families in southeastern England were waking for the day, the survivors of A and D companies reversed the German second line and waited for a counter-attack.

---

39 SHC, Unofficial Battalion History, p.33.
40 Ibid.

The initial assault completed, the battalion now faced the difficult task of consolidating and holding the position. As it stood, they had outpaced the battalions on both their right and left flanks. On their right flank to the south, the 20th Durham Light Infantry struggled to reach their final objective. This left A Company's flank in the air. The Durhams encountered difficult resistance, particularly from enemy snipers and machine guns, that were picking off their officers and stalled their attack at the Blue Line.[41] To protect their gains, C Company, under Second Lieutenant Stedman, came up and connected Jordan and Jehovah trenches together by linking up shell holes on the right as a makeshift defensive trench to protect the battalion's right flank. On the left, the 1st North Staffordshires had to pull back due to their left flank being up in the air, further exposing the 8th Queen's in the salient at the front of the division. As such, D Company on the left got to work linking together the two battalions using shell holes and uncut wire. They spent most of the day trying to improve their position and to connect with the battalions to the north and south to create one unified line of defense in case of the expected counter-attack.

Compounding the situation now were the wounded. The battalion had paid a heavy price. Though resistance from each of their objectives was fairly minimal, they were under German artillery fire from 3:50 am onwards, shells that were both accurate and deadly. Both the company commanders leading the assault, captains Yandell and Rider, were wounded. Also wounded were lieutenants Millard, Lake, and Stedman and Company Sergeant Major Waller. Second Lieutenant Green and Sergeant Mowbray had been killed, along with at least two dozen others. As the day continued 200 wounded accumulated along a front hundreds of yards deep. Many were unable to walk; nearly all were struck by shrapnel, which meant horrific wounds from flying steel shrapnel balls and jagged shell casings, the latter that could rip men apart. Dr Charles Lodge Patch set up his aid station by the battalion headquarters in Image Crescent Trench but had to figure out a way to get his stretcher bearers to collect the wounded while under shellfire. It proved not only to be difficult, but potentially murderous duty for his bearers.

At battalion headquarters, Peirs and Hamilton had their own trouble. The Germans were not only bombarding the battalion to their front, but were specifically laying down heavy fire to the rear to upset communications

---

41 TNA, WO 95/2639/1, 20th Battalion, Durham Light Infantry War Diary, 31 August 1917.

and to prevent reinforcements from coming up. At dusk, two additional burdens presented themselves. It began to rain and the trenches and shell holes that the battalion was sheltering in began to fill with water, their sides eroding into slimy, muddy mess that caused the men additional difficulty in reinforcing them. The enemy led a disorganised counter-attack, which the battalion called up artillery support to break up. On their right flank, the 20th Durhams' situation proved precarious.

As the Durhams struggled, battalion headquarters dispatched Lieutenant Albert Frost and twenty men with rations for those in the front lines. Frost was a former ranker who did three years in the Scots Guards before accepting a commission in April 1917 in the Queen's. A veteran with service in an elite regiment, Frost was now in his first engagement as an officer and leading his small detachment forward along the right side of the battalion line. To his front, he could hear firing and see SOS signals for friendly artillery to batter the German counter-attack that formed. As his men gingerly made their way forward with rations, Frost ran into a panicked soldier of the Durhams who told him that one of their positions had just fallen to a German counter-attack. Without flinching, Frost ordered his men to drop their rations, unsling their rifles and to attack. They took the position through hand-to-hand combat and thwarted the counter-attack. Frost earned a Military Cross for his initiative and bravery.

As dawn broke on 1 August, the Queen's continued to hold. The rain was coming down in torrents and their trenches and shell holes flooded. The battalion medical officer, along with some bearers borrowed from the 8th West Kents, attempted to find the wounded, some of whom were drowning in the holes they had dragged themselves into for protection.[42] The work was endless, with hundreds of wounded men, including the officers who commanded A, D, and B companies. William Yandell, who led D Company, had a gunshot wound to the chest. A 32-year-old foreman gardener from Taunton, Yandell had served in the Royal Fusiliers before gaining his commission and joining a battalion full of officers from elite backgrounds. Having earned a blighty, he would never command a company at the front again.[43] His fellow company commander, Frank Rider, also earned a ticket home through three

---

42 SHC, Unofficial Battalion History, p.34.
43 TNA, WO 339/41659.

gunshot wounds to his thighs that miraculously caused no bone or nerve damage.[44]

As Yandell and Rider made the laborious journey back on their stretchers, Second Lieutenant E.J. Millard fought for his life with a gunshot wound to his abdomen. Millard was a salesman by profession who volunteered in September 1915 with the Royal Fusiliers. He became a quartermaster sergeant in the 18th Battalion when he was recommended for a commission in 1916. Dr Lodge Patch did his best to stabilise him for his evacuation to 32 Casualty Clearing Station, where he lived for an agonizing two days before dying and being interred at Brandhoek Military Cemetery. He died a bachelor, leaving behind a writing case with a note in it saying 'If this case should be found, will finder kindly send same to my father.'[45] The torment of Millard and his family was shared by dozens of others as severely wounded men suffered their last agonizing moments in the muddy morass of their captured German trenches, men now fighting for their lives and begging for help as the rain poured.

Though the morning of 1 August allowed for brief respite, the enemy continued to shell their position in the afternoon and did so for the rest of the day. No place was spared; the battalion headquarters, in fact, came under particularly heavy shelling. Peirs was nearby when his adjutant, Guy Hamilton, was killed standing outside of their dugout organising the battalion's relief after dark. Hamilton was a 19-year-old officer who came to war from Brighton College via the Inns of Court Officer Training Corps.[46] He had been wounded in April 1917 and had only just rejoined the battalion on 11 July.[47] He was described afterwards as 'an ideal adjutant, being fearless, hardworking, quick and most conscientious, besides having a very high sense of duty.'[48]

Hamilton died while organising the battalion's relief by the 9th East Surreys the night of 1 August. By this point the men of the 8th Queen's had been awake for two days and had been hunkered down in the mud for twenty-four hours as it rained continuously. The men that came out of the line looked

44 TNA, WO 339/40711.
45 TNA, WO 339/63563.
46 *Illustrated War News*, 21 April 1915, p.46.
47 *Yorkshire Evening Post*, 8 August 1917, p.3.
48 Brighton College Roll of Honour, https://www.brightoncollegeremembers.com/roll-of-honour/1863.

to the East Surreys like a mob of troglodytes, 'coated with mud and soaked to the skin, many too bleeding from wounds in the knees caused by barbed wire, as the Battalion was wearing shorts, and all so tired that they could hardly drag themselves along.'[49] Their losses were brutal: 12 officers and 293 other ranks killed, wounded, or missing. Though an agonising experience and no doubt one that would be relived by the survivors for the rest of their lives, the battalion had accomplished something that it had not done before. They planned and executed a complex attack and took their objectives. They held their position until relieved. They suffered for it, but they stood firm in appalling conditions. Immediately after getting his men settled at Micmac Camp, Peirs wrote to his mother on the morning of 2 August before settling in for some sleep in his tent,

> I am about to go to bed but I just write to let you know that I have been in & am now out of the great strafe all serene. The Battn. did well & took all its objectives. I was in command as the C.O. stayed out. The weather is vile & the trenches we have made absolutely filthy. I am covered in mud & must wash.[50]

The major had reason for serenity; his men did their duty under his leadership. A few months later, he attached a rosette to his DSO ribbon for his role in seeing the job through.

* * *

The attack to the south of Shrewsbury Forest was the only major action fought by the 8th Queen's in 1917. Most of their time at the front was spent in routine trench duty with periods of rest behind the lines. In their one attack, three things can be observed from their experiences and their performance. First, that they carefully planned a battle at the division, brigade, and battalion level that was vastly more sophisticated than any other action they had fought – or would fight – over the course of the war. If one compares this attack to Loos, then the idea of an evolution in tactical sophistication is instantly apparent. At Loos they engaged in an open order daytime assault,

---

49 SHC, Unofficial Battalion History, p.34.
50 Peirs to his mother, 2 August 1917.

in waves, with no artillery preparation or support. There they had no detailed operational orders and the attack was essentially unplanned. Though the situations were different – the attack at Loos being a follow-up to a structured attack the previous day – the level of sophistication of the 31 July attack is impressive. The planning details reveal thoughtfulness and good staff work. The battalion's action itself demonstrates a significant payoff for their months of training since 1916 and sophistication in their new tactical scheme, which was well rehearsed.

Second, when it came to the attack itself, the men were able to take their objectives with proper artillery support. The timetable for the attack worked and they sustained few casualties from enemy resistance. Their planning paid off and they were lucky to not have severe impediments to hold up their assault teams. It was not hyperbole or pathological positivism for Peirs to write home of their success; in a war that so far had robbed them of any distinct battlefield success, they had as close to it as they would come in taking Jordan and Jehovah trenches. Limited objectives could be taken by highly trained soldiers working with artillery to both diminish and limit enemy resistance until those assaulting soldiers were basically on top of their opponents.

Peirs was also serene in another fashion. He was confident and proud of what his men accomplished, despite their losses. This was the battalion's first major attack since Loos. For those veterans still with the battalion, there was a sense of insecurity, doubt, and, for some, survivor's guilt. In this attack, they proved to both the army and to themselves that they had what it took to be successful soldiers. For Peirs, he succeeded in pulling off an attack with men under his command that would make Colonel Fairtlough proud.[51] The 8th Queen's had come into their own as part of a division that Peirs wrote to his sister proudly was 'getting a reputation for strafing.'[52]

Finally, and less positively, the attack demonstrated that success still came at a grave cost. Preventing high casualties for attackers in the open when the enemy's artillery was zeroed on their path of assault was nearly impossible. From the moment they assembled at the tapeline, the battalion took casualties from shrapnel and high explosive artillery shells. Once they achieved their

---

51 This and the preceding sentences are paraphrased from a comment on the manuscript by Jenna Fleming.
52 Peirs to Odile, 3 August 1917.

objectives, they then came under punishing fire as they tried to consolidate, all the while dealing with environmental conditions that made the situation much worse. The terrain was churned up and boggy and the addition of heavy rain ushered in unpredictable suffering due to the environment in which these men had to fight. The image of wounded men drowning in shell holes is enough to sober any intemperate analysis of their success. Yes, the British Army was learning, but men were still being killed in droves and required to fight in conditions that were dispiriting and demoralising at best, foundationally disillusioning at worst. Perhaps the most significant factor to the survival of the battalion after Third Ypres was not their success, but the fact that they only had to endure those conditions for a few days before then being pulled out of the line and rested. Peirs's assessment of their service being 'long periods of absolute boredom with short intervals of paralysing terror' proved to be a reality in 1917.[53]

At Micmac Camp and then Dickebusch, the battalion rested and took on drafts to replenish their depleted ranks. Their role at Third Ypres was not finished, but they did not take centre stage again. Instead, they joined the chorus of battalions that were rotated up the line in support positions. Their job was to hold the line, a boring job that they were used to, but one that was hardly easy. They were gassed on and off, the Germans keeping up pressure and certainly not allowing them to go quietly. Peirs wrote to his sister about their conditions with his usual wry humor:

We are living underground in a big system of tunnels, which are now some little way behind the line. They are really a number of narrow passages about 3 ft wide & never more than 5 ft 9 high & usually much less. They are a really large system as there must be at least 250 men here including several brigade staffs dressing stations etc. We are fairly comfortable as we have what was a Brigade Hqrs, though the bloke in charge of the tunnels tried to turn me out, as he wanted it for his office. However he didn't get it, though we let him live with us as a compromise. We have also got electric light & an electric fan which are very excellent, though for the last 2 days the engine has broken down & we have been distinctly stuffy. We come to the surface occasionally to see if the war is

---

53 Peirs to his father, 10 November 1915.

going on, but otherwise do nothing in particular & it is no place to take a country walk.[54]

It is just as well that they were kept in support. The battalion was recovering from their attack and many of the men were new. Many of the officers were also replacements. Peirs noticed the difference between the new officers and the old, a difference that had crept into battalions gradually as more men were promoted from the ranks. Peirs, the temporary officer solicitor, wrote home to his father, also a solicitor 'We are being swamped with a number of new 2nd Loots. They are men who were sent home earlier in the year to take commissions from the ranks & it remains to be seen how they pan out. Someone has just sadly remarked that they are not even as respectable as solicitors.'[55]

Rotated in and out of trenches in late summer, the battalion's fate was already determined by GHQ. On 20 September, they were taken out of the trenches east of Ypres for the last time and went into rest camp. There they played football and cricket. Notably, they were beaten at cricket by an Australian team.[56] After three months in Belgium, they received orders to prepare to embark south to a quieter theatre at the Somme. The battalion left by train, and 'the Ypres Salient was thus left for the last time and no one regretted it or ever wished to return to it.'[57] For the divisions remaining or who would be moved to the salient, their part in Third Ypres was yet to be played. For the 24th Division, their time was done, and they looked forward to a more hospitable place to hold the line in France opposite Saint-Quentin, a quiet sector since the German withdrawal to the Hindenburg Line earlier in 1917.

---

54 Peirs to Odd, 18 August 1917.
55 Peirs to his father, 21 August 1917.
56 SHC, Unofficial Battalion History, p.35.
57 Ibid.

Chapter 7

Survival

The landscape to the east of Péronne is charming and ubiquitously agrarian. The narrow country roads lead from village to village, bisecting fields either muddily ploughed or abundantly green, depending upon the season. The villages are largely quaint and uncommercialised. Often there is a church with a belfry and spire, a bus stop on the main road, and commonly a crucifix or a war memorial at an intersection. There are also cemeteries, most of which are in remote locations along the roads, or in the distance sitting adjacent to a field. These are the only prominent reminders of the fact that this land was once fought over by great armies and spoilt by them, left in rubble and ruin. The scars of that contest are nearly all gone now – the villages rebuilt and the locals leading peaceful lives. If it was not for the shells and shell fragments that come out of the ground, this could be any other agricultural area in northern Europe.

We are conscious of its history because of the winding river that gives the region its name: the Somme. The river itself is undeserving of its grim and tragic connotation, but it will be forever linked to the two horrific battles waged here in 1916 and 1918. The region is burdened by its history. Once the great armies departed, the people here reclaimed their villages and dealt with the wreckage left behind. Their history is often forgotten when we write about the Somme; it is a history of the people, too, who filled in the trenches and shell holes and rebuilt the villages that stand a testament to the resilience of their spirit to recover from the twentieth century's worst human tragedies. As British, Australian, and Canadian tourists go in search of the battles their ancestors fought, the French villagers of Picardy go about their daily lives in a place that relives the traumas of the past by the busload. Such is the fate of all battles remembered and their battlefields memorialised. Such is the fate of all who live in areas scarred by war.

It is easy now to forget the extent of the absolute destruction wrought by the war. It is also easy to forget that this destruction was also largely deliberate. Years of shelling turned villages into rubble redoubts and pastoral ridges to ramparts. After the British and French offensive at the Somme in 1916 – the Fourth Army's great meatgrinder of attritional battles – the German army withdrew to the Hindenburg Line in April 1917. As they pulled back, they devastated from Péronne to Saint-Quentin so that the British Army, in their tepid advance forward, had little remaining of military value. These wrecked villages became artillery placements and ammunition dumps. Those nearer the front, facing the enemy, became redoubts linked together by remote outposts in the farms beyond their reach. The whole region, by 1918, was an army encampment stretching from Amiens to the no man's land opposite Saint-Quentin. It was a vast sea of military men and material spanning dozens of miles in depth.

It was in this landscape of ruins, training camps, and trenches that the 8ᵗʰ Queen's moved into in the waning weeks of September 1917. Along with the rest of the Fifth Army, the battalion came south from Ypres to rest, regroup, and retrain. For the remainder of the year, the battalion's war diary reflects trench rotation, working parties, patrols, and training. Officers and men rotated in and out of leave; new faces came into the battalion to replace those that had been lost at Ypres. Major Peirs left for Aldershot in October, where he went to Senior Officer Training School. Twice decorated with a DSO, Peirs was now being trained to command a battalion. By November, the battalion had familiarity with their new home, a section of small villages fortified by outposts and trenches, stretching from Hargicourt to Le Verguier. Peirs's trench map still has his blue pencil marks of the routes taken by the battalion up and down the line. Unlike their service at the salient, this was easy duty.

It was the battalion's third Christmas abroad. For their CO, Archibald Tringham, it was an opportunity to go home on leave to be with his family. His wife had lost her brother in the war and suffered from a prolonged illness. Tringham had commanded the battalion for two years and had often temporarily commanded brigades when needed. At 48, he was still a very fit man, but the prolonged stress of both the front and his family situation was bound to have taken its toll, and rest at home was certainly both warranted and needed. On Christmas Eve, the battalion carried on their training. On Christmas Day they attended divine service and in the days following rotated their companies for their annual celebratory dinners. Then they rotated back into training and working parties, the same as they had throughout the autumn. It was a dull winter.

The battalion's convivial medical officer certainly found the winter routine of their new sector one of comparative comfort. Dr Charles Lodge Patch was a chatty officer who liked to play cards over drinks with his fellow officers. Born in India in 1887, he qualified as a doctor after medical school at the University of Edinburgh, served in the pre-war Indian Medical Service, and then transferred to the RAMC where he joined the 8th Queen's at the Somme. Peirs recommended him for the MC after he displayed gallantry in treating the wounded during the attack on Shrewsbury Forest in 1917. Lodge Patch described February 1918 as a 'very comfortable time … After three years of war, one had learnt the art of making oneself comfortable under adverse circumstances.'[1] The enemy was quiet and rotations in and out of trenches were no more dramatic than extended working parties interrupted by the occasional mortar shell. Behind the lines, officers and men lived in comfort. The army had put up Adrian huts, which they nicknamed 'Snow Palaces' that included an officer's club with a full bar and a performance hut, the 'Daly Theatre', named after the commander of the 24th Division.[2] Lodge Patch recalled how cushy this spot of the war was for him, replete with drinks, dancing, gambling, and dinner parties, 'every night was a night of feasting and wining in February '18.'[3]

This level of comfort and consistency was unique. There is a sense of a 'calm before the storm' to Lodge Patch's recollection. There is also, however, a bit of the memoirist's penchant for building tension and telling a good war story. While Lodge Patch centres his recollection on comfort, if we move away from the 'milk and honey' officers' mess of the 8th Queen's and consider the war as a whole, a grimmer picture emerges for the BEF and the Fifth Army. The battalion's unofficial historian recalled:

> The opening of the year 1918 found the B.E.F. somewhat disqui-
> eted. The great efforts of the previous year, from which so much
> had been hoped, had been made and made apparently in vain. The
> Russians had deserted us; the German divisions on the Western

---

1   IWM, Doc. 11129, Papers of Captain Charles Lodge Patch MC, Memoir, p.1.
2   Ibid, p.2.
3   Ibid.

Front were daily getting more numerous, and the enemy were openly boasting that at last their time had come, when they would burst the barrier of the West and sweep us into the sea. The British Army felt like an athlete who has put his whole strength into what he hoped would be a victorios [*sic*] spurt, but who after all finds that he has misjudged his distance, and that his opponent is again at his shoulder and is rapidly gaining on him. It is true that these considerations may not have been apparent to every soldier, but, what was self-evident to all, was that the war was still going on as strong as ever, that we had had no comfort or glimpse of civ-ilization for 3 months, and that there were too many confounded working parties.[4]

If we pull the lens out from the officer's card table, the situation facing the BEF as a whole at the start of 1918 was far different than the year previously. The Fifth Army had been battered at Third Ypres. Despite their hard fight-ing, there was no end to the war in sight. Indeed, there was a growing suspi-cion that they were vulnerable. German divisions had been transferred from east to west with a purpose. From GHQ all the way down to the divisions in the front lines, there was a deep suspicion of a major German offensive.[5]

Was the Fifth Army ready to resist such an attack? Two significant factors indicate that it was not. The first was a general manpower crisis that faced the BEF in the winter of 1918.[6] Attrition had taken its toll and there were not enough trained men available to replenish losses. As a result, infantry brigades became leaner by reducing their complement from four battalions to three. This affected the 8th Queen's directly as they took on men from a disbanded battalion (3/4th Queen's) and were transferred out of the 72nd Brigade to join the 17th Brigade in February.[7] There they joined the 1st Royal Fusiliers and the 3rd Rifle Brigade under the command of Brigadier General Percy Stone. Just as significant as the reorganisation of brigades, was a new

---

4   SHC, Unofficial Battalion History, p.40.
5   Beckett, Bowman, and Connelly, *The British Army and the First World War*, pp.349–50. Additionally, Lodge Patch's memoir is quite clear that officers within the battalion believed this to be true.
6   David Stevenson, *With Our Backs to the Wall* (Cambridge, MA: Harvard University Press, 2011), p.49.
7   SHC, Unofficial Battalion History, p.40.

defensive scheme put into place by GHQ and implemented by Fifth Army commander General Hubert Gough.

Similar to German defense in depth tactics, the Fifth Army designed their own system at the Somme. The new defensive system consisted of three areas to resist a potential attack. The first was a forward zone. This amounted to a collection of remote outposts that directly faced the enemy. The second was the battle zone, where the enemy was to be drawn into, engaged and defeated, and finally, a rear zone, which amounted to the emergency brake on any German attack. The forward zone's job was to harass, slow down, and break up enemy attacks. The bloodied enemy, now more hesitant in their assault, would be met by stiffer resistance in the battle zone thousands of yards deep, and there defeated through counter-attack. The system was logical if the defenders were well-trained, had consistent orders, clear lines of communication, and knew what they were doing. Unfortunately, this was not the case. 'The over-arching concept of the system was never fully understood by the BEF as a whole, once again revealing a disturbing inability to disseminate information clearly and thoroughly.'[8] Moreover, for officers and men who had been principally attacking for most of their experience in the war, a complex defensive scheme was beyond their capacity to fully grasp and implement effectively in just a few months.[9]

So, when the 8th Queen's went up the line near Bernes in February 1918, they were in a new brigade attempting to implement a new system of defence in an area that they were only really beginning to know. The colour-coded system of vulnerable forward positions placed strain on officers who were unaccustomed to thinking in terms of complex defensive preparations. Writing a few years afterwards, the battalion's first historian recalled their precarious situation.

> The whole of the 5th Army was desperately digging itself in, and was trying to do too much; too many lines were hastily dug, and none were continuously good. One really good line out of reach of a preliminary bombardment would have been worth all our rainbow coloured, hastily wired, spitlocked trenches.[10]

---

8   Beckett, Bowman and Connely, *The British Army and the First World War*, p.351.
9   Ibid.
10 SHC, Unofficial Battalion History, p.40.

Battalions were asked to master their new trenches, improve their positions, patrol regularly, and if in the forward zone, to hold out indefinitely in the event of an attack by the enemy. Though the scheme looked logical on the maps at army HQ, for the brigades rotating in and out of their zones, there was a serious concern about how the scheme would work if tested.

The Calm

The 8th Queen's moved into rest at Hancourt in February. Warm huts awaited them and notably they were reviewed by Gough and his commanding officer, Field Marshal Haig. Peirs shook hands with the BEF's commander, finding 'Duggy's hand a little clammy.'[11] Their position overall was comfortable; officers had evening drinks in their club and gambled after dinner. Peirs planted a garden and fretted over his flowers. By early March, he began to see the fruits of his labour, writing to his beloved mother that the 'snowdrops have become gigantic, as they ought seeing that they are planted in an old manure heap, & the most pessimistic of the periwinkles are in full bloom.'[12] As he found comfort in his gardening, rumours circulated of an impending German attack to coincide with the milder weather that had brought forth the spring flowers in his manure heap.

It is a good thing that the battalion had a month of relative peace considering what awaited them next. With peaceful hobbies came a sense of hopefulness. Gardens, card-playing, music, and games were ways of maintaining their sense of humanity in trying times. Down time was a powerful reminder that life would return to normal if they survived their time in uniform. Throughout his long service on the Western Front, Peirs wrote regularly to his parents and sisters, their emotional bonds maintained through family affection, joking, and gossip.[13] Like many of his fellow officers and men, his family supported him with books and magazines, delicacies, equipment, tobacco and more. Writing to his mother about his makeshift rockery and pessimistic periwinkles was a comfort to him as well as her. Through the flowers of spring that were poking out of his manure heap, there is an unintended metaphor for what they had all been through. Hopefully his fussing

---

11 Peirs to his mother, 16 February 1918.
12 Peirs to his mother, 3 March 1918.
13 For more on the importance of families to supporting men's emotional health during the war, see Michael Roper, *The Secret Battle*, Chapter 2.

over his flowers brought a smile to the older woman's face at her son's attempts at making the best out of a bad lot.

Her dutiful son had now finally achieved battalion command. After two and a half years commanding the 8th Queen's, Archibald Tringham was transferred to command the Fifth Army's entrenching battalions. After church parade on 3 March, Tringham left the battalion and Peirs took over. Three years after his first temporary command of the battalion at Loos, the 32-year-old officer had proven himself time and time again. The DSO ribbon and rosette adornment upon his tunic breast indicated his bravery and coolness under fire. The unabashed confidence his fellow officers had in his abilities was perhaps the greatest testament to his leadership. Peirs was a fighting Kitchener-battalion officer who had grown into his role. Like many other citizen-soldier battalion commanders in the British Army, his was hard-earned, well-deserved, and a long time coming.

At the beginning of March, the battalion moved from Hancourt to Montrécourt, where they were in corps reserve. There they trained and played games. On the 12th, they went into brigade reserve at Vendelles, a small French village in the forward zone. Directly to their front was the fortified village of Le Verguier, the last real bastion in their section of line before the Germans opposite. Recent intelligence indicated that if there was an attack, it would take place soon. No doubt the rumours of an impending attack were met with both trepidation and a sense of cautious confidence; the veterans in the battalion knew how to fight and the newbies had spent months training. Thus, when the battalion rotated from support into their front-line positions at Le Verguier, the officers and men did so on high alert for enemy activity.

At some point coming up the line, Peirs injured his foot and the wound had turned septic. The battalion medical officer, Captain Lodge Patch, recommended that he stay behind with the baggage at Bernes while the battalion went up the line. Peirs's right hand man, Major Reginald Rowland, took command of the battalion and moved them up the line to Le Verguier.

The Position

The 8th Queen's relieved the 1st Royal Fusiliers on the evening of 18 March 1918. They marched up the Vendelles road and set up their battalion HQ in Le Verguier. Two companies, B and D, took their positions in a semi-circle along the northern and eastern edge of the village. Their positions were at the top of a slope that led down into a valley. In good weather, the edge of the village provides a vast vista and one can instantly understand why it was a defensive position. B and D companies split their platoons into the forts and posts on the outskirts of the village. The forts themselves were the ruins of buildings now reinforced with sandbags, wire, and machine guns. Below in their cellars were dugouts to protect their garrison from bombardment and from gas. As they took to their posts, the officers directed their men into positions and checked their stores. The outgoing officers of the 1st Royal Fusiliers kept them up to date on the situation to the front. Anticipation breeds anxiety; in the best of times, these feelings can be euphoric and energising. In this instance there was a sinking feeling that their battalion was in for it as they settled into their new positions.

The other two companies – A and C – passed through the village and made their way down the hill to the forward outposts at the extreme front of the 24th Division. They trekked towards the Grand Priel Farm where they separated. A Company established their headquarters at Graham Post, positioning its platoons to the front at their forward outposts. The outposts consisted of a group of strongpoints that were meant to be mutually supporting. C Company made their way north-east to Shepherd's Copse. This outpost consisted of a string of small redoubts covering about 75 yards along a ridge between Le Verguier and Villeret. One of C Company's officers, Claude Piesse, recalled that his post was poorly provisioned with only spare rifle ammunition, no grenades, and water so tainted by petrol that the men refused to drink it.[14] According to the British defensive scheme, these outposts served a singular purpose: to delay the enemy as long as possible by breaking up their attacks. If Piesse's recollection is accurate, then his platoon certainly did not have much to provide sustained resistance.[15]

That being written, the forward outposts' tactical intention was subject to debate at the highest level of the Fifth Army. On paper, the outposts to the front of the 24th Division appeared to be exposed and vulnerable to be rushed, surrounded, and cut off in the event of a major attack. Indeed, this was noted by General Hubert Gough, who instructed XIX Corps Commander

---

14 IWM, Doc. 18591, Papers of Lieutenant Claude Piesse. Piesse mentions the tainted water twice in his memoir, once as kerosene and the other as petrol.

15 There is a lack of evidence to suggest that the remaining outposts were also so poorly provisioned.

General Herbert Watts to ask 24th Division Commander General Arthur Daly about the justification for outposts positioned so far forward. In this game of general officer telephone, Watts expressed his concern that A and C companies' position at Le Verguier 'were "isolated" and likely to be "scuppered"' in the event of an attack. Daly indicated that the purpose of the outpost companies was to break up an enemy attack. If they delayed such an attack, then they justified the decision to keep them there. He accepted full responsibility if those companies were scuppered. General Watts concurred and informed the army commander of the rationale to keep the outposts where they were.[16]

To the north of the 8th Queen's was 199th Brigade (66th Division) at Villeret. To the south, on the right flank, was the 17th Brigade's other forward unit, the 3rd Battalion, Rifle Brigade. Brigadier General Stone distributed the Rifles in a deep formation with a flexible reserve that could rush to a crisis point if needed. This matched their flatter terrain well; if the Rifles were forced to withdraw, they could do so back towards the fortified village of Le Verguier. Indeed, the village was not only the brigade's central island of defence, but it proved to be an essential component of the 24th Division's defensive scheme and officers were instructed that it was 'on no account to be evacuated.' [17] Though the specifics vary as to how this was to be done, the assumption was made clear to Peirs that he was not to abandon his position, but to hold the village and to await a British counter-attack to rescue his beleaguered command should it come under attack.[18]

As they relieved the Royal Fusiliers on the night of 18 March, the Queen's patrols reported that there was considerable movement behind enemy lines.[19] The following days, more patrols went out from the outposts under orders to instigate a fight with any enemy encountered in no man's land with the hope of capturing and interrogating enemy prisoners. Dawn broke on 19 March with heavy fog impeding visibility. The weather was relatively warm and daybreak was both dewy and thickly translucent, before the mid-morning sun burned off the mist. Anticipating an attack, British artillery shelled German lines

---

16 TNA, CAB 45/191, A.C. Daly to James Edmonds, 5 January 1927. It should be noted that the general is confused about the conduct of these outposts – he credits them for holding out for twenty-four hours under attack, which while true of the village itself, is not what happened to A and C companies.

17 TNA, CAB 45/193, Folder P, Peirs to Edmonds, 18 February 1927.

18 Ibid.

19 TNA, WO 95/2205/3, 17th Brigade War Diary, 18 March 1918.

on the 20th; yet all was quiet, eerily so, behind their own lines. Peirs was still with the baggage at Bernes, literally with his foot up. Major Rowland was in command at the battalion HQ dugout with his adjutant Lieutenant Donnell and the medical officer, Lodge Patch, playing bridge until midnight. The company officers went through the usual motions, inspecting their lines, and rotating between duty and rest.

As the night of 20 March turned to the morning of 21 March, their positions became once again blanketed in thick fog. Patrols went out from the forward posts so that they could feel for enemy activity. No threat was found, but there were noises to the east in Ascension Wood. Lieutenant Field of A Company took a patrol out to investigate and returned at 4:00 am with nothing to report.[20] His men could not see anything in the fog, but kept alert together as best they could for sounds to the east.

The Storm

Opposite Le Verguier, the German army prepared for an offensive so large it was meant to be war winning. The Spring Offensive, or Kaiserschlacht, was the brainchild of the First Quartermaster of the German army, General Erich Ludendorff. Noting the effectiveness of penetrative infantry tactics in Italy and against Russia, he devised a series of offensives against both the British and the French armies that were intended to win the war before American military might could come to the fore on the Western Front. The first of these attacks – Operation Michael – focused on the Saint-Quentin sector, where the Fifth Army attempted to implement their new defensive scheme. The first offensive came with an immense assemblage of firepower and concentration of manpower: it involved 6,400 cannon, 3,500 mortars, and 30 divisions attacking along a 50-mile front.[21]

North of Saint-Quentin, German divisions targeted the British 66th and 24th divisions. The Prussian 4 Garde-Infanterie-Division (4 GID) was charged with attacking between the fortified villages of Villeret and Le Verguier. The 4 Garde was a crack division that 'regarded themselves as the soldierly backbone of a weakening army, which had been exhausted by almost four years of devastating battle experience, tottering morale and deficient

20 TNA, WO 95/2208/2, 8th Queen's War Diary, 21 March 1918.
21 Jerry Murland, *Retreat and Rearguard* (Barnsley, South Yorkshire: Pen & Sword, 2014), p.12, p.26.

supplied of men and material.'[22] To their south, responsible for taking the village of Le Verguier itself, was the 208th Infanterie Division. This division had suffered heavy losses in 1917, but it was reconstituted and rested for the attack. Both divisions were tasked with breaking through the British defences in the forward zone and pushing back through their battle zone to advance on Péronne as soon as possible.

None of this was known to the 8th Queen's or to the 3rd Rifles as they manned their outposts in the heavy fog of 21 March. The German divisions were trained to do exactly what General Gough feared: to encircle the advance positions and scupper them, before then moving forward through the battle zone. The topography was advantageous to the attacker. Le Verguier was a strongpoint, but if the enemy broke through the flanks, the village could be easily encircled. Moreover, the outposts were too far from the main village to maintain effective command and control of the battalion as a whole. For example, Shepherd's Copse was well over a mile away from battalion HQ. At Priel Crater, A Company was closer, but their forward positions were also extended beyond easy communication. If telephone lines were severed, communication would be difficult; in order to get runners back to battalion HQ they had to go over ground and up a significant hill to reach the nearest fort, exposed to enemy fire. To walk briskly from either position to the village now takes at least fifteen to twenty minutes. If a runner had an impediment of fog or the discombobulating sensory effects from shelling, not to mention if they were wearing a gas mask, it is easy to see how such a journey could become arduous, if not impossible.

At 4:30 am the sentries of A and C companies looked above the parapet of their outpost trenches and saw flashes in the sky to the east and explosions behind them as German shells landed in Le Verguier. Though these men were no strangers to shellfire, this was the most concentrated bombardment they had ever heard. Oddly, the shells were all ranged far behind and the forward positions were left untouched. The ground shook with the concussions and men at their posts braced themselves under attack. Junior officers instructed their men to listen and look to the east. As dawn broke, the sentries kept their watch, but the fog was so dense that they could scarcely see 20 feet

---

22 Sebastian Laudan, '"Tag X – Durchbruch" The German Advance from the Saint-Quentin Canal 21 March 1918', *Stand To!*, No. 111 (January 2018).

to their front. The bombardment to the rear persisted, the fog lay thickly unabated, and the men stood to on their firestep ready to repel the enemy.

The situation was very different in the village behind. The shelling was severe and was a mixture of high explosive, shrapnel, and gas shells that forced men into their dugouts. Private E.F. Harrison recalled, 'I had always thought that the bombardment would develop gradually but the full force was almost instantaneous … One moment we were walking along like normal, the next there were shells busting all about all. We all ran like mad for cover.'[23] A lull in the bombardment came at 6:00 am and the battalion HQ moved to a better position along the sunken road at the southeast corner of the village.[24] There they were protected by a steep bank and a deep dugout that also afforded Major Rowland and his adjutant Lieutenant Donnell an underground telephone cable with a direct line to their brigade HQ in nearby Vendelles. The telephone cable was more than just a way to report information; it was also a lifeline to call in artillery support or reinforcements, as well as to get a grasp of their overall situation on their flanks.

To illustrate how different the situation was within the village compared to the outposts, when a runner arrived from A Company to headquarters at 7:00 am, he was surprised to find that the battalion staff were all wearing their respirators – and had been for an hour – as the situation at Priel Crater was relatively quiet.[25] The runner's arrival also indicated that the forward companies had lost their ability to contact battalion headquarters by telephone. By 7:00 am, the forward outposts were now isolated from their battalion HQ, as well as from one another.[26]

With the village under bombardment, both A and C companies sent out patrols to ascertain the situation to their front. The fog made visibility poor and as late as 9:00 am there was nothing unusual to report. Around 10:30, however, four men from C Company came running south–east towards A Company headquarters in the Priel Crater. They were being hotly pursued by the enemy. Just as they arrived, A Company came under German machine

23 Quoted in Martin Middlebrook, *The Kaiser's Battle* (Barnsley, South Yorkshire: Pen & Sword, 2016), p.148.
24 TNA, WO 95/2208/2, 8th Queen's War Diary, 21 March 1918.
25 SHC, Unofficial Battalion History, p.42. This sense of surprise raises an interesting question as the men in C and A companies surely would have been able to hear the barrage to their rear, but the heavy fog likely obscured the severity of it upon the village.
26 Ibid.

gun fire from the north. A and C companies were divided as German soldiers worked their way around the outposts. Risking complete encirclement, A Company's HQ withdrew with the remaining men to Orchard Post on the eastern outskirts of the Le Verguier. In the confusion, they left behind men in the outposts under the command of lieutenants May and Tomley, both of whom put up a stiff fight before their positions were overwhelmed and captured.[27] The enemy was able to get extremely close to their positions and then pounce on them using the fog as cover. For the defenders, they were left shooting into a void until enemy infantry were on top of them. Rather than being able to mutually support one another, the outposts became small islands of resistance before falling. Still, part of A Company was able to get out and make their way back to the village.

The situation to the north at Shepherd's Copse was worse, however. Being even further away from the village HQ, Shepherd's Copse was particularly vulnerable to the type of fate that befell A Company to the south. Situated atop a ridge with multiple machine gun posts, Shepherd's Copse was not a terrible position for defence. However, the trenches appeared to be in poor order and there was a visual impediment – an earthen mound – to the east that obstructed the view. On a clear day this would have been a significant factor for the defenders, but on 21 March this was unlikely as they could not see very far in the fog anyway, perhaps only 10–20 yards clearly. The more significant drawback was the position's isolation from the village. Within minutes of the German attack by the 5 Garde-Regiment zu Fuß, C Company was completely cut off from communication with both A Company to the south as well as their battalion headquarters in the village. Their whole system of support ended as soon as the attack began.

There is some confusion, if not contradiction, in the historical record of what fate befell C Company.[28] Their position was isolated and deeply blanketed in fog when it came under repeated attacks, roughly around 10:00 am. What is consistent in the different accounts is that German assault parties worked their way around the outposts under the cover of fog, cutting off

---

27 TNA, WO 339/102702, Percy Edward May; WO 339/94927 William Price Tomley. There are statements by lieutenants May and Tomley in their service records on their capture.

28 There are two accounts of the fate of C Company in *Stand To!, the Journal of the Western Front Association*. See Sebastian Laudan, '"Tag X – Durchbruch" The German Advance from the Saint-Quentin Canal 21 March 1918,' *Stand To!*, No. 111, January 2018, and David Baker, 'John Sayer VC: A Forgotten Hero', *Stand To!*, No. 80, September 2007.

most of C Company from the rest of the battalion. Then they reduced the garrison with bombs before taking the position and moving on.[29] The best account of the fate of C Company from British sources comes from one of its officers, Second Lieutenant Claude Piesse, who was in command of one of the remote outposts with twenty-two men.[30] Piesse indicated that the position held out for up to two hours until their ammunition expired and every man was killed or wounded.[31] In several post-war documents, Piesse indicated that his command held off the German advance stridently.[32]

It was also from his outpost that Piesse observed an exceptional act of valour. Lance Corporal John Sayer was a married father of six children from Islington who had trained as a machine gunner and had been with the battalion since 1917. Assigned to C Company, Sayer's position was at the junction of two communication trenches when the German guardsmen began their attack. Sayer used his rifle at first and then his bayonet to hold off repeated attacks by the enemy and, by holding his position, delayed the Germans from encircling the company. Sayer held out until he was severely wounded and captured. Piesse recounted that Sayer almost single-handedly saved his outpost from being immediately surrounded.

Piesse wrote to Colonel Peirs from his prisoner of war camp later in 1918, the former lance corporal having died in a German hospital at Le Cateau. Later Piesse and Peirs recommended Sayer for a posthumous Victoria Cross.[33] Piesse wrote, 'L/C/ Sayer showed throughout the upmost contempt

---

29 The battalion war diary is unspecific on what happened to C Company, yet specific about A Company, which indicates that there was not a clear indication of what happed both at the time and afterwards. Based on the surviving information and research done by Sebastian Laudan, this general statement of German tactics seems to be correct across the varying accounts.

30 Liddell Hart Centre for Military Archives, King's College London, Lh2P/79/1–3, Report of Claude Piesse to Basil Liddell Hart, 1. In his account in the IWM, he indicates he had fifteen men under his command. See also IWM, Piesse Memoir, p.11.

31 Claude Piesse, Copy of his recommendation for Lance Corporal Sayer's VC, 24 February 1919. This copy was gratefully provided to the author by Susanna Monseau.

32 IWM, Doc. 18591, Papers of Lieutenant C.L. Piesse; Liddell Hart Centre for Military Archives, King's College London, Lh2P/79/1–3. Both collections have reminiscences by Piesse and are consistent in most of the details of the morning attack.

33 The citation reads: 'For most conspicuous bravery, determination and ability displayed on 21 March, 1918, at Le Vergiuer, when holding for two hours, in the face of incessant attacks, the flank of a small isolated post. Owing to the mist the enemy approached the post from both sides to within 30 yards before being discovered. Lance-Corporal Sayer, however, on his own initiative and without assistance, beat off a succession of flank attacks and inflicted heavy casualties on the enemy. Though attacked by rifle and machine-gun fire, bayonet

for danger and the enemy – he inspired everyone by his conduct, and by his actions undoubtedly enabled my post to hold out as long as it did for nearly two hours, that is just until the mist rose about Noon.'[34] Piesse credited Sayer with not only slowing the German attack, but also with saving Le Verguier itself. In his account, Sayer kills many German soldiers and exhibits 'almost incredible bravery.' Piesse was a fierce defender of his men's actions at Shepherd's Copse and spearheaded the eventual posthumous VC for Sayer.[35]

Ultimately, though, C Company's outposts were each encircled in the fog and fell. There has been discrepancy about how – and specifically when – these positions were reduced. Recent research by Sebastian Laudan into the 6 Kompanie 5 Garde-Regiment zu Fuß indicates that the Copse was taken through infiltration around the flanks followed by a careful use of grenades that kept the men in C Company pinned down in their trenches. German soldiers then rushed the position. When they got there, they found perhaps fifty to sixty unwounded and stunned Tommies, who were taken prisoner. According to German records, few men were wounded in the attack and the resistance was light before the position fell quickly.[36] Laudan argues that the more significant resistance came from the south near the Grand Priel Farm and Ascension Wood area, which was where parts of A Company fought a rearguard action in their withdrawal to the village.

So, there are two different accounts; one has the posts falling relatively quickly without much resistance, and the other has the positions holding for nearly two hours until nearly every man was wounded or killed. In Piesse's definitive words, 'The [his] post was never surrendered.'[37] How do we reconcile these two accounts and why do they differ so significantly? First, the sources themselves come from mostly first-person testimony that is subject

---

and bombs, he repulsed all attacks, killing many and wounding others. During the whole time he was continuously exposed to rifle and machine-gun fire, but he showed the utmost contempt of danger, and his conduct was an inspiration to all. His skilful [*sic*] use of fire of all description enabled the post to hold out till nearly all the garrison had been killed and himself wounded and captured. He subsequently died as a result of wounds at Le Cateau.' *The London Gazette*, 6 June 1919, No. 31395.

34 Claude Piesse, Copy of his recommendation for Lance Corporal Sayer's VC, 24 February 1919. This copy was gratefully provided to the author by Susanna Monseau.

35 Letter from H.J.C. Peirs to Claude Piesse, 27 August 1918. A copy of this letter was gratefully provided to the author by Susanna Monseau.

36 Sebastian Laudan, '"Tag X – Durchbruch," The German Advance from the Saint-Quentin Canal 21 March 1918', *Stand To!*, No. 111.

37 See TNA, WO 339/102286, 'Statement regarding circumstances that led to capture'.

to the fog of war. Claude Piesse's account is focused on two main factors: the fact that his platoon fought bravely to the last and then later his account of Sayer's heroism.[38] Piesse manned one of the outposts for his company, a fairly limited position, and is relatively unspecific about the circumstances of his own platoon's actions that morning in their outpost. When considered with the poor visibility and the fact that he did not keep the time during the attack, not to mention the disorienting trauma of his wounding, then his account certainly invites scrutiny.[39]

There is another aspect at play. Piesse's account is consistent that his men made their last stand heroically.[40] Thus, when he wrote his story of Shepherd's Copse, he described it as a futile, but brave defense against all possible odds. His outpost fell only after every man was killed or wounded. This is part of the reason he placed such emphasis on the fact that he had specific written orders to hold until the very last. Clearly, the officers of A Company to the south had a different understanding – or interpretation – of their duty; they put up resistance until it was no longer practical to do so and then withdrew to fight again from the next line of defence. Why each company had a different response to their orders is something we do not know, but Piesse's written account concludes 'I was and am quite satisfied that I pulled my weight'. but then later casts doubt on his own actions by writing 'I sometimes think I failed in my duty.'[41] For Piesse, the question of C Company's fate clearly haunted him afterwards.

It is also certainly possible that some of C Company's outposts held out longer than others – visibility was extremely limited.[42] If we look beyond Piesse's account, there is another interpretation of the events at Shepherd's Copse from one of C Company's other subalterns, Arthur Claude Nye, which offers an additional interpretation. In his service record there is a brief account of Second Lieutenant Nye's capture. Like Piesse, he was in command of a

---

38 The Sayer account is not present in Piesse's Prisoner of War Statement in his service record. See TNA, WO 229/102286, 'Statement regarding circumstances that led to capture'.

39 IWM, Doc. 18591, Papers of Lieutenant C.L. Piesse, Piesse memoir, 'Addenda'. In this document he indicates the poor visibility, the poorly provisioned trench he was tasked with holding, and that he did not keep the time during the attack.

40 Stephanie Barczewski, *Heroic Failure and the British* (New Haven, CT: Yale University Press, 2016), Chapter 5 offers insight into the cultural importance of the last stand.

41 IWM, Doc. 18591, Papers of Lieutenant C.L. Piesse, Piesse Memoir, p.11.

42 Laudan's account indicates precise times, whereas the British eyewitness sources consulted for this account are not as precise.

front-line post when the bombardment began at 4:00 am. He explains that the Germans approached their position in heavy fog (or 'mist' as he called it) around 11.00 am. They met with the Germans with heavy fire from both their rifles as well as their Lewis gun, briefly delaying the enemy attack to their front. He then wrote, 'When the mist cleared, the enemy were observed to have established themselves in our rear, rapidly increasing in numbers and resulting eventually in our capture just before noon.'[43] Surrounded, Nye was captured unharmed with the rest of his men.

There is a possible middle ground between these interpretations. There was clearly confusion and it is likely that some positions fell while others resisted more stridently. It is also possible that Piesse was not in a very good position to grasp the full situation of his entire company. He was in a trench and it was foggy, as he indicates. Especially if we consider the other sources involved, it is unlikely that C Company slowed the entire German advance for two full hours; as Piesse indicates in his memoir, the enemy were already working their way around his position before they came under direct attack – a fact validated by his fellow officer Arthur Nye.[44] As they were being surrounded, they fired their weapons at the sounds around them, so thick was the fog.[45] The account of Nye, as simple as it is, gives us another depiction of the attack. The enemy felt forward for resistance, likely cautiously between 10:00 and 11:00 am, the fog being an impediment to the attacker as well as the defender.[46] Then they surrounded the outposts before grenading the garrison into surrendering and moving on to Priel Wood. Indeed, Piesse himself was wounded by one of those grenade fragments in the neck and lost consciousness before being taken into captivity. As he was taken away, Sayer lay on a German stretcher having fought off the enemy as valiantly he could for as long as he could.

The discrepancy of sources and their vagueness towards the amount of time these posts held out certainly does not necessarily diminish Sayer's actions or Piesse's account. It indicates an essential truth of history: that it

---

43 TNA, WO 339/102835, Arthur's Claude Nye. PoW Statement of A.C. Nye, 7 January 1919.
44 IWM, Doc. 18591, Papers of Lieutenant C.L. Piesse, Memoir p.10. Piesse writes as follows:
   'In London acter [*sic* after] the war my OC Col Peirs and I tried to coordinate times and came to the conclusion that the front line was attacked before the outposts. Certainly we in the outpost fired in the direction of marching feet long before we were attacked'.
45 IWM, Doc. 18591, Papers of Lieutenant C.L. Piesse, Piesse Memoir, Addenda.
46 Martin Middlebrook, *The Kaiser's Battle*, p.181.

is difficult to reconstruct the exact timeline of chaotic actions from sources that often differ.

What we can say for certain is that by noon, both of the forward companies had lost most of their strength, their outposts were surrounded and the bulk of their men had been killed, wounded, or captured. In the process, both A and C companies had slowed the German advance for at least an hour as the enemy had to take each position and then consolidate their gains and prisoners. As they did so, they also alarmed the village to prepare for an attack. This was, after all, the tactical purpose of these positions. Though the outposts were ripe plums for the taking, the village itself was the whole tree and proved to be a more formidable obstacle. After reducing the outposts, the Germans paused their attack to mop up, reorganise, and take their prisoners to the rear. The fog had been both helpful but also an impediment to their organisation of the attack and they needed to regroup. To the north, the 4 GID advanced towards Villeret and into the valley between the two villages, taking resistance as they entered Priel Wood. To the south, the 208th ID made slow progress against the 3rd Battalion, Rifle Brigade, who were being pushed back from the east and south upon their support positions. By midday, as the fog lifted, it was clear that Le Verguier was at risk on three sides. The weight of two German divisions now readied themselves to try to envelop and bag the 17th Infantry Brigade.

The Defence

As A and C companies fought for their lives that morning, the rest of the battalion sheltered in the village under the weight of the bombardment. The battalion's medical officer, Charles Lodge Patch, left the battalion headquarters to make his way north of the village to his RAMC aid station at Piumel Quarry. The shelling being heavy, he quickly lost his way in the village. Disoriented and unable to see clearly in his gas mask, he lifted it up to take a look around and inhaled a mouthful of phosgene. His lungs now reacting to the gas, he laboured forward until he reached the advance aid post. Once there, he found a wounded officer from C Company, no doubt saying to him panickily that the post to their front was 'full of Boche.'[47] Indeed, Lodge Patch looked over the top of his position and saw German field guns being

---

47 This could indicate that not every officer in C Company had the same understanding to hold to the last man.

pulled up onto the hill opposite the quarry. He ordered the withdrawal of his aid post with all the equipment, personnel, and wounded they could carry. The Germans had clearly overrun the advance positions and were now streaming into the valley north of the village, dividing the Queen's from the 66th Division to the north.[48]

As the village braced for attack, there was a firm grasp of the precarity of the situation back at 17th Brigade HQ in Vendelles, where Brigadier General Percy Stone carefully orchestrated his two forward battalions' resistance. On the right flank of the village, the 3rd Battalion, Rifle Brigade, were in a good defensive position with forward outposts and a continuous line of the trenches near Cooker's Quarry. It is here that they slowly fell back and managed to beat off several enemy attacks throughout the day, protecting the southern flank of the village, at least temporarily. As they did so, Stone ordered a company of the 1st Royal Fusiliers up to the Le Verguier Switch as a second line of defence for if/when the Rifles had to withdraw. It was a shrewd tactical decision to protect the right flank of the village. As he did so, he called back to 24th Division HQ for reinforcements, who dispatched dismounted cavalry to Vendelles in case a rapid counter-attack was needed if the village fell.[49]

In the early afternoon, there was a lull in the bombardment. German units were preparing for their next attack.[50] During the lull, Captain Lodge Patch visited B Company at Fort Dyce to the north of the village to check on their wounded. He was greeted with tea and whisky by the subalterns in command. They indicated that the fort had been attacked several times so far 'in a halfhearted manner', but that they were able to beat off each attack with Lewis guns and musketry. Lodge Patch recalled, 'it was obvious that the situation was fairly desperate, but every man with whom I spoke, had made up his mind that he was going to give Jerry more Hell the next time they came over.'[51] Steeled by whisky and the bravado of B Company's officers, Lodge Patch continued his tour of the lines. When he got back to HQ in the early afternoon, he learned that Fort Dyce was again under attack, as well as Fort Bell to the north.[52] The main assault on Le Verguier had begun.

---

48 IWM, Papers of Captain Charles Lodge Patch MC, Memoir, pp.7–8.
49 TNA, WO 95/2205/3, 17th Brigade War Diary, 21 March 1918.
50 IWM, Papers of Captain Charles Lodge Patch MC, Memoir, p.9.
51 Ibid.
52 He incorrectly states that the forts fell that afternoon.

As the Germans pressed the north of the village, the 8th Battalion's commanding officer hobbled up a communications trench with his stick in his hand and negotiated a path forward through miles of British lines. Indeed, the ordeal of Jack Peirs began before daybreak, when he came under bombardment snug in his billet at Bernes. As was his custom before going into action, he wrote his mother a brief and obscure letter telling her that he was well. He then put on his boots and called for his servant to get his kit ready. Ashplant in hand, he got up from his bunk and instantly felt the sharp pain from his infected foot. He gritted his teeth and grabbed his box respirator.

It took him hours, but Peirs reached Vendelles by mid-afternoon and then made his way forward to Le Verguier as the village was under attack.[53] Arriving at HQ in the sunken road, he met Major Rowland, who briefed him as to the situation. The outposts had fallen, and A and C companies were nearly completely lost. The village's northern flank, in particular, was in danger of being up in the air as 199th Brigade came under intense pressure to withdraw. Peirs assessed the situation personally and watched as men retreated north towards Jeancourt. He recalled later, rather mildly, 'I saw them go, and was rather annoyed, as my left flank in Le Verguier was left bare.'[54] Lodge Patch was nearby and with his medical orderlies and bearers, 'hurled vitriolis curses after them, but the withdrawal went on.'[55] Peirs witnessed the 2/7th Manchesters, who had been rushed up to plug a gap to the north that morning, falling back after taking 70 per cent casualties. They withdrew along with the rest of their brigade.[56]

---

53 The times of Peirs's arrival vary within the source materials – anywhere from 3:00 to 7:00 pm, but there is one clue from Peirs himself that helps us ascertain the timing. He wrote to Shaw Sparrow after the war that he observed watching the 66th Division withdraw towards Jeancourt to the north, which puts his arrival in late afternoon. This is consistent with the unofficial battalion history, but not with the war diary. See Peirs to Shaw Sparrow, 2 February 1921.

54 The British Library, MS 48204A, Shaw Sparrow Papers, Letter from Peirs to Shaw Sparrow, 2 February 1921.

55 IWM, Papers of Captain Charles Lodge Patch MC, Memoir, p.10. Peirs also recalled seeing them withdraw in his letter to Shaw Sparrow.

56 TNA, WO 95/3145/2, 2/7th Manchester Regiment War Diary, 21 March 1918; TNA, CAB 45 192 Somme. Letter from Richard Bond to General James Edmonds, 6 January 1927. Bond indicates that the 2/7th Manchesters should have been moved up overnight to support the position but instead sustained heavy casualties moving up under bombardment on the 21st and were unable to provide robust support on the flank as a result.

As 66th Division withdrew, the enemy now had a clear approach to the north of the village. Moving south from Brose Wood, the first main German attack came at Piumel Post and then Forts Bell, Dyce, and Orchard Post to the north and northeast. Notably, these forts were able to repel repeated attacks. The men had clear fields of fire for their rifles and Lewis guns and, as Peirs wrote, 'the enemy was not in any way inclined to face rifle fire and in the experience of my Battalion when fired at he shut up & tried to find a way round.'[57] With the northern flank exposed, it was only a matter of time before the enemy worked their way around, no matter the marksmanship. Le Verguier had become a peninsula of resistance.

The crisis continued and was felt on both sides of the 17th Brigade's front. To the south, the 3rd Battalion, Rifle Brigade put up doughty resistance, but were pushed back towards the Le Verguier Switch.[58] They had been in action all day. In the village centre, the 17th Trench Mortar Battery responded to each attack from the north with a hail of mortar support. They expended 1,500 shells 'mostly at close range, and in the fighting at close quarters many of these were thrown by hand.'[59] The fact that they ended up hurling mortar shells at their opponents surely indicates a sense of desperation difficult to capture in official sources.

Though the 8th Queen's Battalion war diary is mum on what unfolded in the early evening – say after 5:30 pm when the Manchesters retreated – Lodge Patch gives us a desperate account in his memoir.[60] His prose can be easily confused with a medal citation for valour.

> The night of the 21st-22nd was a veritable Nightmare. Colonel Peirs our C.O. was indefatigable. He was a sick man, and I had left him behind, when the Battalion came into the line, as he was suffering from a badly inflamed foot, and could hardly walk. But the first signs of the Hun attack, brought him post haste from Vendelles to LeVerguier, and the morale of the battalion was increased, at once by his arrival. Time after time, one Company Commander after another would rush into the Headquarter Sap to say that his post

---

57 TNA, CAB 45/193, Somme, Peirs to Edmonds, 18 February 1927.
58 TNA, WO 95/2205–3, 17th Brigade War Diary, 21 March 1918.
59 TNA, CAB 45/193, Somme, Stone to Edmonds, 1 November 1927.
60 The timings of all the sources are subject to dispute, except perhaps for the brigade war diary, which does not have a lot of specifics about what was happening inside of the village.

had been occupied by the Boche, and each time the Colonel would go out with him, gather together what men were left, fix up a Lewis Gun here, a Covering Party there, and order a dozen men to attack with grenades from another direction. The Huns would be thrown out and the fort retaken; but this could not go on indefinitely.[61]

Expending energy and ammunition, the beleaguered garrison of Le Verguier found themselves by nightfall in the unenviable position of being surrounded. Having taken a beating, the enemy abated their attacks at night and bombarded the village to further reduce resistance. By midnight, the surviving men of the 8th Queen's had been awake and either under bombardment or in battle for nearly twenty hours; their minds and bodies no doubt were at breaking point, yet they had to endure another night of shelling.

As it did the day before, dawn came with a heavy fog. The enemy's verey lights indicated that they were closing in on all three sides to the remaining forts in the village.[62] Fearing and anticipating encirclement, Peirs ordered the battalion's papers burned. Orderlies at headquarters piled up the boxes and poured kerosene on them. Documents aflame, Lieutenant Donnell 'our merry Irish adjutant cracked many jokes over the annoyance, that the G and A, and particularly the Q Branches of the Division had given us in their frequent references to these same documents.'[63] Indeed, they brewed tea on the pyre for the beleaguered and exhausted staff who had been awake for twenty-seven hours. Over breakfast, they heard German shooting to the north-west at 6:30 am. Then bullets hit the parapet of the sunken road and the HQ staff threw aside their typewriters and grabbed their rifles, fighting off an enemy approach to their left. Clerks and cooks desperately emptied their rifles at the approaching Germans in the fog.

The attack on the battalion headquarters in the sunken road indicated that the centre of the village had fallen and was in enemy hands. All that remained was Fort Greathead and the battalion HQ along the sunken road at the southern end of the village. At 9:30 am, Peirs climbed the embankment and, under cover of the fog, walked towards Fort Lee. Noting that the

---

61 IWM, Papers of Captain Charles Lodge Patch MC, Memoir, p.10.
62 SHC, Unofficial Battalion History, p.42.
63 IWM, Papers of Captain Charles Lodge Patch MC, Memoir, p.11.

position had fallen, he hastened to his headquarters and gave the order to withdraw immediately along the road if they could. He wrote afterwards,

> We were in a fog and nearly surrounded & incidentally quite defenceless & it weighed considerably with me whether I might get out with the two companies I still had & save them for another day or wait and chance my luck. I chose the former alternative, but I very much doubt whether I should have done so had I been a regular soldier with my career dependent on my obeying orders.[64]

Though his remarks come with the context of hindsight, there is an element of his battlefield thinking present. His orders were to hold Le Verguier at all costs. With a significant portion of his men killed, wounded, or captured, he decided that the rump of the battalion was better served fighting it out than in a prison camp. His mind was exhausted by a day's worth of shelling and fighting – his body tired and his foot sore – but his instinct proved right. He ordered a Lewis gun team to cover the garrison from the embankment and then led his 200 or so men to the south-west.

It is with a degree of conspicuous irony that the fog that led to the destruction of two of the battalion's companies on 21 March aided in the survival of the remaining two companies the next day. German soldiers had pushed their way through Le Verguier tentatively and were regrouping for their attack on the sunken road when the battalion withdrew. Both the road itself and the fog offered a natural screen for the battalion's escape. Peirs and his men walked out of their battered shell of a village and into the next line of defences held by the 1st Royal Fusiliers at the outskirts of Vendelles. As they approached, the fusiliers listened and heard British voices in the fog before seeing the outline of their helmets and the shouts of nervous subalterns for them not to fire. Peirs fell into their friendly trench then limped up to his brigade headquarters and reported the loss of the village to his CO Percy Stone. He was not sure if he was to be sacked for disobeying his orders or decorated. There was no time for praise or for censure; the enemy would resume their attack soon. For now, Peirs and the remaining garrison of Le Verguier had survived.

---

64 TNA, CAB 45/193, Somme, Peirs to Edmonds, 18 February 1927.

In Retreat

The remaining 200 men came inside the wire of the 17th Brigade's position and immediately reinforced the 1st Royal Fusiliers manning the trenches to the east of Vendelles. Then the brigade received orders from the 24th Division for a general withdrawal to Bernes, and then to Montecourt some 7 miles away. The battle had fundamentally changed from that of trench warfare to manoeuvring in open countryside. In the words of Brigadier General Stone:

> This ended the first phase of the Battle – the prolonged resistance against overwhelming odds and Artillery in our Battle Zone. It was to start again early the next morning, but from now onwards we were to fight in the open – against the same odds, but having suffered severe casualties, exhausted by fighting and loss of sleep, with little Artillery support, and having lost nearly all our fighting equipment except the rifle.[65]

The 17th Brigade began its withdrawal towards the River Somme, which was the line to be held at all costs in the event of a retirement.[66] The overall situation was one of confusion, especially for those in high command, as the many pieces on the battlefield map continued to move. For our understanding, the most important aspect is that the Fifth Army was in retreat and its units were expected to fight a rearguard action until the front stabilised. This was done so according to lines of resistance where units paused, assessed the situation, dug in, and then skirmished to stave off a general route of the division and the army as a whole.

The overall strategic situation was not clear cut at the brigade or battalion level, however. Instead, officers were busy trying to pack up and get their men moving. When orders came to withdraw from Vendelles, the remaining men of the Queen's fell in with the rest of the brigade and marched towards Montecourt. They passed through Bernes, where the scene was desperate, 'many dumps of valuable R.E. materials were being burnt to prevent them falling into the hands of the enemy … A vendor of the E.F. Canteen was giving away whole boxes of cigarettes, bottles of whisky, and tins of salmon

65 TNA, WO 95/2205/4, Report on Operations from 21 March to 6 April, 1918, p.7.
66 Murland, *Retreat and Rearguard*, p.145.

and sausages to the troops who passed by.'[67] With handfuls of loot, the men moved overland across the fields as German artillery had zeroed in on the roads.[68] The landscape around them was pockmarked with shell holes and in places was littered with dead horses, shattered wagons, and detritus shed by retreating men. Compounding their difficulty, enemy airplanes strafed infantry who had taken to the fields to avoid shelling.[69] Once at Montecourt, the battalion went out on patrol to look for the approaching enemy, which did not materialise. At nightfall they rested. They had been either under fire or in action since 4:00 am the previous day, thirty-nine hours awake and under threat. The men took their rations and slept as well as they could for a few hours.

Their rest was short. At 3:15 am orders came for 17th Brigade to move towards Douvrieux.[70] There they took out their entrenching tools and again began digging rough trenches in their new positions. Footsore, with aching arms and backs, the men were then ordered to move again to cross the Somme at Falvy, their efforts at entrenching ultimately futile. Wearily, they marched 10 miles to the crossing, the 3rd Rifles covering them and skirmishing with the German vanguard that was close enough to harass their rear. Once across the river, they halted and had their first hot meal in days at Pargnvy. As they ate, the 8th Division came up and moved through them to form part of the rearguard defending the retreating Fifth Army. Throughout the night they were sniped at and strafed by distant machine gun fire. On the morning of the 24th, they again moved back to Licourt and from there took positions on the outskirts of Omiécourt. The 24th Division was now thrust into the active battle zone. Their job was to plug a gap and repulse any enemy attack between Omiécourt and Pertain.

The battalion established itself to the east of the village astride the road leading to Hyencourt, a space of about 100 yards or so, where they began digging for cover. Initially the brigade was under orders to support a French attack to the south, but their allies never appeared. Instead, the 50th Division came towards them in retreat and passed through their lines on either side of the road. On their heels were the Germans, who established themselves in Pertain and begin shelling Omiécourt and peppering the shallow trenches

67 IWM, Papers of Captain Charles Lodge Patch MC, Memoir, p.20.
68 SHC, Unofficial Battalion History, p.43.
69 IWM, Papers of Captain Charles Lodge Patch MC, Memoir, p.21.
70 WO 95/2205/3, 17th Brigade War Diary, 23 March 1918.

of the 8th Queen's with machine gun and sniper fire. Then they attacked in column along the road. As they came up, the battalion's remaining Lewis guns thwarted them, breaking up the advance and forcing them back into Pertain. 'The killing was good that day, and the Kaiser was paying heavily in blood for his gains on that part of the line anyway,' wrote Lodge Patch.[71] After abandoning their direct assault, the Germans began bombarding their position and then pressed their attack on the right flank of the Queen's, which, too, was repulsed. The situation grew hotter and more desperate by mid-afternoon.

Leading from the front, Peirs was exposed. While giving orders, he was wounded by shell fragment in the forearm.[72] Though the bone shattered, he stayed with his men. Sergeant Walter Hitchcock captured the moment in his memory:

> Major Peirs had just been wounded, we were standing on top of the trench when they put some shells over, and I was in the bottom of the trench, quick! He stood there, and he broke his arm, so I said to him 'Would you like me to send somebody back to the dressing station?' he said, 'No, no. I want you to take a machine gun over to that cross-roads' this was after he was wounded, 'if the Germans come down there, they've all got to come down that road.' I said, 'We haven't got a machine gun, and we haven't got a machine gunner, Sir.' so he said, 'Well, do the best you can.' Nothing was done, I didn't do anything at all, there was nothing I could do.[73]

With the enemy pressing in on their flanks, and with his men down to their last rounds, Peirs ordered the battalion back into Omiecourt, and from there to Chaulnes, where they dug in and awaited the next attack. With his arm dressed, at nightfall Peirs was evacuated and Major Rowland took command. Once again, the Queen's had been called upon to blunt the enemy advance. Now at Chaulnes, they were again ordered to hold at all costs. For the remaining men – now only a makeshift and shallow company – this was a

---

71 IWM, Papers of Captain Charles Lodge Patch MC, Memoir, p.38.
72 Ibid., p.41.
73 Memoirs of Walter Hitchcock, https://walterhitchcock-ww1.blogspot.com/.

grim but not entirely unexpected order. There was one silver lining as Lodge Patch recalled mirthfully that 'Chaulnes was a glorious place to ransack.'[74]

At 7:00 am on 26 March, the Germans attacked again and the Queen's held, checking their advance with rifle fire. After a brisk firefight, orders came to withdraw towards Lihons with the object being Vrély. The 24th Division as a whole withdrew; the 17th Brigade, still in action, did not begin to leave until after 11:00 am and then fought a rearguard action back to their next position.[75] They moved across the grim 1916 Somme battlefields, but the fields were impassable due to shell holes and the brigade kept to the road. No doubt survivors recalled a bitter irony to passing over such hard-fought ground near where many in the battalion had lost their lives two years before.[76] After being checked at Chaulnes, the Germans began making their way to the south, trying to get around the 17th Brigade and cut them off. Their flank threatened, they continued the withdrawal to Vrély, harassed by machine gun fire on the march. Arriving in the village, the brigade scraped together a defensive line between the Vrély-Warvillers and the Vrély-Méharicourt roads facing south where the enemy had been working their way around. They dug in as the day turned to evening and then found billets in the village. Brigadier General Stone had found stragglers from other units in the village and placed them in the 17th Brigade's trenches overnight so that his men could rest in the village.[77] The village's inhabitants had fled, and brigade's cooks slaughtered and cooked some of their animals 'on the principle of better us than the enemy.'[78]

The next morning, the Germans renewed their attack from the south. The enemy advanced in extended order. With clear fields of fire, the brigade held its ground and stopped their advance. Having lost their momentum, the Germans resorted to their usual tactic of bombardment. Thankfully, the night was quiet and the men were able to sleep a little in their trenches. Their rest was short, however, and the enemy attacked at dawn on 28 March. Like the previous day, this attack was thwarted, but the Germans had learned their lesson and instead of repeatedly attacking, they began moving to both the north and south to surround the village, as they did at Le Verguier.

---

74 IWM, Papers of Captain Charles Lodge Patch MC, Memoir, p.44.
75 Edmonds, *Military Operations in France and Belgium 1918, Vol. 1*, p.503.
76 SHC, Unofficial Battalion History, p.44.
77 Ibid., p.45.
78 Ibid.

Their flank threatened, the brigade withdrew towards Caix, with the enemy hot on their heels. At Caix they found French soldiers holding positions along the road supported by a battery of 75s firing at the advancing Germans. As they retreated past the beleaguered Poilus, they were cheered by their allies and were met warmly with cheers for the remnants of the battalion.[79] They continued to Villers-aux-Erables, where they halted. It began to rain. Then they received word for the retreat to continue to Castel.

The battalion had retreated 14 miles under threat and in heavy rain. To say that they were exhausted and at their wits end is an understatement. Between 21 March and 5 April, they had lost 20 officers and 388 men.[80] The whole of the battalion consisted now of 200 men that were a mix of the Queen's and stragglers they had accumulated during the retreat. They had precious few hours of sleep and both their food and water had been inadequate. The only good meal and night of sleep was on the 26th, just before they then endured the longest and most arduous march of the entire retreat. They had fought a rearguard action the entire way and had never been out of the sound – if not the sights – of the advancing enemy. It is almost unfathomable the level of endurance necessary for the remaining men to keep going and perform their duty in such a situation.

All around them were signs of desperation. There were hastily thrown up barricades along roads and slit trenches to cover their retreat. Wagons and trucks were left on the side of the road, dismantled by artillery or mechanical failure. Hodge-podge units and stragglers were all around, makeshift aid posts with wounded awaiting evacuation, men pilfering supply dumps so they would not end up in the hands of the enemy, and piles of supplies ablaze. The battalion had performed as well as possible, but courage came at the cost of most of their officers and men; the survivors now slept uneasily at Castel on the 28th, no doubt fearing that this was the end of the line.

Mercifully, though, the pace of the enemy's advance had slackened. The Queen's were ordered to Hailles to defend the river crossing there. There they took to billets and had a quiet night before resuming their defense on the 30th. The enemy attempted to push on their southern flank, but was thwarted by a British cavalry attack, indicative of the changing character

---

79 Ibid.
80 TNA, WO 95/2205/4, 17th Brigade War Diary, 7 April 1918, Summary of Casualties 21 March to 5 April. Numbers are as follows: KIA 5 officers, 23 other ranks; WIA 7 officers, 23 other ranks; MIA 10 officers, 259 other ranks.

of the Western Front.[81] If you had said to these men but two weeks earlier that they would witness such a thing, they would have laughed. Now the cavalry was engaged and helping to stop the enemy advance. At Hailles, they rested before being ordered north towards Amiens, reinforcing Boves and then defending the line east of the city to Gentilles, where they had a quiet few days. Though still subject to shelling, the situation was not as desperate and the battalion passively held their position until being pulled out by the 58th Division on 5 April. Major Rowland collected his broken battalion and marched them out of the line. Their role in the Kaiser's Battle was over. Though they had earned praise for their fighting ability and endurance, it came at a severe cost. Like so many units who survived Operation Michael, they would never really be the same again.

* * *

One of the difficulties in writing military history comes through the process of making sense of events that at the time were anything but clear. The written records largely give us points on a map, some information about casualties and unit strength, and an indication of the time that significant events happened, though the latter is often contested. Eyewitness reports tell us something of the emotional chaos of these events, but these reports are confusing and do not always match the official documents. The challenge for the historian's judgment is in balancing the two types of sources and reconstructing an event, nearly as it happened. The above reconstruction endeavours to do just that; to make sense of the situation that befell the 8th Queen's over a ten-day period in 1918.

What it reveals is a battalion that was put in an unenviable position and was caught in a desperate situation that increased in tempo and severity by the minute. The early hours of the Kaiserschlacht saw two companies of the Queen's fight a desperate and confusing action in which they were surrounded and reduced by the enemy. Those outposts achieved their desired result, which was to delay the enemy attack, and by doing so, sounded the alarm for the remaining companies to be at their post and ready to defend the village.[82] In the village, B and D companies, along with the stragglers who

---

81 SHC, Unofficial History, p.46.
82 TNA, CAB 45/191, Somme, Letter from A.C. Daly to General James Edmonds, 5 January 1927.

got away from A and C, held the line as units were being pushed back along the Fifth Army front, an act of defiance that was a testament to their training and coolness as they came under repeated attack. Musketry, machine guns, close support of mortars, and effective leadership mattered. Of course, they were not in it alone and also had the support of a veteran brigade commander who managed their resistance as best one could under the circumstances. Despite ultimately failing to hold the village, the battalion and brigade made the right decisions and corrected their setback to the opening attack with determination. In reality, with their flanks collapsing, the battalion and brigade did the best they could at the only militarily sensible position open to them – delaying the enemy and preventing a panicky rout – suffering greatly as a result. This is why Le Verguier became a symbol of their heroism; it represented much about the peculiar heroic desperation inscribed in the Queen's motto – 'Even in defeat there can be triumph.'[83]

The events afterwards, however, are enough to sober such talk of triumph. For a week, the battalion was pushed back from village to village, every morning under threat and every afternoon uncertain of where they would sleep for that night – whether it would be in a village further back or a prisoner of war corral behind the lines of the advancing German army. Three years of static war had been upended by the Kaiserschlacht; as the battalion marched dozens of miles back in their rearguard action they realised that something was changing around them in their desperate struggle for survival. They also demonstrated, again, their training. At each village they dug in and repulsed the enemy. At each, they then packed up and retreated in as orderly a fashion as possible, before then turning again to fight. No doubt they witnessed panic and felt fear; but they were adaptatively elastic and ultimately successful in the one thing that mattered for infantry battalions of the unlucky Fifth Army – they survived.

These are the conclusions we can draw about the performance of the battalion as it faced its most unrelenting period of trial during the war. But we should also think in terms of what the sources do not reveal. They do not reveal the confusion of 21 March at Le Verguier. For officers, some were confused in their duty, dislocated, distracted by the twin limitations of fog and the fervour of combat. For men, their confusion was compounded by the

---

83 *Vel Exuviae Triumphant*, 'The Chapel of the Queen's Royal Surrey Regiment', https://www.queensroyalsurreys.org.uk/chapels/chapels-index/holy-spirit-chapel/holy-spirit-5.shtml.

uncertainty of not being in the know – not having a clear understanding of what was happening. Their eyes were on their kill zones through their sights. After the village fell, the uncertainty continued and became more miserable. Men missed meals and were dehydrated. Men saw demoralised stragglers around and burning debris from deliberate destruction. They saw an orderly retreat hang by a thin thread – not every unit around them was reacting the same as their brigade. They took on men from random units who lost their way. They were strafed by snipers, aircraft, and unseen enemy machine guns and mortars. They took casualties the whole way as they retreated, leaving many men behind to uncertain fates. They saw their officers and NCOs reduced to a rump of experienced men upon whose shoulders their future rested. It would take the battalion months to figure out exactly what happened; it would take some of them a lifetime to understand their own role in the events in which they lived through at Le Verguier and in the great retreat that followed.

Chapter 8

Endurance

As the 24th Division fought their way back to Amiens during the Spring Offensive, 18-year-old Private A.J. Abraham marched out of the gates of Hillsborough Barracks in Sheffield. For the past five months, Abraham had been training in a battalion of underage recruits bound for overseas service. On 31 March 1918, his unit departed their training barracks for the last time. The German breakthrough in France led to hundreds of undertrained men rushing to the front ahead of their nineteenth birthdays. As Abraham marched through Sheffield, thousands of civilians turned out to cheer the boys before they entrained for London and then to Folkstone. There he was billeted in a house with no beds, his messmates sleeping on the bare floor under their army blankets. The next day they boarded their troopship and steamed for Boulogne, their vessel flanked by Royal Navy destroyers. At his depot in France, he learned that he had been posted to a battered service battalion just pulled out of the line, the 8th Queen's.[1]

At Pende, Abraham greeted the survivors of Le Verguier. He and his young comrades brought the battalion up to fighting strength. Abraham was mustered into No. 4 Platoon, A Company, where he met Sergeant John Feist.[2] His new NCO was a hardened veteran with a bullet gouge on the butt of his rifle to prove it, the latter a scar from Le Verguier.[3] Abraham also met his company commander, Edward Abdy Fellowes, one of the original officers of the battalion and a man with extensive combat experience. Immediately, Abraham and his fellow replacements were put into training in drill and marksmanship. Within a week, he was promoted to lance corporal, recalling 'we youngsters made up more than ninety percent of the battalion … and my career as a non-commissioned officer had started.'[4] One of his earliest

---

1   IWM, Doc. 546, Papers of A.J. Abraham, Memoir, pp.8–12.
2   He misspells Feist's name in his memoir.
3   IWM, Doc. 546, Papers of A.J. Abraham, Memoir, p.14.
4   Ibid., pp.19–20.

duties was escorting his section to the sergeant tailor's workshop so that they could have their service uniform trousers converted to shorts, a particular affectation of their divisional commander, Major General Arthur Daly.[5] The tailor did his duty to the letter; the men's trousers were converted to shorts. According to Abraham, the tailor's orders only pertained to trousers and so he refused to hem their long underwear. The men were left with their legs only half converted to divisional standards.

Whether it was the sewing of unit patches or trouser conversion, sartorial initiation was one of the first rituals of entering a new battalion and getting used to the way in which they did things. And like all new drafts, Abraham had a steep learning curve ahead of him to adjust to the front and learn as much as he could from the few old salts still remaining in the battalion. Thankfully, these new soldiers were eased into this transition as the battalion was in no shape to fight. The division as a whole had to be reconstituted after the Spring Offensive nearly destroyed it. What was left of the old 8th Queen's was only a fragment of its former self and it was now replenished with inexperienced soldiers who made up the bulk of its ranks. Thus, the grimly realistic pattern of re-training and rebuilding the battalion – a pattern imperfectly perfected since Loos, the Somme, Ypres, and now Le Verguier – repeated itself.

Unknown to Abraham in his tender eighteen years were the realities that necessitated rebuilding a service battalion. Of its original officers who left Blackdown in August 1915, the 8th had only three left. Not all the officers who originally led the battalion had been killed, of course, but nearly every one of them had been wounded at least once or invalided for a period with disease. By 1918, the old soldiers remaining had once been replacements themselves for men lost at Loos, the salient, or the Somme. By April 1918, the battalion had suffered 604 men killed in action and over twice that number wounded or hospitalised due to their service.[6] Though Abraham had heard something of the Kaiser's battle from his new chums over the brazier, he certainly did not know what a long arc the battalion took from Loos to Le Verguier. As he was growing up, the 8th Queen's was shedding men in battle. Now he joined the legacy of a bloodied but unbroken chain of men whose lives were forever altered by the experience of soldiery on the western front.

---

5   Ibid., p.23.
6   Commonwealth War Graves Commission, https://www.cwgc.org/.

Abraham was fortunate in his commander, Edward Fellowes. Fellowes was an experienced officer who had risen to company command. Commissioned at 19 immediately out of Marlborough OTC, Fellowes was the son of a barrister and grew up in a townhouse in South Kensington. In August 1914, he was bound for Merton College, Oxford but instead took a commission as a second lieutenant. Serving as a platoon subaltern, he was wounded by shrapnel in May 1916, a shell fragment gouging out a section of his back including part of his first lumbar vertebra.[7] Turning septic, he was sent home and convalesced for the rest of 1916 before then returning to the battalion in 1917, when he took command of B Company at Third Ypres. After a stint of staff duty, he returned to the 8th Queen's and took command of A Company in April 1918. His company had been one of the two wrecked at Le Verguier and it was his job to rebuild it with his novice soldiers. At 22 years of age, he was not that much older than Abraham, but three years of commanding men on the Western Front revealed a vast gulf of experience between the two.

Reconstituting the battalion came in three phases. The first was through rigorous training. Once the rump of Le Verguier veterans arrived in Pende in early April, a draft of 299 other ranks met them that was swiftly followed by 85 more men and 5 officers.[8] Most of the new men had no combat experience and their training had been cut short in England. Like Abraham, they were rushed to France. The task fell to more experienced officers and NCOs to immediately began training these men to use their rifles and in the pragmatic business of squad and platoon tactics.

As the battalion replenished its ranks in April, word had got out about their stand at Le Verguier. In the local press in Surrey, the battalion was held up as a heroic example of British fortitude with such headlines as 'The Queen's in Action: Breathless Heroism and West Surreys [*sic*] Fight to the Last Man',[9] 'The Heroic Queen's',[10] and 'Worn out with Killing: How the Queen's West Surrey's Fought.'[11] Reading about one of his battalions in the press, the honorary colonel of the regiment, E.O. Hamilton, wrote to the battalion's commanding officer 'I wish to send you & the Battn. my hearty congratulations at the noble way you have kept up & added to the record of

7   TNA, WO 339/1468.
8   SHC, Unofficial Battalion History, p.47.
9   *Croydon Advertiser*, 30 March 1918.
10   *Surrey Mirror and County Post*, 5 April 1918, p.3.
11   *The Hampshire Telegraph*, 29 March 1918, p.5.

the Regt.'[12] Within days of their stand at Le Verguier, the narrative had been set that amidst the turmoil of the British retreat, the 8th Queen's had performed an act of exceptional gallantry. The reality, as we have seen, is more complicated: gallantry came at a severe cost and ultimately their position fell. Pushed back, the battalion kept fighting, shedding more men along the way, but surviving. The grim realism of attrition meant that there were few men remaining from Le Verguier to receive such commendations. Yet, for the hundreds of new men filling out the company rosters, they understood that their new battalion had a deserved reputation that they were expected to live up to.

The second stage of rebuilding the battalion was to acclimate the new men to the Western Front. Mid-May found the battalion back in routine trench duty at Maroc, trenches they knew all too well near the old Loos battlefield. The battalion sheltered in bombed out houses in reserve before then moving into front line trenches.[13] Rumours swirled about the enemy possibly attacking as part of a new phase of their spring offensives – specifically this time as a gas attack – but these proved unfounded. Instead, they were in a relatively quiet section of line, one occasionally interrupted through shelling, usually in response to British shelling of German lines.[14] They took casualties and for the replacement officers and men, this was their first tour of the trenches, not to mention for most their first exposure to artillery. It was also their first exposure to gas as a British gas attack blew back into the battalion's trench, notably with no casualties reported.[15] When they came out of the line, they went directly back into training.

Trenches, gunfire, and gas garnered experience and with it came confidence in their duties. In June, the battalion rotated back into trenches, but this time more aggressively in spirit. They began patrolling in no man's land to dominate their front; to be aggressive with the enemy and for officers to instill the right offensive attitude in their new men. Unfortunately, this aggressiveness was tempered by the uncontrollable factor of a pandemic; by mid-month influenza raced through the battalion, reducing its trench strength by half 'and of the remainder many were very unfit.'[16] It was the

---

12 TNA, WO 95/2208/2, 8th Queen's War Diary, April 1918, Appendix 15.
13 IWM, Papers of A.J. Abraham, Memoir, p.21.
14 TNA, WO 95/2208/2, 8th Queen's War Diary, 12–18 May 1918.
15 TNA, WO 95/2208/2, 8th Queen's War Diary, 14 May 1918.
16 SHC, Unofficial Battalion History, p.48.

first wave of the 1918 influenza.[17] Most of the men who fell sick came back to the battalion within a week, but it was still clearly surprising how quickly the disease came on and spread through the unit.

At the end of June, Peirs returned to the battalion. He had recovered from his gunshot wound at the Prince of Wales Hospital for Officers in what is now the elegant Landmark Hotel in Marylebone. His convalescence came with visits to family and his office, which was located only a few miles away in London. His channel crossing was marred by unpleasantness; his hair oil bottle burst in his saddlebag and he was unable to sleep due to his pajamas smelling strongly of cantharides. When he arrived in France, the battalion was not where he was expecting it to be and he had to labour to find them, as he complained to his mother.[18] Recovering from his wound and the ordeal of the Spring Offensive, Peirs appeared unchanged. He was surprised at how young the battalion was compared to the one he had left; he wrote to his father of the new draft of men that 'most of whom are quite good, but one or two are still very juvenile & do not seem to be more than 16.' Still, he was confident that they would make for effective soldiers, 'it is only a question of time, & I gather they have come on amazingly since they joined us 2 months ago.'[19]

In July, the battalion took to trenches in Les Brebis, again near the old Loos battlefield where they had had their first bloodletting nearly three years before. The weather was fine; when they rotated out of the line, there was training and sports. Morale was high. Peirs wrote to his sister:

> I have been very busy the last few days & though we are out of the line, the weather has been beautiful & I have taken the Battalion out all & every day to get them away from their billets, which are extremely uninteresting, to some lovely country about 4 miles off, where we do a little battlefighting & sleep a lot. The men or rather boys seem to enjoy themselves out there & we got them some cricket & various odds & ends of games.[20]

---

17 Though a milder version generally to what came later in the year during the second wave of the virus.

18 Peirs to his mother, 24 June 1918.

19 Peirs to his father, 2 July 1918.

20 Peirs to Olive, 17 July 1918.

Once back in the line, they actively patrolled and there was sporadic, but at times heavy, artillery activity. On 23 July, a patrol carried out a daylight raid against the German front lines. Sneaking through high grass, they were shocked to discover that the front line trench was empty. Three days later, a patrol under Second Lieutenant F.F. Reeves consisting of twenty raiders and three double Lewis gun sections – fifty men in total – went out in force to the German first line of trenches. In heavy rain and using the Lewis guns as cover, they entered the enemy's front line trench. Still empty, they pressed to their support lines under cover of bombardment. There, they killed an enemy sentry and took his shoulder straps for identification. The Germans retaliated and the patrol hunkered down in the German first line trench until the bombardment abated. Six men were wounded, three of whom by friendly artillery as the British barrage fell short. Though the raid had limited success, it was helpful for intelligence to know the strength of the German front line and have an identification. Reeves was awarded the Military Cross for his actions.

Further honours came for the battalion as they were relieved and reviewed by their new corps commander, Lieutenant General Sir Alymer Hunter-Weston. The charismatic and controversial general handed out decorations for the distinguished survivors of Le Verguier. Second Lieutenant C.F. Olley received the Military Cross and Company Sergeant Major W. Hayward and Sergeant E.L. Blay received Distinguished Conduct Medals. Three further sergeants – Fear, Feist, and Jefferies – along with privates Wheeler, Williams, and West, received Military Medals.[21] This congratulatory moment came with the news that their brigade commander, P.V.P. Stone, was leaving. His farewell message revealed the task yet awaiting them: 'There is much yet to be accomplished, and I know you will keep these great traditions, and the memory of our fallen comrades forever in your thoughts and by your further splendid efforts to bring the nation to Victory and Peace.'[22] Stone himself deserved much praise for his brigade management during the Kaiser's battle. He was succeeded by Brigadier General George Thorpe.

Decorations and heroic farewell messages from generals are sometimes seen with a measure of cynicism, but they are both poignant and important gestures. They represented an acknowledgement of bravery, both exceptional

---

21 TNA, WO 95/2208/2, 8th Queen's War Diary, 31 July 1918.
22 TNA, WO 95/2208/2, 8th Queen's War Diary, Appendices, July 1918.

and ordinary, and showed the men within the battalion that they were capable of meeting and exceeding the test of combat. They brought honour to the battalion and helped it cope with losses. Stone's emphasis on fallen comrades and regimental tradition is also something we should not overlook as boilerplate. He was a hard-fighting brigadier who led his men in one of the most challenging rearguard actions for the British Army of the war. He maintained control, instilled discipline, and, crucially, did not panic in the face of a constantly changing battlefield. His units held out, and for many, survived the ordeal. Those who remained were now the bearers of the memory of the fallen, whom Stone evoked to instill the last bit of determination in his old brigade to stick it out. As Stone himself wrote to Peirs proudly from the front, 'the old Brigade has beaten all records, and won the whole name for that Division. We are still at it!'[23] As the tide of the war now changed, it would be up to every infantry brigade to do its duty and see the war through.

Indeed, the Queen's raid on an empty German trench revealed some of the cracks in the German defences all along the line. Though the Kaiserschlacht had decimated units in both the British and French armies, it had also been extremely costly on the attacking German divisions. Germany's manpower advantage at the start of the offensives now became a deficit.[24] Soldiers – and in particular officers – were not easily replaced. Early summer brought not only more offensives, but also influenza, which did not discriminate in its victims according to nationality. The German army simply could not sustain these types of losses, especially with an allied army that was growing in strength due to American intervention.

That strength was demonstrated in July. Not only did the allies withstand the final brunt of the German offensives, they stopped them in their tracks at the Second Battle of the Marne. The effective counter-attack led by French and American forces demonstrated that the steam had run out of the German offensives and the momentum had shifted. With victory at the Second Marne, the overall allied commander, Marshal Ferdinand Foch, with steely determination, implemented the aggressive strategy he had been champing at the bit to pursue for the last four years of war. As the fifth year of the war began in August 1918, all armies were directed to move forward in

---

23 Peirs Papers, Percy Stone to Peirs, 4 April 1918.
24 Jonathan Boff, *Winning and Losing on the Western Front*, p.22.

a series of combined efforts to break the German army and force a decision on the western front.

Though the tide had turned, the reconstituted 8th Queen's remained at Les Brebis rotating in and out of their familiar trenches for the rest of the summer. As Peirs wrote to his father, 'Everyone seems to be pushing the Bosch except us, & we continue to lead our placid existence.'[25] They patrolled and carried on as they had been doing while armies to the south were fighting more heavily. After Le Verguier, the key thing was to get their drafts ready for battle. As the battalion's historian summarised, 'We had been very fortunate passing the whole summer in such a quiet part of the line, ample time had been given us to complete the training of new officers and men and to restore the high state of efficiency which the battalion had attained prior to 21st March.' He continued that they 'were now ready to undertake the more strenuous tasks in front of it.'[26] Though spared the initial attacks of the BEF in the late summer of 1918, the 24th Division would soon face the final campaign of their service during the war.

The Beginning of the End

The strategic situation on the Western Front changed dramatically after the Second Battle of the Marne in July. Foch's counteroffensive used the French and American armies to destroy the German momentum of 1918 and shift the initiative to the allies.[27] Following up on the success of the battle of Hamel in July, the BEF planned and executed its most successful attack using combined arms at Amiens on 8 August 1918. The attack came as a shock to the German high command, Ludendorff famously dubbing it the 'black day' of the German army.[28] Thus, what became known as the Hundred Days Offensive was the impetus of victory on the Western Front, as allied armies had figured out a means of fighting the war to its conclusion, whether that was in 1918 or the following year.

This specific strategic view was one that was likely unknown to the officers and men of the battalion, but there was a sense that the tide had turned. As early as 1916 at the Somme, Peirs had written home that he believed the Germans to be wavering. Though that general impression

---

25 Peirs to his father, 25 August 1918.
26 SHC, Unofficial Battalion History, p.51.
27 Boff, *Winning and Losing*, pp.22–3.
28 Neiberg, *Fighting the Great War*, p.343.

proved inaccurate then, it did hint at something more important; that the more the allies pressured the Germans, the more their material resources would matter to the eventual outcome of the war. The longer the war lasted, the greater the advantage to the allies. Moreover, by early autumn it was appearing that Germany would be left alone to wage war against the nation/ empires that now opposed it. By September, the Austro-Hungarian Empire was in retreat and the Ottoman Army reeling in the Middle East. Peace would come to the other fronts in just a matter of time, leaving Germany alone to either continue fighting or to ask for terms. It was an unenviable and untenable position.

For the German army on the Western Front specifically, the situation was dire in September and downright hopeless by October. Most notably, the British First and Fourth armies penetrated the Hindenburg Line at Canal du Nord. On 2 October, the German high command, OHL, briefed leaders of the Reichstag that the war was lost and to seek favourable peace terms. The feeling was that if they negotiated from a place of strength – or we should say where they still had some strength left – they might get more favuorable terms, in particular, from the Americans.[29] This was not to be the case and the war went on until Germany had to accept whatever terms the allies dictated to them or else face an invasion of their home nation in 1919. Rested and ready, the 8th Queen's moved into the line to see out their last campaign of the war. The battalion had served in some capacity in each of the major campaigns on the Western Front since 1915. It was fitting they would now see the job through to the end.

Back up the Line

Having spent the previous six months retraining and rebuilding, the battalion moved into active combat operations. In early October, the 24th Division transferred out of Hunter-Weston's VIII Corps with a note from the mustachioed old pusher that he would 'watch its doings, and the career of each individual in the Division with the greatest personal interest.'[30] The division then entered the Third Army, which along with the British First and Fourth armies, was part of a 40 mile offensive to break the German army.

29 Edmonds, *Military Operations in France & Belgium, 1918, Vol. 5*, p.143.
30 TNA, WO 95/2208/2, 8th Queen's War Diary. Letter from General Sir Alymer Hunter-Weston to General Daly, 30 September 1918. For distribution to officers and men and enclosed in the 8th Queen's War Diary, Appendix II.

At the end of September, General Julian Byng's Third Army broke the German lines at Canal du Nord and were now pressing their advantage towards Cambrai.[31]

The 24th Division entrained on 1 October and went into training at Le Souich. This was a new part of the front for the battalion. When they departed for Havrincourt on 6 October, they entered the XVII Corps in exchange for the 57th Division.[32] From there they advanced towards Anneux. Arriving then at Rumilly, they saw flames from the east at Cambrai, where the enemy had set fire to the town before evacuating it.[33] On 8 October, they came up in reserve as their corps pressed forward, pushing the withdrawing Germans to the south of Cambrai. The Third Army took 1,200 prisoners.[34] The next objective for the army was to advance on the River Selle, which despite its diminutive size, proved a formidable obstacle that the Germans would not give up lightly.[35]

The overall situation demanded that the allies continued pushing. On 10 October, Foch handed Field Marshal Haig a directive indicating that there were to be three coordinated operations to pressure the Germans; one in Belgium, one in France along the Solesmes-Watigny front, and one to the south at the Aisne Meuse.[36] Haig was to continue pushing the Fourth, Third, and First armies towards the River Selle. As the Third Army moved forward, it encountered stiffer German resistance the closer the attacking divisions got to the river. Still, significant advance was made, XVII Corps sending its vanguard forward as fighting cyclists.[37] The 8th Battalion now advanced with the 17th Brigade and took a position on the southwest outskirts of Rieux-en-Cambrésis, a small village to the west of the Selle.

There they encountered a defensive rearguard position that essentially amounted to machine gun nests at strategic points to cut up approaching infantry.[38] The defenders knew the lay of the land, so areas of assembly and approach for attacking infantry had been zeroed by their artillery, which was fiercely accurate. Both infantry and cavalry had come through on the 10th

---

31 Edmonds, *Military Operations in France & Belgium, 1918, Vol. 5*, Chapter 11.
32 Ibid., p.208.
33 TNA, WO 95/2208/2, 8th Queen's War Diary, 8 October 1918.
34 Edmonds, *Military Operations in France & Belgium, 1918, Vol. 5*, p.210.
35 Boff, *Winning and Losing*, p.31.
36 Edmonds, *Military Operations in France & Belgium, 1918, Vol. 5*, p.232.
37 Ibid., p.242.
38 IWM, Papers of A.J. Abraham, Memoir, p.103.

and took significant casualties as they encountered German resistance. On the morning of 11 October, the approach to the village 'showed all the signs of recent combat, dead horses, discarded equipment, fresh shell holes, etc.'[39] All signs indicated that the positions would come at a cost.

It was the task of A Company to press forward and reduce any resistance remaining in Rieux. The company went up the main street, but was immediately shelled. They moved into artillery formation and turned east out of town to continue their approach. Advancing through the enemy barrage, they came under machine gun fire from nests along the top of a gentle slope. German snipers targeted their officers and NCOs.[40] Adding to the maelstrom, an enemy plane dropped flares on their position, marking them for shelling, which soon came down upon their advance.[41] As resistance increased, Second Lieutenant Ronald Brooks attempted to get his men around the enemy positions to reduce the machine gun nests from their flank. Brooks was a 19-year-old officer commissioned straight from Haileybury, where he was a star cricketer.[42] He was the younger brother of Lieutenant Joseph Brooks, who had served in the battalion in 1915 and 1916 before then transferring to the Royal Flying Corps. Peirs was quite fond of the older brother and no doubt paternalistically looked after Ronald the same way he did his brother Jo. Brooks and his platoon felt their way forward, the young man personally leading their attempt to get at the enemy. He took Sergeant Cole and Lance Corporal Abraham with him, crawling forward through a beet field with only the leaves of the crops for cover.[43] Cole was hit, exclaiming to Lieutenant Brooks 'Oh sir, I'm dead.'[44] Brooks crawled to his aid, rolled him over, and then said to Abraham, lying to his right, 'By God, he really is.' With few men at his disposal and the platoon already taking heavy casualties, Brooks withdrew his remaining men.

---

39 Ibid., p.95.
40 Ibid., p.96.
41 Ibid., p.98.
42 Brooks's ability as a first-class Cricketer earned him a Wikipedia page: https://en.wikipedia. org/wiki/Ronald_Brooks. Interestingly, he was recommissioned in the Second World War.
43 IWM, Papers of A.J. Abraham, Memoir, p.98. Abraham names this fellow as Sergeant Carr but there is no record of a Carr in the battalion in 1918. There is a Sergeant Harold Cole, however, who fought in this engagement and was killed on 11 October. Harold Cole was 21 and from Reading. He was awarded the Military Medal in November 1917 and a Bar in September 1918.
44 IWM, Papers of A.J. Abraham, Memoir, p.99.

As A Company attempted to take the German machine guns beyond the town, the rest of the battalion came up and attempted to establish a line and push through the village. As A Company fought their brave, but ultimately failed attack, C and D companies pressed through the village and mopped up resistance there. The appearance of two captured British tanks being used by the enemy furthered the confusion and thwarted their advance beyond the village.[45] All along the line, British battalions faced the same stiff resistance from the German rearguard, who had chosen their ground carefully. It was decided by 17th Brigade to hold up the attack and wait for the next day for artillery support.

The difficulties faced in the attack on Riuex are typical in battles of encounter and demonstrate the new reality of the mobile war on the Western Front. Their brigade had advanced quickly over the previous days. There was little intelligence as to what was in front of the battalion as it moved forward into the village. There was no time to bring up artillery and to come up with a significant fire plan for support, especially as they did not know exactly what was in front of them. Once they entered the village, resistance proved heavy from the ridge beyond, and the battalion had to withdraw. That evening they understood the situation better: the enemy were holding the Selle with artillery and machine guns and would put up a stiff fight to cover their withdrawal. As such, a new way approaching the tactical problem needed to be developed. That evening, the Queen's were ordered to press the attack and advance towards St Aubert and then to the river beyond the next day.

The battalion bedded down in cellars in Rieux. Shortly after daybreak, aerial intelligence reported that the enemy was retiring and that the Queen's were to follow.[46] The battalion assembled into artillery formation at 11:00 am and then advanced the 3 miles eastward towards Villers-en-Cauchies. They made the journey in about an hour and a half, their progress slowed a bit by artillery shelling which became heavy as they approached the village. Peirs sent men into the town to clear out any remaining German observers and to cut the telephone wires that ran east from the village in case there were spotters in the buildings.[47] Once in the village, he received orders that they

---

45 SHC, Unofficial Battalion History, p.52.
46 Ibid.
47 Ibid.

were to continue their attack that evening towards the east bank of the Selle. Peirs and his company commanders left the battalion and moved forward to scout the route of their advance and the position they were to take. He left behind his adjutant, Captain Fellowes, to bring up the battalion to their jumping off point near Montrécourt Wood. As the battalion marched up the line, orders were received that they were to attack under cover of a barrage timed for 6:30 pm.

In order for a barrage to cover infantry, they needed sufficient time to get into position and to be able to move towards the barrage under its cover. At the Selle, the barrage began before the battalion had arrived and had time to assemble. Peirs decided not to rush the attack, but in the process, the Germans retaliated with their own artillery and the battalion was forced into cover where they were, taking casualties. He then ordered B and C companies forward, who were able to reach the river and attempt to ford it. The water was too deep. A patrol of C Company found a way forward along a broken 6-inch railway bridge, but encountered resistance from machine guns on the eastern bank and were driven back. The situation was extremely tense as indicated by an unusually desperate sentence in the war diary, 'the number of men that could be thrown across by the broken bridge was insufficient to deal with the enemy counter-attacks, and it was therefore decided to hold the bridges from the W. side.'[48] The battalion held the western bank before their relief the next evening.

The situation on the 13th was as such. The 8th Queen's had advanced and held the western bank of the Selle with two companies holding at first one, but now two possible bridgeheads built by the Royal Engineers further south, while the enemy continued to shell their position to prevent them from crossing the river.[49] Before dawn, the bombardment was so thick that it necessitated the removal of the battalion headquarters – along with the unfortunate A Company that had suffered at Riuex – to a sunken road 400 yards to the rear. This only led to a temporary reprieve as this position soon came under bombardment with high explosive and mustard gas shells. Lance Corporal Abraham recalled trying to get some rest in a dugout carved into the bank of the road. He and his chum Cornell awoke, pulled their blanket

48 TNA, WO 95/2208/2, 8th Queen's War Diary, 12 October 1918.
49 Ibid, 11–12 October 1918.

aside, and then promptly vomited on the road after inhaling gas.[50] The men around them were also symptomatic. Peirs, his adjutant, Edward Fellowes, and 120 other men had been exposed, their eyes and skin already feeling the irritation of the sulfur mustard. Their symptoms got worse as the day went on. Their skin became itchy, blistered, and generally irritated, their eyes looked like oysters, and they began wheezing and sneezing. Some, like Abraham, were vomiting. Peirs and the officers were evacuated by stretcher. Those who could walk made their way back the next day, blinded and guided by the quartermaster sergeant.[51]

The rest of the battalion held their position at the river. On the 13th, the enemy attempted to cross in order to counter-attack against B and C companies, but they were repulsed.[52] At nightfall, the rest of the battalion came out of the line. Relieved, they limped with their casualties back to Rieux. There the battalion reorganised itself into three companies, as most of A Company had been gassed and C Company bore the brunt of casualties in the Selle attack.[53] Among their dead was Lieutenant Evelyn Dorrell, who had already in the war suffered wounds to his wrist, forearm, and face before then recovering and making his way back to the battalion in time for his mortal wounding at the Selle and dying in the very last weeks of the war.[54]

As it stood, the 8th Queen's had been in action for three days, pushing the German rearguard towards the Selle and holding the bank of the river against attack. In the process, they lost an entire company of men, as well as most their headquarters staff as gas casualties. Peirs and Fellowes evacuated to a hospital on the coast. Blinded from gas, the colonel still managed to write to his father of the ordeal in which they had just been through, noting 'where I have been lately he [the enemy] is still putting up a very good show & has plenty of ammunition to spare. I had a very interesting week before I got gassed, as we had one or two scraps & chased him for about 8 miles in

50 IWM, Papers of A.J. Abraham, Memoir, p.105.
51 Ibid, p.107.
52 SHC, Unofficial Battalion History, p.53.
53 SHC, Unofficial Battalion History, p.54; TNA, WO 95/2208/2, 8th Queen's War Diary, 12–13 October 1918.
54 TNA, WO 374/20340, Dorrell was the younger brother of Second Lieutenant Harold George Dorrell, who was killed in action in April 1916.

the time.'[55] Unlike the Spring Offensive, he was glad to be the one doing the chasing and itching to get back to his battalion to see the war end.

The Final Push

Having most of their headquarters in hospital, the brigade shifted command of the battalion to Major Harry Hamilton Hebden MC, from the Royal Fusiliers as temporary CO. He inherited a reduced battalion full of young soldiers who had just had their first baptism of fire. The battalion had not slept for forty-eight hours and needed rest. In addition to attacking against machine gun placements, they were also under gas and high explosive shelling for over a day. Though their field kitchens advanced with the battalion and they had their rations to eat when they could, they were physically exhausted. Compounding – or we should say working in tandem with exhaustion – was their sense of mental fatigue. They needed rest to rehabilitate rattled men.

The battalion left Riuex and went to the Cambrai area, where they reconstituted and trained for the next fortnight. For men who had just been on a real attack, the mock tactical demonstration no doubt seemed both very raw and deeply ironic. On 19 October, they were inspected by their brigade commander, Brigadier General George Thorpe CMG DSO, a Boer War veteran who was in his first major combat command after years of helping to plan the war as a staff officer. While they trained in assault tactics and pontoon bridging, their former commanding officer's eyes healed and Peirs played billiards and golf from his resort hospital on the coast with the rest of the convalescing battalion staff.[56] Peirs was itching to get back to his men. He wrote to his sister Cecily: 'At present I am in hospital with gas but expect to go back in a day or two.... after a little more acclimatising I shall go and seek my lambs again and I fancy they will take a good deal of finding as no one seems to stop more than a day or two in one place at the moment.'[57] Four days later he was still in hospital, but hopeful for a reunion with his men, especially as they were advancing so quickly and pushing the retreating Germans. He wrote to his father, 'I am much better now & expect to go back in a couple of days, as the effects of the gas have nearly gone… I am

---

55 Peirs to his father, 18 October 1918.
56 Peirs to his father, 14 October 1918.
57 Peirs to Cecily, 20 October 1918.

rather wondering what the Battalion is doing. They can't be far from the push mentioned in to-day's papers but whether they are in it I don't know.'[58] Peirs and Fellowes returned on 31 October, just in time to receive news that Austria-Hungary had surrendered.[59]

With Germany shedding allies – as well as prisoners on the Western Front – the end of the war came into sight for those who were fighting it. Still, November proved a bloody month as the allies continued their pressure on Germany. On 3 November, the 8th Queen's were back at the front with orders to attack the following day. They were to pass through the 73rd Brigade and take the sister villages of Wargines-le-Petit and le-Grand. The situation changed, however, and the enemy withdrew further. The 73rd Brigade pursued and took both villages before then being held up by high ground to the east.[60] Orders now came to move the next day through the 73rd Brigade at Wargines and then press the enemy further.

The battalion bivouacked that night, sleeping out in the open as they had in manoeuvres back at home in 1915. Three years of trench warfare had changed the context. They were no longer the hodgepodge assortment of eager volunteers; most of those men were all gone. The battalion was now full of men who were schoolboys when the war began, not men with wives and growing children at home. In seven months, not only had the battalion been completely rebuilt, but the character of the war had completely changed. When 1918 began, they were rotating in and out of trenches as they had since October 1915. The Spring Offensives changed all of that. Now, they had been advancing for the past three weeks, pushing an enemy that fought fiercely but desperately in the face of their momentum. They were sleeping rough and in a different place nightly. They also had the confidence of men who finally felt like they were winning the war.

All that training, all those parades, and all those manoeuvres and field days were paying off. On 5 November, the battalion assembled at 4:00 am and advanced towards Wargines-le-Petit. The weather was vile with mist and rain. With the 1st Royal Fusiliers on their left and the Guards Division on the right, they moved through the 73rd Brigade and pressed forward. They were

58 Peirs to his father, 24 October 1918.
59 Peirs Papers, message to Peirs and the battalion, 31 October 1918.
60 TNA, WO 95/2208/2, 8th Queen's War Diary, 3–4 November 1918.

under humane orders: if significant opposition was encountered, they were not to press the advance but to call up artillery support.[61] At 7:00 am they advanced out of Wargines and towards Saint-Waast. By 10:00 am, the battalion was at the outskirts of Saint-Waast, an advance of 3.5 miles, their line extending to the south to the outskirts of Le Pissotiau. There they encountered enemy machine guns and halted. Later, they came under shelling. They bedded down in their position and held it overnight. The next day – 6 November – they cleared both villages, Saint-Waast causing some casualties for the battalion from both machine guns and gas. Among the wounded was Second Lieutenant Charles Abel Field, a 23-year-old manufacturing clerk from Hertfordshire.[62] He was a well-liked officer who had been promoted from the ranks. Field was also one officers from A Company who managed to survive Le Verguier, bearing a bullet hole in his helmet from a near miss.[63] His luck ran out at Saint-Waast and he died of his wounds the day after the Armistice, his personal effects taken from him while he was in hospital.[64]

Thursday, 7 November was the last time the battalion was in action. In their final four days of fighting, they took thirty-eight casualties, which was a comparatively low cost for the miles they gained from the enemy. The next day they marched out of Le Pissotiau. A high-velocity gun shelled them as they passed the Château de Rametz. Scattering off the road, the battalion bitterly took their final casualties of the war from a gun miles away lobbing high explosives at map coordinates that some German staff officer believed essential to their dying war effort. In Bavai they found billets. The village was chock-full of civilians who were friendly and relieved that the Germans were gone. After four years of occupation, they greeted their new British inhabitants warmly.

The battalion held church parade on Sunday, 10 November. It was the feast of Saint Leo the Great. This peacemaking pope is known to have personally persuaded Atilla the Hun to turn back his invasion of Italy, thus saving Rome from certain destruction. The next morning, the brigade major sent notice to battalion commanders of the Armistice. At 11:00 am, the officers and men of the 8th Queen's heard the sound of artillery stop. Silence

---

61 TNA, WO 95/2208/2, 8th Queen's War Diary, 5 November 1918.
62 Clapham War Memorials, 'Charles Abel Field', https://sites.google.com/site/claphamwarmemorials/home/holy-trinity-clapham-common/charles-abel-field
63 IWM, Papers of A.J. Abraham, Memoir, p.84.
64 TNA, WO 339/89000.

was their first indication of survival. The cacophony of violence was over; their war was over. They were too tired to celebrate and there was 'not a drip of drink in the battalion' anyway.[65] They had been in action and marching for a week and needed rest to recover their humanity and process the peace. Feeling laconic, Lieutenant Colonel H.J.C. Peirs DSO lit his pipe and sat down to write to his father. The sum of his resigned reflection amounted to the simplest of exasperated declarations, 'So that's that.'[66]

---

65 SHC, Unofficial Battalion History, p.55.
66 Peirs to his father, 11 November 1918.

Chapter 9

Remembering

The Armistice came to weary men. Their ordeal was over, but their service was not. As November went into December, their commanding officer kept them busy with drills and instructional lectures that, no doubt, increased rather than distracted from the tedium of waiting for demobilisation. They moved from drafty billets to drafty billets, eventually settling by December in more comfortable accommodation that included a concert hall. Officers arranged football and rugby matches with other battalions, granted passes for the men to visit local towns, and generally tried to keep order as best as possible. When Christmas 1918 came, the men ate their dinners together and celebrated as much their own survival as the holiday. It was the last time they formally messed together until their reunions after the war.

The New Year celebration turned out to be more eventful than one would anticipate. On 30 December, the officers of the 17th Brigade dined with a typed menu of courses named for their former battles. A course of 'plie frite Montecourt' was followed by 'dindon roti Le Verguier'. The somewhat grand meal for Western Front standards came with a full programme of entertainment and ended with liqueurs and coffee. New Year's Day saw the battalion officers again dining in style with an elaborately illustrated menu that was signed by the twenty-six in attendance, the memento kept by Peirs with his letters after the war. Their dining rituals have an element of whimsy that can be seen in hindsight as a transitory moment between the army and their return to civilian life at home. At the cusp of their demobilisation, they dined fancily as relieved men. They had survived.

It would take months, but demobilisation came. The first historian of the 8th Queen's ends his account of their service as such: 'in the last week of June the 8th Service Battalion "The Queen's" was finally disembodied after being in existence for nearly 5 years. It is in the hope that all record of its glorious achievements will not be lost that the above account has been penned.'[1] Though catalogued as an anonymous writer in the Surrey History Centre, the author was possibly Captain Edward Fellowes MC, who served in combat with the battalion interruptedly from its departure at Blackdown until the bitter ending at Bavai on Armistice Day.[2] He went from being a teenage subaltern right out of public school to a decorated veteran who had commanded an infantry company. Fellowes finished the war as adjutant of the battalion and for some reason in the early 1920s he possibly wrote the battalion's story in the First World War. Whether Fellowes or another officer, the author of the history saw his experience as one that was bound to the men around him. It is quite telling that instead of writing a personal account – a memoir or such of his service – the author wrote on behalf of the battalion as a whole. Like many unit historians, he was likely bound by a sense of duty to the men he was memorialising to get the details of their service right and to pay tribute to what they all went through together.[3]

The last words of the battalion history echo with sentiments common in the post-war years, especially felt by veterans, and more than hint at the memorial motivations in penning a history. The author picked a curious word for their demobilisation – he called it a disembodiment – which might have been an intentional word choice, or perhaps one that just came to mind. It is, however, a perfect word. A battalion is a living body of men who work together and share in both their stalwartness and their suffering. At its embodiment in 1914, the Queen's consisted of a group of diverse volunteers who were united in wanting to do their duty as they saw it. By 1916, that cohort had been reduced by attrition. In the final year of the war, the battalion was nearly entirely full of new men who replaced those transferred, were captured, invalided, or killed. Every man who rotated into the battalion replaced another who had worn the paschal lamb on his cap. Indeed, a service battalion was something embodied by rotation: what shaped its character were the officers and NCOs who instilled a standard of discipline and by example helped the men to carry on. Unlike some other battalions,

---

1 SHC, Unofficial Battalion History, p.59.
2 Fellowes has similar handwriting to that of the author of the history. Some pages of the battalion history are on House of Commons stationary. Fellowes worked for the House of Commons after the war and eventually became the Clerk of the House of Commons. In addition to the stationary and the handwriting, Fellowes was one of the few officers who was with the battalion for the duration of the war, with the exception of his convalescence for his wounds/illness.
3 Jenna Fleming encouraged this observation.

the 8th Queen's was fortunate to have a leadership culture embodied in 1914 that remained intact in 1918. The last two officers demobilised were of the first two commissioned: it was Peirs and Fellowes and their two batmen (unfortunately unnamed) who handed in the battalion's stores in June 1919. When they did so, they completed the mission of all the men in the battalion, both living and dead. At that moment their duty was complete.

What they had been through was a life-altering experience. It is perhaps cheap to reduce such a thing as a world war to this contemporary nomenclature, but it is hard for us now to conceptualise how vastly different their lives were 1914–19 compared to what came before and then what came after. For all who served and survived, their lives by the 1920s essentially had three important phases: before the war, when they came into their adulthoods; the war itself, which was the great diversion or interrupter of their lives; and then what came afterwards. For any Briton of the war generation, the afterwards meant adjusting back to civilian life – or not adjusting – finding a career, for some a family, and negotiating the interwar years as best they could. The outbreak of the Second World War meant, of course, that they had another interruption, one that for most was less all-encompassing than the first, since they were now too old to fight. Yet it did not stop them from doing their part; Peirs, Peter Bye, and Fellowes notably commanded contingents of the Home Guard. But their war would always be the first one and they would go to their graves with an identity that they shared with all who rotated in and out of the 8th Battalion, The Queen's. Old men might forget, but none who served could truly shed the war or its remembrances afterwards.

After a period of transitionary demobilisation during the winter of 1918, the men of the battalion eventually returned home. From then onwards the question turned to how they would remember their experiences. Neither the 8th Queen's nor their brigades or division had an official book-length history. Their story, so much as it was known, remained solely their own, confined to the veterans who served. Of course, there were reunions of the battalion and many of the men participated in Armistice Day remembrance activities in their various locales, but there was nothing exceptional about the way in which the history of the battalion passed into memory. Their story is the same – or a similar one – to many other Kitchener battalions who saw through their service on the Western Front. Theirs is the story of the common soldier who did their part in the war and then came home as citizens reconstituting their identity and lives after being at the front.

This is not to say that their service was completely forgotten, but that it was remembered principally by the battalion's veterans alone. Still, there were three tangible ways in which veterans found meaning in their war experiences afterwards. The first is through official recognition and commemoration. The second is through engagement with the war's history as it was being written in the 1920s. The third is through reflection and testimony, where men attempted to make sense of their service. To this, we can add a fourth element, but one that mostly came after the last of the battalion's survivors died. Through family stories and digital storytelling, some of the battalion's history has been preserved.

Official Acts

The end of the war was the beginning of the battle over its legacy. Essentially, the 1920s were a period of memorialisation and coalescence over the war's social meaning in Britain. Across Britain, households and communities mourned dearly the war dead and sought to make sense of the loss of over 700,000 men. Almost immediately, local committees formed to erect memorials to the fallen, beginning a culture of commemoration that continues until this day. Local memorialisation tied directly into the national rites that by 1920 were established with recognition of Armistice Day at the Cenotaph in Whitehall and the internment of the Unknown Warrior in Westminster Abbey. Across the nation, memorials became centres for remembrance rituals that firmly placed the fallen at the centre of the story of the war. The popular history of the First World War in Britain since then has been demonstrated through living rituals and expressions geared towards honouring the war dead. Of course, the fallen were only one part of the war's story. Vastly more soldiers returned from the war's fronts and were demobilised back into civilian life than those who died. Some returned home with disabilities or with war wounds that required rehabilitation or significant accommodation. Whether these wounds were physical or mental (or both), the post-war lives of veterans and their families bore the scars of war service in the decades beyond.

In fact, Peirs's father, Hugh Vaughan Peirs, was a central figure in the creation of the Carshalton War Memorial, near where the family lived in the village.[4] The local memorial commission began their work in 1916 and had

---

4   Andrew Arnold, *Their Name Liveth Evermore*, p.12.

a proposal ready by January 1919. Hugh's hopes met some criticism from his only son when he wrote to him in January 1919 with the committee's ideas. The 8th Queen's commanding officer indicated that it was too early to commemorate, and he advised his father to 'wait till the men now serving have a say.'[5] Tellingly, Peirs believed that memorials were all fine and good, but that the survivors needed to be accommodated for as well as the war dead. He advocated for establishing veterans' clubs:

> What is to my mind required in the future in every village is a club for all men who have served the country in an active capacity in the war. There is no question that such a system would retain the Esprit de Corps of the army & be of infinite benefit to the nation in a number of ways.[6]

The tension between Peirs and his father over commemoration reflected a general trend in the interwar period of how the war would be remembered. Was it the place of the grieving to remember it mostly through the cult of the fallen? Or did that emphasis on the dead belie the war experiences of those still living, who found virtue in comradeship during the war and wished to commemorate, even celebrate, their hard-fought victory? Peirs's desire for living memorials – clubs for veterans – was a sensible and positive approach to the latter, while also giving men with similar experiences a chance to decompress and deal with their war experiences together in a supportive environment of fellowship. The Carshalton War Memorial went forward as planned and father and son dutifully attended its unveiling in 1921.

The war dead remained central to the commemorative efforts of the 1920s. One aspect of solemnity was the creation of permanent burial places in France and Belgium and the reinternment of soldiers in Imperial War Graves Commission cemeteries. The missing, some of whom were in unknown graves, were further honoured with their names on memorials such as the Thiepval Memorial or at the Menin Gate. For the men of the 8th Queen's, the Loos Memorial at Dud Corner is a particularly important place, commemorating ninety-four men who died in 1915 and whose graves

---

5   Peirs to his father, 14 January 1919.
6   Ibid. Indeed, Peirs eventually had a role in the formation of Toc H, which came out of one such club active during the war. See Steve Smith, 'The First Committee Members', https://tochcentenary.com.

are unknown. In all, 712 men of the battalion were buried or memorialised abroad.[7] The identification of the war dead and their being laid to rest among their comrades was the first official act of memorialisation. Back in blighty, the war dead were commemorated on local memorials mostly across the south of England. The small villages, in particular, felt acutely the war's losses due to the intimate family and friendship networks that spanned generations.

The mid-1920s saw two acts of memorialisation for the 24th Division. The first was the division's monument in Battersea Park. Sculpted by the war artist Eric Kennington, the memorial was unveiled on 4 October 1924 with remarks from the division's mid-war commander, Major General Sir John Capper. The modernist memorial depicts three soldiers upon a plinth with interlocking hands and a serpent intertwined around their feet, impeding their ability to move. One of the likenesses was of Kennington's friend, the war poet Robert Graves. Carved into the plinth are the badges of the constituent units of the division, the Queen's one of nineteen others who served in the division. Notably, officers and men of the battalion were there for the unveiling, including the last two commanders of the battalion, Peirs and Reginald Rowland. The memorial commemorates both the 35,000 men who were killed, wounded, and missing from the division, as well as the spirit of soldiers at the front through three comrades. Kennington's monument is a moving reminder of the intimacy of their service.

The dedication of the 24th Division's memorial came with a somewhat complicated backstory. The initial war memorial committee was formed in the early 1920s and consisted of former officers of the division. The secretary of the committee was Peirs's cousin, P.T. Chevallier, and the committee held at least one meeting at the law office of Ellis Peirs & Co.[8] The committee debated in 1921 whether there would be a war memorial erected in England or one in France. Ultimately, the London memorial took priority.[9]

Early on, the committee was in contact with the mayor of Le Verguier, Charles Severin. The division's memorial committee identified Le Verguier as a possible site for memorialisation because of the stand made by the 17th Brigade on 21–22 March 1918. That desperate moment became indicative of their service in the war; they had shown tenacity, competence, and had

---

7   Commonwealth War Graves Commission, www.cwgc.org.
8   P.T. Chevallier to Colonel Stone, 22 November 1921. The correspondence of the committee was gratefully provided by M. Henri Severin.
9   Ibid.

maintained order. Le Verguier's mayor and some members of the committee were keen for a memorial to the 24th Division in the French village. In 1921, Brigadier General Stone visited Le Verguier on behalf of the committee and met with the mayor to ascertain the needs of the community and whether it was appropriate for a memorial to be built there in honor of the division. In 1922, the committee debated the location – France or England – ultimately, they decided to survey the surviving officers of the division for their input. They voted four to one for a memorial in London so that it could be accessible to the grieving.[10] At the same time, the committee also believed that something should be done for the village of Le Verguier.

At the division's annual reunion dinner in 1924, Major General Sir John Capper put forward a proposal that the memorial committee do something for the village. He committed £250 of his own money with the understanding that the officers of the division pitch in matching funds.[11] The committee then queried the mayor of Le Verguier as to how they could help the community. It was ultimately decided that the division contribute a belfry for the local church, the bells of which would be in honour of the war dead. Extra funds then went to the cost of rebuilding the local school and community building in the centre of the village.

On 3 October 1926 a dedication ceremony was held in Le Verguier. In attendance were officers and men of the division, including Capper, who presided over the dedication and wreath-laying. There was a guard of honour consisting of former officers and rankers, who wore civilian suits, bowler hats, and stood at attention with their MCs or DCMs on their breasts. French schoolchildren stood in gratitude at the front of the crowd. Mayor Severin wore his tricolour sash and addressed the crowd from a school balcony. At the foot of the village war memorial, a wreath and plaque were laid for the division and their defence of the village. The central street leading out of the village was renamed, Rue de la 24 ème Division Britannique. Eventually, the bells rang out from the hilltop church down into the valley, the sound passing the remnants of trench lines and dugouts, now turned back into fields that harvested spent shells by the thousands, fields in which men of the 8th Queen's had fought, bled, and died to hold.

---

10 P.T. Chevallier, Minutes of the Memorial Committee, 19 May 1922.
11 P.T. Chevallier to officers of the 24th Division, 7 November 1924.

Other Remembrances

Archives reflect only a select number of documents that do not encompass a complete picture. In terms of the 8th Battalion, there is quite a bit of official paperwork that survived the war. The war diaries are all intact and accessible. Some officer and other ranks' service records, though incomplete, give a general impression of the types of experiences by men in the battalion, though, through fragments of official paperwork. Individual families have maintained something of the memory of their loved ones: whether it is a photograph, medal collection, sporadic letters, or oral history, the war waged by the 8th Battalion survives in at least a few families' collective memories in Britain. In the twentieth century, there were a few attempts to engage with the legacy of the war through the battalion's unique history. These tell us something about the way in which history was written and the story that those who lived through the war wanted remembered.

There were two attempts at writing the battalion's official history after the war. The first, mentioned at the beginning of the chapter, is the unofficial battalion history written by one of its long-term officers in the early 1920s. It is the most comprehensive narrative of the unit before this book was written. The other is a chapter in H.C. Wylly's *History of The Queen's Royal (West Surrey) Regiment in the Great War*. It is a summary account of the unit's actions that was likely based upon the unofficial history, as there are narrative similarities between the two. Though Second Lieutenant Claude Piesse described Wylly's work as 'a fairy tale', the chapter gets the basics right, but it is unspecific.[12] Like many other Kitchener battalions, the record of the 8th Service Battalion remained alive mostly in the memories of its veterans and the grieving families of the war dead.

In the 1920s, former officers did wade-in to discuss the war record of the battalion in the official history of British military operations on the Western Front. The tremendous effort to write the official history of the war was spearheaded by Brigadier General Sir James Edmonds. While it was being written, Edmonds was keen on corresponding with former officers of the particular campaigns in which he was writing. As he compiled their feedback, the official history incorporated suggestions and nuances of those who were involved in the events described. A number of officers within the battalion, as well as staff officers of the 72nd and 17th brigades and the 24th

---

12 David Baker, 'John Sayer VC: A Forgotten Hero Reassessed', *Stand To!*, No. 80, p.11.

Division wrote to Edmonds with their feedback. Peirs and Brigadier General Stone, in particular, wrote extensively on Le Verguier and the exact circumstances of the events of 21–22 March 1918. Notably, Peirs also wrote to Shaw Sparrow regarding his book *The 5ᵗʰ Army in March 1918* (1921) offering 'a few points of correction' to the author's account.[13] The battalion's former colonel engaged with the war's history as it was written and was particularly careful at preserving the memory of his battalion's war record.

At least four of the battalion's soldiers penned war memoirs, of varying types, that have survived, all of which reside in the Imperial War Museum. The first to do so was the battalion's medical officer, Charles Lodge Patch. Written immediately after the events described and initially drafted upon army medical forms, Lodge Patch's account first appeared in his school magazine in 1919. There is evidence that he tried to publish the account at greater length that year, but to no avail, probably as the war books market had begun to turn against war memoirs in the mid-1920s. His account is a vivid tribute to the officers and men with which he served, particularly the former, through the harrowing two weeks after the 21 March attack on Le Verguier. Joining Lodge Patch in the Imperial War Museum are the fragmented recollections of Claude Piesse, describing his war experiences in 1917–18. The third is the memoir of Lance Corporal Abraham. His account is very different than that of Lodge Patch. It was written after the mid-1960s. Distance from the war gives it both a quality of perspective, but also, a degree of un-specificity that comes from the merging of many events together in memory to tell a good story. Still, it is a very vivid account of what it was like to be a ranker in the battalion after it was reconstituted in April 1918 and the 'warts and all' approach makes it a very distinctive document from the accounts of officers. Joining Abraham was E.G. Nurse, another common soldier in the battalion, whose typed diary and short but vivid account of the retreat from Le Verguier is a useful contrast to the official war diary.[14] Through Abraham and Nurse, we have the common soldier's struggle not just against the Germans, but also to keep up morale in the face of the many discomforts of life in the line for the unprivileged mass of soldiers. Lodge Patch, Abraham, and Nurse had a similar motivation to write; to leave behind a personal account

---

13 The British Library, MS 48204A, The Shaw Sparrow Papers, Peirs to Sparrow, 2 February 1921.

14 IWM, 81/23/1, Papers of E.G. Nurse.

of a hard-fighting service battalion. Their work stands in contrast to that of the unofficial history, which was meant to encompass the experiences of the whole, rather than that of individuals. Put together, a portrait of the battalion emerges from the bottom up to the very top.

Of course, the most significant set of personal papers from the battalion – to date – is the correspondence which became the genesis for this book. The Peirs/Dracopoli family saved the colonel's correspondence and ephemera. His letters span the battalion's entire service on the Western Front, and were held in a Harrods department store box and saved by Peirs's widow, Eirene. One envelope of ephemera was simply marked on the outside by her 'interesting for posterity.' Within the collection are several typed transcriptions, indicating that at some point either Peirs or someone in his family went back through the correspondence and contemplated transcribing it, perhaps for publication. Had the family not dutifully saved and curated the materials and then shown a desire for their use and publication online, we would know far less about the inner workings of the battalion and the transformation of a civilian solicitor into a competent commander.

Microhistory and Memory

We began this story with Peirs and it is fitting that we should end with him, too. After a brief pulmonary illness, Jack Peirs died in May 1943 at his home in St Albans. His war-time funeral was held at St Michael's church and the mourners sang 'He who would valiant be' as they commemorated the life of the thrice awarded DSO, who died a member of the Home Guard, whilst Britain was at war again with Germany. His ashes were taken from the church through to the memorial garden. From there, they went to his final resting place, the churchyard at Aspall Hall, with the rest of the Chevallier family. He was remembered by his local paper as a 'charming personality' and as a man with 'a high sense of public duty'. Traits that no doubt he wanted emphasised.[15] He left behind his wife and widow; Eirene kept his uniformed portrait on the wall of her flat in Chelsea for the rest of her life.

Peirs also left behind hundreds of men who served alongside of him, some of whom turned out to mourn their colonel at St Albans alongside his family. The battalion was Peirs's second family and a source of great devotion for him during the war and beyond. Though he would have had a comfortable

---

15 Peirs Papers, Peirs obituary clipping.

life as a solicitor in his father's firm had he not served, the experience commanding a battalion on the Western Front is what made his life distinctive and exceptional. His journey from middle-class solicitor to soldier, from novice militia officer to war hero, as he trudged through the war from Loos to Le Verguier, is one of emotional fortitude, competency in command, and resilience. He was wounded three times. He came under countless barrages. He led men in attacks, exposing himself to repeated danger. And he walked miles up the line on a blood-poisoned foot to inspire his men to hold to the last in the midst of the Kaiserschlacht. As exceptional as Peirs's experience was, he also exhibited the type of heroism that was common on the Western Front – pluck, or the ability to adjust and to carry on with a droll cheerfulness despite it all.

It is easy to see the pluck and to miss the pathos in Peirs's letters and his war record. He was a man who was raised in a classist imperial society that valued privileged men like Peirs, who were public school athletes and well-heeled professionals. This is not meant to be derisive, but it is a reminder that behind the war hero was a society that valued the attributes he exhibited and encouraged them through an officer class that defined itself in terms of perseverance, stoicism, and sense of duty. Peirs was no bore, indeed, he exuded personality; he was sarcastically quick to make fun of staff officers or incompetents and he seemed to live for family and society gossip. He was paternalistic towards his working-class men, referring to them as his 'lambs', a leadership model that now looks condescending in its classism. He was, in short, a real-life human with flaws and prejudices. He was also an admired leader of men in a terrible war.[16]

Indeed, after his death, he was remembered not for his contribution to the law, but for his service at the front. In that spirit, the battalion's ever loyal medical officer Charles Lodge Patch published the final tribute to his life under the headline 'Peirs of Le Verguier'. In it he wrote that Peirs was 'a non-professional soldier who fought one of the greatest holding actions of the Great War.' Bidding farewell to his commander, he continued, 'Good-bye, Peirs! Many an officer, many a man, have been waiting to welcome you these twenty-five years and more – all those, in fact, whose deeds are enshrined

---

16 Meghan O'Donnell has a nice short piece on historicising Peirs: https://jackpeirs.org/commentary/3456/

in that memorial at the little village of Le Verguier.'[17] Thus the battalion's former commander was remembered not for his lively letters fretting about staff officers or French civilians cheating the battalion, but instead for one day of his hundreds of days in service where he rose to the occasion of his command and exceeded it.

Battalions are, of course, more than their officers, though they often reflect the morale of the officers in command. This book has been an attempt to tell the story of an average battalion of citizens who throughout their time at the front grew into soldiers. It is not the story of the men, principally, but a collective story about what was required of men on the Western Front and how they adapted and changed to meet the challenges in front of them. This was no easy task. From its very first battle, the battalion suffered terrible casualties. It was reconstituted again and again. Even when not in battle, it suffered casualties from snipers and mortars, from diseases and exposure. Hundreds lost their lives; over 1,000 wounds sustained. Some never recovered from their physical or mental scars. The war's legacy carried forward, literally, on their bodies, within their lungs, and inside of their heads. The experience of being a part of the battalion was one that carried forward until the last one of the 8th Battalion's veterans died. Their legacy still carries over for some of the families of these common men who fought a very uncommon war. Men who went to war with varying perspectives, backgrounds, and motivations, but shared one thing in common: their battalion.

---

17 Lodge Patch, 'Peirs of Le Vergiuer' clipping, Peirs Papers.

Afterword

As one writes a book, it tends to change a bit. This one changed to meet the source materials available and the research limitations due to the Covid-19 Pandemic. It only tells part of the story; we have some central characters and a major arc to the story, but we do not understand fully what is happening in conversations between chums over the brazier. That is a story harder to tell; we know the history of the battalion, we have some good sources and characters within it, but the vast majority of the men's thoughts and feelings about their service have gone with them to their graves. Such is the great limitation of writing history, especially during a pandemic; such is the limitation of writing about a group of several thousand men.

That caveat being written, this book aims to show how the war was fought by the lowest but most significant group unit identity. To demonstrate how a battalion fought and changed over the course of the war. The war record of the battalion reveals certain simple truths that reveal a different story to the usual mud, blood, and futility school of the infantryman's war on the Western Front. Here we have a story where the officers and men of the 8th Queen's became better soldiers as they grew in experience. The war became more complex and increased in its challenges, but so, too, did their tactics and ability to meet those challenges. The battalion that crossed the Lens-La Bassée road on 26 September 1915 was not the same battalion that crossed the Selle in October 1918, literally as well as figuratively. These men learned how to be soldiers as the battalion learned how to fight a modern war. This book has tried to demonstrate the challenges of service so that the reader can understand and appreciate what went into fighting the war from the ground up.

Of course, this book is also part of a commemorative genre of war stories roughly categorised as the unit history. In writing it, I have been conscious of the commemorative impulse, while also trying to push the boundaries of the genre. Professional historians are meant to be detached from their sources no matter the difficulty. In writing this story, it was hard not to be drawn into the lives of the men of this battalion, particularly as the sense of loss is so palpable and the sense of sacrifice so acute. The battalion did the job it was called upon to do, but at a tremendous cost. As Maud Fairtlough wrote to Hugh Vaughan Peirs in 1919, 'I think of those … who served with my husband. He would be proud of the battalion he trained but one can hardly bear to think of all they have gone through.'[1] For the men who survived, they carried with them the conflicted feelings of their war memories. For grieving families like the Fairtloughs, they wrestled with understanding the meaning of the war as they solemnly commemorated the war dead. It is conscious of the burden of the war's memory that I have tried preserve the war record of the 8th Queen's from the fragments left behind by the battalion's officers and men. In the end, I hope that it can be of interest for posterity.

---

1   Peirs Papers, Maud Fairtlough to Hugh Vaughan Peirs, 30 March 1919.

Bibliography

Manuscript Sources

The British Library (BL)

MS 48204A, The Shaw Sparrow Papers

Imperial War Museum (IWM)

Department of Documents

Doc. 546, Papers of A.J. Abraham

Doc. 12610, Papers of E.V.H. Fairtlough

Doc. 824, Papers of R.E. Lambert

Doc. 15123, Papers of D.O. Lee

Doc. 4612, Papers of E.G. Nurse

Doc. 11129, Papers of C.J. Lodge Patch MC

Doc. 18591, Papers of C.L. Piesse

Doc. 111442, Papers of K.F.B. Tower

HU 115890

Liddell Hart Centre for Military Archives (LHC)

Lh2P/79/1-3, Claude Piesse Letters

The National Archives (TNA)

CAB 45 Correspondence with the Official Historian

WO 95 War Diaries

WO 158 Operational Files

WO 339/374 Officers Service Records

WO 363 'Burnt Records' for Other Ranks.

WO 372 Medal Cards

Special Collections, Musselman Library, Gettysburg College

MS-250 The First World War Letters of H.J.C. Peirs

The Surrey History Centre (SHC)
ESR Papers of the East Surrey Regiment
QRWS Papers of the Queen's Royal West Surrey Regiment

Newspapers and Periodicals
The Civil & Military Gazette
Dorking and Leatherhead Advertiser
The London Gazette
The Malvernian
The Surrey Mirror
The Surrey Advertiser
The Surrey Comet
The Thanet Advertiser
Western Daily Press

Websites
https://www.jackpeirs.org
https://www.queensroyalsurreys.org.uk
https://www.surreyinthegreatwar.org.uk
https://www.awm.gov.au
https://www.cwgc.org
https://www.livesofthefirstworldwar.iwm.org.uk
https://www.longlongtrail.co.uk
https://www.brightoncollegeremembers.com
https://tochcentenary.com
https://ww1geek.com
https://theconversation.com
https://walterhitchcock-ww1.blogspot.com
https://www.iwm.org.uk

Secondary Sources
Arnold, Andrew. *Their Name Liveth for Evermore: Carshalton's First World War Roll of Honour.* Stroud: The History Press, 2014.

Atkinson, Christopher, *The History of the Eighth Battalion The Queen's Own Royal West Kent Regiment, 1914–1919.* London: Hazel, Watson & Winey, LD. 1921.

Atter, Nigel. *In the Shadow of Bois Hugo: The 8th Lincolns at the Battle of Loos.* Solihill, West Midlands: Helion & Co., 2017.

Attwell, W.A. *Laurence Attwell's Letters from the Front.* Barnsley, South Yorkshire: Pen & Sword, 2005.

Audoin-Rouseau, Stephane and Annette Becker. *14–18: Understanding the Great War.* New York: Hill and Wang, 2000.

Baker, David. 'John Sayer VC: A Forgotten Hero', *Stand To!*, No. 80, September 2007.

Barczewski, Stephanie. *Heroic Failure and the British.* New Haven, CT: Yale University Press, 2016.

Beckett, Ian. Bowman, Timothy and Connelly, Mark. *The British Army and the First World War.* Cambridge: Cambridge University Press, 2017.

Bennett, Kirsty. Middleton, Imogen, Page, Michael and Warren, Juliet (eds.). *In the Shadow of the Great War: Surrey 1914–1922.* Cheltenham, Gloucestershire: The History Press, 2019.

Boff, Jonathan. *Winning and Losing on the Western Front.* Cambridge: Cambridge University Press, 2012.

Boswell, F.A. *With a Reservist in France.* London: Routledge, 1917.

Bourke, Joanna. *Dismembering the Male.* London: Reaktion, 1999.

Braybon, Gail (ed.). *Evidence, History, and the Great War.* New York: Berghahn Books, 2003.

Cecil, Hugh and Liddle, Peter (eds.). *Facing Armageddon.* London: Leo Cooper, 1996.

Chapman, Guy. *A Passionate Prodigality.* London: Ivor Nicholson & Watson, 1933.

Cherry, Niall. *Most Unfavourable Ground: The Battle of Loos 1915.* Solihull: Helion & Company, 2005.

Clayton, Anthony. *The British Officer.* London: Routledge, 2013.

Connelly, Mark and Goebel, Stefan. *Ypres.* Oxford: Oxford University Press, 2018.

Corrigan, Gordon. *Loos 1915.* Stroud, Gloucestershire: Spellmont, 2006.

Douie, Charles. *The Weary Road.* London: John Murray, 1929.

Doyle, Peter. *Loos 1915.* Stroud, Gloucestershire: Spellmont, 2012.

Dracopoli, Marco. 'A New Officer for a New Army: The Leadership of Major Hugh J.C. Peirs in the Great War'. *The Gettysburg Historical Journal*: Vol. 13, Article 6.

Doughty Robert. *Pyrrhic Victory: French Strategy and Operations in the Great War.* Cambridge, MA: The Belknap Press, 2005.

Edmonds, Charles. *A Subaltern's War.* London: Peter Davies, 1929.

Edmonds, Sir J.E. *History of the Great War: Military Operations in France & Belgium.* (Uckfield, East Sussex: The Naval & Military Press/Imperial War Museum), Volumes 1915 (2), 1916 (1–2), 1917 (1–3), 1918 (1–4).

Eksteins, Modris. *Rites of Spring.* New York: Mariner Books, 2000.

Farrar-Hockley, Anthony. *Goughie: The Life of Sir Hubert Gough.* London: Hart-Davis, MacGibbon, 1975.

Fox, Aimee. *Learning to Fight: Military Innovation and Change in the British Army, 1914–1918.* Cambridge: Cambridge University Press, 2018.

Frayn, Andrew. *Writing Disenchantment.* Manchester: Manchester University Press, 2014.

French, David. *Military Identities.* Oxford: Oxford University Press, 2008.

Fuller, J.G. *Troop Morale and Popular Culture in the British and Dominion Armies 1914–1918.* Oxford: Clarendon, 1991.

Gerwarth, Robert. *The Vanquished*. New York: Farrar, Strauss and Giroux, 2016.

Gibbs, Philip. *Realities of War*. London: Heinemann, 1920.

Gilbert, Martin. *The First World War*. New York: Henry Holt and Company, 1994.

Gough, Hubert. *The Fifth Army*. London: Hodder and Stoughton, 1931.

Graves, Robert. *Good-bye to All That*. London: Jonathan Cape, 1929.

Gregory, Adrian. *The Last Great War*. Oxford: Oxford University Press, 2008.

Griffith, Paddy. *Battle Tactics of the Western Front*. New Haven: Yale University Press, 1994.

Haig, Douglas. *War Diaries & Letters*. Editors Gary Sheffield and John Bourne. London: Weidenfeld and Nicholson, 2005.

Hamilton, R.G.A. *The War Diary of the Master of Belhaven*. London: John Murray, 1924.

Hamilton, Richard and Herwig, Holger. *Decisions for War*. Cambridge: Cambridge University Press, 2004.

Hay, Ian. *The First Hundred Thousand*. London: Blackwood, 1916.

Hodgkinson, Peter. *British Infantry Battalion Commanders in the First World War*. Farnham, Surrey: Ashgate, 2015.

Holmes, Richard. *Tommy*. London: Harper, 2005.

Humphries, Mark Osborne and Maker, John (eds.). *Germany's Western Front: Translations from the German Official History of the Great War: Volume II – 1915*. Waterloo, Ontario: Wilfrid Laurier University Press, 2010.

Hynes, Samuel. *A War Imagined*. London: Pimlico, 1992.

Jones, Simon. *World War I Gas Warfare Tactics and Equipment*. Botley, Oxford. Osprey, 2007.

Jones, Spencer. *From Boer War to World War*. Norman, OK: Oklahoma University Press, 2012.

Jones, Spencer (ed). *Courage without Glory: The British Army on the Western Front in 1915*. Solihill: Helion & Company, 2005.

Keegan, John. *The Face of Battle*. New York: Viking, 1976.

Kramer, Alan. *Dynamic of Destruction*. Oxford: Oxford University Press, 2007.

Laudan, Sebastian. '"Tag X – Durchbruch" The German Advance from the Saint-Quentin Canal 21 March 1918', *Stand To!*, No. 111, January 2018.

Lloyd, Nick. 'With Faith and Without Fear: Sir Douglas Haig's Command of First Army During 1915' in *Journal of Military History*, Vol. 71, No. 4, October 2007.

Lloyd, Nick. *Loos 1915*. Stroud, Gloucestershire: Tempus, 2006.

Lloyd, Nick. 'Lord Kitchener and "the Russian News": Reconsidering the Origins of the Battle of Loos' in *Defence Studies*. Vol. 5, No. 3, September 2005.

Lloyd, Nick. *Passchendaele*. New York: Basic Books, 2017.

Lucas, Michael. *The Journey's End Battalion: The 9th East Surrey in the Great War*. Barnsley, South Yorkshire: Pen & Sword, 2012.

McCartney, Helen. *Citizen Soldiers*. Cambridge: Cambridge University Press, 2005.

McCartney, Helen. 'The First World War Soldier and his contemporary image in Britain'. *International Affairs*, 90:2, 2014.

MacDonald, Lyn. *1915: The End of Innocence*. London: Penguin, 1997.

MacGill, Patrick. *The Great Push*. London: Herbert Jenkins, 1916.

Macleod, Jenny and Purseigle, Peirre (eds.). *Uncovered Fields: Perspectives in First World War Studies* (Leiden: Brill: 2004).

Manning, Frederic. *Her Privates We.* London: Serpent's Tail, 1999.

Meyer, Jessica. *Men of War.* London: Palgrave Macmillan, 2011.

Middlebrook, Martin. *The Kaiser's Battle.* Barnsley, South Yorkshire: Pen & Sword, 2016.

Moran, Lord (Charles Wilson). *Anatomy of Courage.* New York: Carroll & Graf Publishers, 2007.

Mosse, George. *Fallen Soldiers.* Oxford: Oxford University Press, 1990.

Murland, Jerry. *Retreat and Rearguard Somme 1918: The Fifth Army in Retreat.* Barnsley, South Yorkshire: Pen & Sword, 2014.

Neiberg, Michael. *Fighting the Great War.* Cambridge, MA: Harvard University Press, 2005.

Overy, Richard. *The Morbid Age.* London: Allen Lane, 2009.

Parker, Peter. *The Old Lie: The Great War and the Public School Ethos.* London: Continuum, 2007.

Philpott, William. *Anglo-French Relations and Strategy on the Western Front, 1914–1918.* London: Macmillan, 1996.

Philpott, William. *Three Armies on the Somme.* New York: Knopf, 2009.

Philpott, William. *War of Attrition.* New York: The Overloook Press, 2014.

Prior, Robin and Wilson, Trevor. *Passchendaele the Untold Story.* New Haven: Yale University Press, 1996.

Prior, Robin and Trevor Wilson. *The Somme.* New Haven: Yale University Press, 2006.

Rawson, Andrew. *Battleground Europe, Loos – Hill 70.* Barnsley, South Yorkshire: Leo Cooper, 2002.

Rawson, Andrew. *Battleground Europe, Loos – Hohenzollern Redoubt.* Barnsley, South Yorkshire: Leo Cooper, 2003.

Reynolds, David. *The Long Shadow.* New York: Simon & Shuster, 2013.

Richards, Anthony. *In their Own Words: Untold Stories of the First World War.* London: Imperial War Museum, 2016.

Roper, Michael. 'Between Manliness and Masculinity: The "War Generation" and the Psychology of Fear in Britain, 1914–1950'. *Journal of British Studies.* No. 441 April 2005.

Roper, Michael. *The Secret Battle.* Manchester: Manchester University Press, 2009.

Senior, Michael. *Haking, a Dutiful Soldier: Lieutenant General Sir Richard Haking XI Corps Commander, 1915–1918.* Barnsley, South Yorkshire: Pen & Sword, 2012.

Sheffield, Gary. *Forgotten Victory.* London: Headline, 2001.

Sheffield, Gary. *Leadership in the Trenches.* London: Palgrave Macmillan, 2000.

Sheldon, Jack. *The German Army on the Western Front: 1915.* Barnsley, South Yorkshire: Pen & Sword, 2012.

Simkins, Peter. *Kitchener's Army.* Barnsley, South Yorkshire: Pen & Sword, 2007.

Stevenson, David. *With Our Backs to the Wall.* Cambridge, MA: Cambridge University Press, 2011.

Stone, David. *The Kaiser's Army.* London: Bloomsbury, 2015.

Strachan, Hew. *The First World War.* New York: Viking, 2003.

Terraine, John. *To Win a War.* New York: Doubleday, 1981.

Terraine, John. *White Heat*. London: Sidgwich & Jackson, 1982.

Todman, Daniel. *The Great War: Myth and Memory*. London: Hambledon Continuum, 2005.

Travers, Tim. *The Killing Ground*. Barnsley, South Yorkshire: Pen & Sword, 2019.

Veitch, Colin. '"Play up! Play up! And Win the War!" Football, the Nation and the First World War'. *Journal of Contemporary History*, Vol. 20, No. 3, July 1985.

Warner, Philip. *The Battle of Loos*. London: William Kimber, 1976.

Watson, Alexander. *Enduring the Great War*. Cambridge: Cambridge University Press, 2008.

Watson, Alexander. 'Self-Deception and Survival: Mental Coping Strategies on the Western Front, 1914–1918'. *Journal of Contemporary History*, Vol. 41, No. 2, April 2006.

Williams, Rhodri. 'Lord Kitchener and the Battle of Loos: French Politics and British Strategy in the Summer of 1915'. In *War Strategy, and International Politics: Essays in Honour of Sir Michael Howard*. Edited by Lawrence Freedman, Paul Hayes, and Robert O'Neill. Oxford: Clarendon Press, 1992.

Winter, Jay. *The Great War and the British People*. New York: Palgrave Macmillan, 2003.

Wohl, Robert. *The Generation of 1914*. Cambridge: Harvard University Press, 1978.

Wylly, H.C. *History of the Queen's Royal (West Surrey) Regiment in the Great War*. Uckfield, UK: Naval and Military Press, 2009.

Index

.